Retracing Inca Steps

Retracing Inca Steps

ADVENTURES IN ANDEAN ETHNOARCHAEOLOGY

DEAN E. ARNOLD

THE UNIVERSITY OF UTAH PRESS
Salt Lake City

The Defiance House Man colophon is a registered trademark of
The University of Utah Press. It is based on a four-foot-tall Ancient
Puebloan pictograph (late PIII) near Glen Canyon, Utah.

Library of Congress Cataloging-in-Publication Data

Names: Arnold, Dean E., 1942- author.
Title: Retracing Inka steps : adventures in ethnoarchaeology / Dean E Arnold.
Description: Salt Lake City : University of Utah Press, [2021] | Includes bibliographical
    references and index.
Identifiers: LCCN 2020036099 (print) | LCCN 2020036100 (ebook) |
    ISBN 9781647690243 (paperback) | ISBN 9781647690250 (ebook)
Subjects: LCSH: Incas—Social life and customs. | Incas—Civilization. | Incas—
    Antiquities. | Anthropology—Fieldwork—Peru—Ayacucho (Department) |
    Ethnoarchaeology—Fieldwork—Peru—Ayacucho (Department) |
    Anthropologists—Biography. | Pottery, Peruvian. | Ayacucho (Peru : Department)—
    Social life and customs. | Ayacucho (Peru : Department)—Antiquities. |
    Peru—Civilization.
Classification: LCC F3429 .A73 2021 (print) | LCC F3429 (ebook) | DDC 985/.019—dc23
LC record available at https://lccn.loc.gov/2020036099
LC ebook record available at https://lccn.loc.gov/2020036100d

Errata and further information on this and other titles available online at
UofUpress.com.

Printed and bound in the United States of America.

Contents

Figures

Acknowledgments

I am deeply grateful to the late Dr. R. T. "Tom" Zuidema whose hospitality and commitment to exposing me and other students to Andean life contributed greatly to my knowledge and understanding of Peru. This experiential approach to learning has left an indelible impact on my knowledge and professional development. Professor Zuidema suggested that I travel to the village of Acos, the source of the exiles that the Incas resettled in Quinua. That journey was an unforgettable experience and inspired me to write this book. The late Dr. Donald W. Lathrap, my dissertation advisor, encouraged me on my subsequent journey toward a PhD, and I was one of only a few of his students who did not write a dissertation on South American archaeology. Dr. William P. "Bill" Mitchell graciously allowed me to put my sleeping bag in his room in Quinua, shared his principal informant with me, and contributed counsel, criticism, and correction for this, and my other publications about Quinua. I owe a great debt to Bill for his practical help and intellectual contribution through many, many conversations and his prolific publications about Quinua that have enriched my understanding of my work there greatly. He graciously read both an early and a later draft of this manuscript and made many helpful comments and criticisms. My experiences in Peru during my Fulbright Lectureship in 1972–1973 have greatly enriched this book especially because of the friendship of my wife and myself with Parker and Beverly (Lait) Anderson who took us to many areas around Cusco such as the ritual *chiaraje* battle that we witnessed on January 1, 1973.

My daughters, Andrea Arnold Carradus and Michelle Arnold Paine, read and critiqued this manuscript twice and made many suggestions that improved it considerably. It has also benefited from the comments of Darrin Pratt, Dr. Timothy Larsen, David Reid, Dr. Laura Montgomery, Emily

Baca Morroquín, Dr. Brian Miller, and my "new girlfriend from Urbana," June, who has now been with me as my wife for more than fifty-two years. Conversations with Dr. Ryan Williams about some of the content presented here have greatly improved this work. Bill and Cindy Koechling (William Koechling Photography, https://500px.com/billkoechling) scanned my 35 mm slides and cleaned and edited them. Chelsea M. Feeney (www.cmcfeeney.com) made the maps. Finally, I dedicate this work to the memory of my late professors and mentors, Dr. James O. Buswell III, Dr. D. W. Lathrap, Dr. F. K. Lehman, and Dr. R. T. Zuidema, whose encouragement helped launch me into a career in anthropology.

Some parts of this work were previously published. Part of the section "A Great Pre-Inca City" in chapter 2 appeared as a blog on the University Press of Colorado website, "Pedestrian Archaeology in the Great Peruvian City of Wari" and is used with permission. https://upcolorado.com/about-us/news-features/item/2949-pedestrian-archaeology-in-wari.

Figures 5.5, 4.3, and 2.4 were previously published as figure 2.1 (p. 17), figure 2.11 (p. 25), and figure 2.12 (p. 29), respectively, in *Ecology of Ceramic Production in an Andean Community* (1993), by Dean E. Arnold, and used with the permission of the Cambridge University Press. The cover image was previously published in black and white as figure 6.4 (p. 151) in *Ceramic Theory and Cultural Process* (1985) by Dean E. Arnold and is used with permission of the Cambridge University Press. Figure 5.5 was originally published as figure 1 (p. 184) in "Ceramic Ecology in the Ayacucho Basin, Peru: Implications for Prehistory," by Dean E. Arnold, in *Current Anthropology* (Vol. 16, 1975) and used with permission. Figures 8.3 and 8.4 were originally published as figure 7 (p. 235), and figure 9 (p. 237) in "Early Inca Expansion and the Incorporation of Local Ethnic Groups: Ethnohistory and Archeological Reconnaissance in the Region of Acos, Department of Cusco, Peru," by Dean E. Arnold, in *Andean Past*, vol. 7 (2005). Figure 9.1 was previously published on page 277 in "Why Are There So Few Christian Anthropologists? Reflections on the Tensions between Christianity and Anthropology," *Perspectives on Science and Christian Faith* 58, no. 4 (2006), and is used with permission (https://network.asa3.org/page/PSCF?)

CHAPTER 1

The Adventure of Fieldwork

It's not the destination, but the journey.

AS A FREE-RANGE KID, I have always loved adventure. Whether climbing forty-foot rock faces in the Dells near my hometown in South Dakota, exploring and mapping the river that ran through it, or poking around abandoned quartzite quarries, the unknown and personally unexplored drew me to the excitement of discovery, all with insatiable curiosity. During travels with my parents in the American West, trails, mines, and piles of mine tailings pulled me deeper into exploring the new and exotic, and helped to stimulate my curiosity about the natural world. Even so, I never thought I would become an anthropologist. As a teenager, I loved learning about rocks and minerals and the places from which they came, and I wanted to know about their origin, context, extraction, and refining. During those trips to the West, my parents lovingly acquiesced to my requests to tour smelters in Montana (copper), Idaho (zinc), and Colorado (gold) to satisfy my curiosity about the relationship of minerals to metal, and allowed me time and space to visit rock shops and search for gemstone minerals such as garnets in Idaho. As a high school junior, I made use of the school's chemistry lab to do analyses of minerals that I had collected on the trips with my parents to the American West, and my project won first place in the high school science fair. The most exciting and adventurous vocations that I could imagine were becoming a mining or metallurgical engineer or a forest ranger, careers that would engage me in the unknown natural world.

In college, I discovered the lure of learning about peoples of the world in faraway places, such as the San (Bushmen), the Andaman Islanders, and the Australian Aborigines. Previously unknown to me, they were so different that I could not imagine they actually existed outside of the textbooks I was reading.

During that first course in anthropology, I became hooked. As a part of the course readings, the professor assigned a book of first-person accounts of fieldwork by different anthropologists. Called *In the Company of Man*, edited by Joseph Casagrande,[1] the essays were eye-opening, but I found some sexually explicit content to be somewhat shocking. I was a naive sophomore whose previous cross-cultural experiences were limited: a trip across western Canada; an afternoon in Tijuana, Mexico; volunteer work on Skid Row in Chicago; and a summer selling books door-to-door by hitchhiking through rural Neshoba County, Mississippi, with its Jim Crow laws. Three years later, four civil rights workers were abducted and murdered there, a shocking event that still causes anxiety when I think of my own naivete at the time.

In graduate school, I was privileged to take a course from Dr. Casagrande, and he served on my PhD dissertation committee. Many years later, the program for his funeral included a passage from the introduction to his book that had touched me so deeply during my first encounter with anthropology. As I see it now, that passage captured what it is like to be an anthropologist, and to live and work in another culture radically different from one's own:

> [Field research is a challenging scientific undertaking, an adventure of both the mind and the spirit.] Immersed in the life around him, the anthropologist may experience an exhilarating sense of coming to understand another people and of being accepted by them. He may also at times undergo a shattering feeling of isolation, of strangeness and disorientation, and yearn for the comfort of accustomed things. Herein lies the dilemma, for he is neither full participant in the life he studies, nor simply a passive background observer of it. He is something of both, a role nicely summarized in the double term, "participant-observer." Not born to the alien culture or committed to it, the anthropologist must stand at a certain psychological and emotional distance from it. If he is an objective scientist, he cannot "go native." Neither can he hold himself aloof and observe human behavior as a naturalist might watch a colony of ants; with fellow humans there is both the possibility and necessity of communication. One's capacity for imaginatively entering into the life of another people becomes a primary qualification

for the anthropologist. For him, the "field" is the fountainhead of knowledge, serving him as both laboratory and library.[2]

Written before gender-inclusive language became important in anthropology, this quote is still *apropos* more than sixty years later. It encapsulates the fieldwork experience, and still expresses the adventure, the challenges, and the complexities of cross-cultural encounters for all anthropologists.

Anthropologists study humanity. Historically, their work has taken them far from home to live with the people they study. This firsthand experience challenges their preconceptions about the world and about their own backgrounds as they enter into the lives of the people in a different culture. Their approach, however, is different from that of the psychologist, sociologist, political scientist, historian, or literary scholar. First and foremost, anthropologists immerse themselves in another culture as a participant in order to see the culture from the insider's perspective, but at the same time, they view it as an observer because they are not a part of the culture, but outside of it. Just as Casagrande said, this twofold complementary approach allows anthropologists to understand a culture from a unique and more objective perspective that helps lessen the ethnocentric biases that they bring from their own culture, while never quite being totally freed from them.

Coming from a small town in South Dakota, I never thought I would end up in South America for anything, much less doing independent research as a graduate student. Even as a budding anthropologist, I had no idea where I wanted to work. Even research in Mexico seemed unimaginable to me. As a result of my research in Yucatán in 1965, I experienced the culture shock of value conflict, and the loneliness of living in another culture. Nevertheless, I discovered that the contemporary Maya still knew and used an unusual clay mineral (palygorskite) that was one of the significant components of the ancient pigment Maya Blue.[3] At the time, the composition of Maya Blue was still a mystery and the source of the palygorskite they used to create it was unknown. The quest to work on Maya Blue, and an exploration of Maya potters' indigenous knowledge, appeared to have unfathomable research potential.[4] Consequently, it seemed that the future location of my research was sealed. But working in South America and studying the indigenous peoples of the Andes did not seem to be even a remote possibility.

Just as any product of North American education, I knew little about the Incas,[5] and even less about the civilizations that preceded them. They had lived in the Andes of South America, but I never dreamed that I would become an anthropologist and study contemporary Andean rural farmers (*campesinos*) who were also potters.[6] Nor did I realize that I would retrace some of the Inca steps across the Andes in a journey that would change me.

My career as an anthropologist took me to distant places, but none as challenging as my first research in the Andes. It was an experience that changed my life, increased my self-awareness, and challenged many of my values, my physical body, and generally what I had thought of as normal. As Casagrande said, it was "an adventure of the mind and the spirit." It pushed my body to its limits because of strange foods, sickness, and working at heights exceeding two miles above sea level, but it also challenged me intellectually, socially, and emotionally. As I see it now, it was a critical part of my journey as an anthropologist. Understanding another culture (even though that knowledge may never be complete) best comes from immersion in a culture through the time-honored and classic anthropological approach of a participant-observer. This methodology, combined with understanding the environment, history, and prehistory of an area, provides a holistic perspective unique in the study of humanity that produces in great insight into human cultural behavior. As I learned during my fieldwork two years previously in Yucatán, my experience in the Andes showed me in a new and dramatic way the importance of such holism.

About a year before I went to Peru, I read a book by Swiss psychiatrist Paul Tournier called *The Adventure of Living*, in which he argued that without risk, there is no adventure.[7] The book had a deep impact on me, and although Tournier was applying this principle to human relationships, it also applies to anthropological fieldwork. One cannot have "an adventure of the mind and the spirit," as Casagrande said, without risk. Unfortunately, I did not make this connection at the time, immersed as I was in the day-to-day experiences of life as a grad student, but now I realize that the emotional and physical risks of travel and research in Peru led to a transformed "mind and spirit."

This book describes my encounter with the people of the Andes but places those experiences within a journey across the Andes. But this work is also a pilgrimage inward, a journey that taught me about myself, my culture, and my own world view, and challenged my comfortable middle-class values by confronting my ethnocentrism. Through these challenges, I learned much about the Andes—a landscape that itself is awe-inspiring, and about the people who inhabit that land, so distant from my previous day-to-day life. In spite of its inherent beauty, the experience of living there was not always pretty, and was not easy, pleasant, or safe. It was not free of embarrassment or mistakes, nor of physical, intellectual, ethical, or moral challenges, but it was transformative in the way that I viewed anthropology, humanity, and, most of all, myself. It was a journey into greater self-awareness and acceptance of worlds that I did not always understand or appreciate. Like many anthropological experiences, it changed my life and left unforgettable memories. I only came to understand its deep emotional and cultural impact on me much later in life, well after my fieldwork experience there had ended.

Doing research is like solving a mystery. One starts with an issue or question and then proceeds to answer that question using a variety of methodologies. In anthropology, the most basic methodology is participant-observation, but other methods are usually called for, because anthropological research involves examining human behavior holistically in its natural setting. This approach also means that behavior is context dependent and, often, research steers one in new unintended directions. These may lead to a dead end or may become so productive and fruitful that the results bear little relationship to the original question being investigated. Too broad a research question will lead one in too many directions and not make a contribution to anything. On the contrary, defining a research question too narrowly and precisely may lead to nothing significant at all.

The original focus of my anthropological research in the Andes was narrow enough to define the kind of data to be collected, but it was impossible to put it in context ahead of time. Rather, I had to be flexible and willing to change due to the logistical, social, cultural, and environmental circumstances. In the quest of following my research question, I discovered new insights about the present and the past, some of which did not occur to me until well after the completion of my fieldwork and subsequent to years of reflection about my experiences.

Most important, my experience in Peru taught me about Andean culture and the interrelationships of its peoples with their prehistory, history, and environment. This experience illustrated a different dimension of the holism of the anthropological approach. Peru is a country of environmental extremes, and understanding its culture requires a grasp of how the environment, prehistory, and history have helped shaped that culture.

Field research in anthropology is never impersonal and always embedded within contexts that are fraught with many challenges that cannot be anticipated. It is never a straight line from a research question to collecting the data to solving the mystery. There are many distractions and sidebars. Such is the trajectory of fieldwork illustrated by this journey.

In retrospect, my journey was one of the first field studies of what became the subdiscipline of archaeology known as "ethnoarchaeology" in the last third of the twentieth century. Traditionally done by archaeologists and most often focused on the formation of the archaeological record, this study constitutes a different and independent trajectory that sought to understand the relationship of material culture (in this case, pottery) to its cultural, environmental, historical, and prehistorical context.

CHAPTER 2

Beginning the Journey

An Aerial Introduction

AS MY PLANE lifted off the tarmac, I peered out my window anxious to view the Peruvian coast that I had missed seeing from my incoming commercial flight. The Pacific Ocean, with its ribbon of surf along a seemingly endless beach, stretched out below me. Mesmerized by the view, I reflected on my journey to Peru so far. It was early February 1967, and I had arrived in Lima only a few days before. In preparation, I had taken a course in South American archaeology, and it opened up an entirely new world for me. Critical for me was learning that the earliest evidence of humanity in South America at the time was discovered in Peru,[1] that many civilizations had preceded the Incas—some by more than three thousand years—and that the country encompassed vast environmental diversity. Not the least of this diversity were the contrasts between the tropical rain forest in the eastern half of Peru, the semiarid high Andes, and the narrow strip of extremely dry western coast that stretched from northern Peru to northern Chile (fig. 2.1). Contrary to what one would expect, this desert and the Andean valleys were actually the homeland of some of the earliest civilizations in all of South America.

Before I left for Peru, I knew little about the complexities of the history, geography, and culture of that distant land. I didn't realize it at the time, but my flight from Lima across the Andes would help remedy this ignorance, providing a lesson in the geography of the Peruvian coast, its link to the ocean that flanked it, and its critical role in the development of civilization there. Peruvian civilization began more than four thousand years ago and culminated in the development of the Inca Empire. The coast was also a part of that empire, and its seemingly lifeless expanse bore a critical relationship with the people, environment, and prehistory of the adjacent Andean highlands.

After reflecting on the scene before me, my thoughts turned inward. How and why did I come to Peru? Why was I flying across the Andes? Thinking about my journey so far, I recognized that a providential series of events led up to my current adventure in anthropology.

During the war in Vietnam in the early 1960s, U.S. policymakers realized that the lack of language and intercultural skills limited our country's understanding of the rest of the world, particularly Southeast Asia. They also deemed Latin America as a critical area because Castro's revolution in Cuba in 1959 had transformed the island into a socialist state, and he was exporting his revolutionary ideology to other parts of the hemisphere. Castro's associate, Ché Guevara, and his guerrillas were fighting the army in the eastern part of Bolivia, and reports also circulated that Castro-inspired rebel groups were attacking military outposts in the jungles of eastern Peru. As a consequence, Congress passed the National Defense Education Act, which funded graduate fellowships for those studying languages and cultures outside of Europe.

I had already done research two years earlier in Yucatán, Mexico, and worked independently learning conversational Spanish and enough Yucatec Maya to collect a large amount of data describing the indigenous knowledge of Maya potters. My supervisor in Yucatán (Dr. Duane Metzger) had left my university (the University of Illinois) for another position, and I had been assigned to a South American archaeologist (Dr. Donald W. Lathrap) as my PhD advisor. Professor Lathrap had excavated in the Upper Amazon in eastern Peru, and he wanted me to gain competence in South American anthropology and archaeology. He was impressed and pleased with what I had done on my own in Yucatán.

Meanwhile, the anthropology department at the University of Illinois had hired a Dutch anthropologist, Dr. R. T. "Tom" Zuidema who was teaching at the University of Huamanga in Ayacucho, Peru. For his first semester, he wanted to supervise the fieldwork of students during his last semester in Ayacucho, and Professor Lathrap wanted me to go to Peru and work with Zuidema. Lathrap suggested that I apply for a National Defense Foreign Language Fellowship, to improve my Spanish in the cultural context of Latin America and write a research proposal about what I wanted to do in Ayacucho.

I proposed to improve my language skills with classroom training and fieldwork in Peru. I had no formal training in Spanish but had learned it doing participant-observation in Yucatán two years previously. Since I had studied modern pottery production in Yucatán, I also proposed to investigate contemporary pottery production in the Ayacucho Valley. Responding to my research interest, Professor Zuidema had wondered whether it was possible to discern the influences of the major cultural and demographic changes in the valley over the last 1,500 years by examining its contemporary pottery. These influences were threefold. First, the valley was the center of the great pre-Inca Wari Empire, which flourished between AD 650 and AD 1050. After the Incas conquered the region four hundred years later, they transported populations (known as *mitimaes*) from more secure areas of their empire into the valley, presumably to pacify it and make it easier to govern.[2] Finally, the oldest Spanish settlement in Peru after Lima and Cusco was in the valley, and undoubtedly one would expect some Spanish influence in the pottery made there as well.

These diverse cultural and historical influences in the Ayacucho Valley and in the pottery-making communities there led to an intriguing research problem. Archaeologists believe that pottery can reflect cultural and demographic changes in the past, but was it possible to see these influences in the contemporary pottery made in the valley? Comparative examples of Inca and Wari pottery were available at the time, and some information about Hispanic ceramic technology and Spanish colonial pottery (Majolica) also existed. I wanted to find out if it was possible to tease out these influences in the traditional pottery made in the valley.

My proposal was approved and I received the fellowship. Meanwhile, three other graduate students had their proposals accepted as well. They focused on the archaeology and contemporary social organization in the Pampas River Valley south of Ayacucho. All of us were slated to leave in early February 1967.

Unfortunately, the administrators of the National Defense Foreign Language Fellowships believed that the funds should not be used for research in the field, but only for study at a U.S. university unless fieldwork was deemed necessary. As a consequence, I had to write to the Department of Education and explain why I wanted to use the second half of my fellowship's first year for fieldwork rather than classroom study, and attach a letter from my PhD supervisor.

As I see it now, university study with readings, classroom lectures, and language classes, as important as they were, focused on knowledge as an abstraction that did not engage me emotionally and experientially with another culture. Because language is indelibly tied to the culture of its speakers, using only the classroom model for learning a language limits one's understanding of its cultural context.

In retrospect, my trip to Peru taught me more linguistic and cultural understanding than any classroom experience or reading could ever have given me. Rather, fieldwork provided a deep understanding of the land and people of Peru, and its history and prehistory deepened my knowledge of Spanish. The experience also taught me about myself, broadening my understanding instead of seeing humanity from my own cultural viewpoint. As I came to see later, my newly enhanced cross-cultural perspective affected everything from intercultural communication to how I viewed negotiation in international diplomacy.

To carry out my proposal, I would be studying the contemporary Andean *campesinos* (peasants) who were potters and whose ancestors had been conquered by the Incas. The Inca Empire dominated the Andes from the early fifteenth century to AD 1533, when they were conquered by the Spanish. Stretching along the spine of the Andes from northern Ecuador to northern Chile and Northwest Argentina, the Incas tied together some of the most hostile and variegated environments on earth into a single state administered by the supreme Inca through their elaborate infrastructure of roads, bridges, and couriers that carried messages to and from their capital. Although sharing some similarities with other New World civilizations like the Aztecs and the Maya, the Inca Empire was unique in its vast extent and its elaborate organization and transportation infrastructure.

Much of Inca civilization ended with the Spanish conquest. In 1532, Francisco Pizzaro landed at Tumbez on what is now the northern coast of Peru, and began to travel into the Andes (fig. 2.1). He eventually reached the town of Cajamarca where he captured the supreme Inca, Atahualpa, and held him for a ransom of gold and silver. After the ransom was paid, Pizzaro executed him in January of 1533.

Returning to the coast, Pizzaro sailed south to what is now Lima, established a settlement there, and then marched overland to the Inca capital of Cusco, arriving there on November 15, 1533. I began my adventure of studying the Andean peoples in Lima 424 years later.

Now, on my way to Ayacucho and seeing the environmental diversity of Peru for myself, I had no idea of the challenges that awaited me. I had studied about Peru, and knew that its coast was a desert, but I was not prepared for the seemingly endless expanse of sand that stretched out as far as I could see. One of the driest deserts on Earth, the Peruvian coast

FIGURE 2.1. Map of Peru and principal cities mentioned in the text. (Map by Chelsea M. Feeney)

astoundingly receives less than a quarter of an inch of precipitation annually, most of it coming as mist and fog.

The cause of this dryness is the rain shadow created by two factors: the Peru-Humboldt Current and the Andes Mountains. The Peru-Humboldt Current is a cold, upwelling current that flows northward from Antarctica along the west coast of South America (fig. 2.1). At the equator, it turns westward toward the central Pacific. But before then, it cools the moisture-laden winds blowing off the Pacific causing them to drop their moisture far out at sea. When these air masses arrive on land, all that remains of their moisture is fog that gets trapped against the western slopes of the Andes, cloaking the coast with overcast skies from May through October.

As the Peru-Humboldt Current moves northward, it flows over the Peru-Chile Trench, one of the deepest ocean trenches in the world. The colder water from its depths mixes with the water from Antarctica with so much dissolved oxygen that it supports a long food chain from microscopic plants and animals to huge colonies of birds and large sea mammals such as whales, sea lions, and dolphins. Harboring an amazing diversity of sea life, this food chain provides a critical resource for human life in contrast to the dry, lifeless sand of the adjacent desert. Four millennia ago, the sea supported large prehistoric populations on the coast that over time developed into some of the world's great civilizations.

The Peru-Chile Trench is the result of the contact of two of the earth's tectonic plates. One, the South American plate, upon which the continent sits, is continually being forced westward because of the magma rising to the surface under the Atlantic Ocean. As it meets the Nazca plate just off the west coast, it is forced upward. In the distant past, this uplift created the Andes, but this contact zone continues to produce a tectonically active landscape, with earthquakes and volcanic activity, and causes the Peruvian coast to rise about one centimeter per year.

One's first reaction to the dry coastal desert is that it is lifeless and therefore would not support much human life. This impression, however, is an illusion. One cannot really understand Peru's prehistory without recognizing the richness of the subsistence resources created by the Peru-Humboldt Current. In fact, coastal Peru is one of the very rare places in the world where the resource base of complex society did not rest primarily on the intensive cultivation of a domesticated plant (such as maize) as a protein source, but rather on maritime resources that provided food for large numbers of people for thousands of years.

Tapping this abundantly rich resource base required little effort by human populations—both ancient and modern. In order to exploit this treasure trove of food, boats were not necessary because prehistoric populations could access these resources easily from the rocks and beaches along the shore. Sea life among the rocks is abundant with mollusks, starfish, and other animals that get trapped there; tuna, anchovies, and other fish are caught farther out to sea.

I witnessed the ease of acquiring these resources when I visited La Punta, a peninsula of land jutting out into the Pacific from the port of Callao, near Lima. I walked out to the end of the jetty and noticed several young men searching for fish, mollusks, and crustaceans among the rocks. One of them carried a long pole with a small net attached to a "Y" at its end. Moving between the rocks, he used the device to net fish and other sea life when the surf splashed among the rocks, and then deposited each catch into a pouch on his belt. Within half an hour, he departed, having obtained sufficient fare for that day.

The Peru-Humboldt Current provides such a phenomenal food source that the countries of Peru, Chile, and Ecuador declared that their sovereign rights to its resources extended two hundred miles from their coasts. The resources within this territorial limit provide protein for the people of modern Peru and support industries such as fishing, canning, and fish protein concentrate, exported for poultry feed.

The sovereignty over the great economic resources of the adjacent ocean was so critical to Peru that its government prevented foreigners from exploiting these riches. In the 1960s and 1970s, the two-hundred-mile limit of Peru's oceanic sovereignty created many international crises because other countries (and the maritime law at the time) recognized a territorial limit of only six miles from the coast. Because of the abundant sea life in the Peru-Humboldt Current, commercial fishermen from countries such as Japan and the United States tried to harvest its abundant aquatic resources, but their boats were boarded by the Peruvian Navy, brought into port, and their crews detained until their infraction could be resolved. Later, the international "Law of the Sea" conference negotiated the size of this oceanic sovereignty, and now most nations of the world not only recognize Peru's control of a two-hundred-mile zone from its coast, but that of most countries with seacoasts.[3]

The only variation in the conditions that sustain this rainless coastal expanse of sand is the "El Niño-Southern Oscillation" (ENSO) effect. "El Niño" refers to "The Christ Child" in Spanish and is so called because it begins in December, a time celebrating the birth of Christ. At irregular intervals, the central Pacific warms, the current that flows eastward at the Equator deflecting the Peru-Humboldt Current to turn westward farther south than usual. This shift brings warm water from the Equator southward along the normally dry coast and produces devastating rains.

When I first learned about El Niño, its effect was said to be infrequent, and expected every twenty years or so. More recently, it has occurred much more often, and the resulting rains have washed away houses and settlements along the coast. Modern populations resiliently recover from these floods, but archaeological research has revealed that such events also devastated ancient societies and destroyed parts of their settlements and irrigation systems. Some societies never recovered and became some of the archaeological sites that dot the Peruvian Coast.

Besides providing a lesson in coastal geography and its link to the adjacent ocean, my flight to Ayacucho also enhanced my understanding of the relationship of the coastal desert to the neighboring highlands. That relationship became evident as the plane climbed higher and passed over the barren foothills along the western slopes of the Andes. Within this transitional zone, one can see tiny threads of water that feed the many rivers that transect the coastal desert. Their origin lies in the high Andes, flowing through deep gorges for most of their length. Where the rivers break out of the foothills, ancient populations used their water for irrigation, often tapping into them before they reached the relatively flat coastal desert. Today, as in antiquity, these irrigation systems provide coastal Peru with its water for agricultural land along its coastal rivers. In the past, such systems supported large populations that were foundational for the development of civilization. Even today, cities along the coast, such as Lima, still depend upon water coming from the Andes.

As the plane rose to pass over the highest portion of the westernmost range, the foothills dropped away, and the rugged peaks got closer. The Andes are the second-highest mountain range in the world, and although their elevation does not match that of the Himalayas, their peaks still look formidable from the air—most of them are stark, barren, and with no evidence of human activity (fig. 2.2).

It was early February and the highlands were in the midst of the rainy season. Unlike the desert coast, different factors influence the weather and climate in the Andes. From November through April, moisture-laden clouds come across the Amazon rainforest from the Atlantic Ocean, bringing heavy rains as they rise to go over the mountains. This weather

FIGURE 2.2. View of the Andes southeast of Lima. A seemingly hostile and difficult environment for humans, this landscape cradled the development of civilization beginning at least three thousand years ago.

pattern cloaks the Andes with heavy clouds during the rainy season, disrupting air traffic between Lima and highland cities and causing many delays and cancellations. As the heavy clouds move westward, less and less moisture remains, and as a result, those areas farther west receive much less rainfall than those farther east. By the time these air masses reach the coast, no moisture remains, leaving both the western foothills of the Andes and the coast rainless—a condition further enhanced by the effect of the Peru-Humboldt Current.

The plane flew in and out of fluffy white clouds with brief glimpses of the seemingly lifeless expanse of the high peaks and valleys. Even with modern aircraft and roads, this variegated topography isolates many parts of the Andes making them difficult to reach.

As we neared our destination and descended closer to the 9,000-foot altitude of Ayacucho, valleys with green crops appeared through gaps in the clouds, along with an occasional village. Finally, as the plane descended more steeply, I got a more sustained look at the broad expanse of a large valley (fig. 2.3).

This expanse was the Ayacucho Valley, a long, highly eroded basin that stretches northwest to southeast. In all of southern Peru, it is one of the

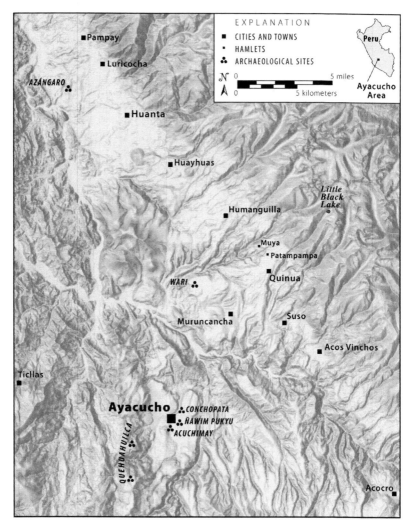

FIGURE 2.3. Map of the Ayacucho Valley showing the towns, archaeological sites, and other locations mentioned in the text. (Map by Chelsea M. Feeney)

few large valleys of relatively low (less than 11,000 feet about sea level) agricultural land located on its gentle slopes below the mountains and in the flood plain on the valley floor (fig. 2.4). Compared to other areas in the southern highlands, conditions here are ideal for maize, the most highly valued crop of native Andeans for many centuries. It can be stored for long periods of time and used for both food and drink. Both today and in antiquity, the valley's agricultural potential supported large, dense populations.

The valley is also an important travel corridor between the central and southern Andes, and from the central Andes to the coast. The highland road linking Lima, Huancayo, and Cusco goes through it, and it is a node for roads to the tropical forest to the east, and to the coast to the west and south. As the only large valley between Lima and the Inca capital of Cusco, it is roughly halfway between the two cities.

This critical position was not lost on Pizzaro and his troops because the first Spanish settlement in Peru outside of Lima and Cusco was established in the valley in 1539. During the early years of Spanish occupation, the puppet Inca ruler, Manco Inca, escaped to the mountains northwest of Cusco, raiding Indian groups allied with the Spanish and disrupting commercial travel.[4] To combat these difficulties and expand control along the highland route between Lima and Cusco, Pizarro directed Capt. Francisco de Cardenas to establish a permanent settlement intermediate between these two cities.[5] During the first few months of 1539, he founded the *Villa of San Juan de La Frontera de Huamanga* ("Village of Saint John of the Huamanga Frontier") on or near what is now the village of Quinua.[6] The settlement occupied a critical defensible position at the base of the steep northern slopes of the Ayacucho Valley, and was located high enough so that the Spanish troops had a commanding view of much of its extent (fig. 2.4). They "held out precariously" against Manco Inca and other local groups who supported the Inca cause until Pizarro sent Vasco Guevara and more soldiers to bolster the settlement's defense and establish Spanish control more firmly.[7]

The weather, however, did not agree with the Spanish, and their perception of the location's advantages lost out to the challenges of the rather miserable mud, fog, and cold of the rainy season.[8] This observation, made by the Spanish centuries ago, was confirmed by my own experience in Quinua, and proved to be a critical factor affecting my research. Rainy and cold weather turned out to be a significant constraint affecting the seasonality of pottery production not only in Quinua but, as I would come to see much later, in the remainder of the Andes and throughout the world.

In addition to the disagreeable climate, the Spanish soldiers were concerned that if war broke out with the local population, the deeply eroded gorges around Quinua would provide few avenues of escape.[9] Consequently, as early as April 25, 1540, the local ruling council in Quinua (the *cabildo*) acted to move the settlement to the floor of the valley to the

FIGURE 2.4. The central portion of the Ayacucho Valley from a position on the mountain above the village of Quinua showing the battlefield of Ayacucho in the bottom center of the image (the light area) and the lighter shapes of the houses of the central portion of the village of Quinua directly above it. The higher portion of the archaeological site of Wari lies in right center of the image, and the city of Ayacucho and its airport (the oblique white area) is seen in the center left of the image on the other side of the valley. The mountain Quehuahuilca is the highest peak on the other side of the valley and is located slightly to the right of center along the top of the mountain ridge.

southwest.[10] The actual change in location, however, may have occurred somewhat later because the official title of the new settlement (*San Juan de la Frontera de Huamanga*) and its status as a city were not granted until 1544. Out of this newly relocated community grew the modern city of Ayacucho.[11]

The new settlement possessed a number of distinct advantages over the original location across the valley. The elevation was lower, and the settlement was closer to good sources of water.[12] The Spanish found that the climate was moderate (neither hot nor cold) and more agreeable than that of Quinua. Further, the land was fertile and would permit rapid adaptation of the fruits and vegetables brought from their homeland.[13] They believed that these characteristics would aid in attracting and keeping new arrivals because a stable European population was necessary to counter the threat of local rebellion and neo-Inca raids.[14]

About a millennium before the Spanish, the valley supported a large population because of its abundant agricultural land and an irrigation technology that raised the elevation at which maize could be cultivated (see the next chapter). Cities developed here during the first few centuries AD, and eventually coalesced into the great urban center of Wari that ruled much of Peru from AD 650–1050 (figs. 2.3 and 2.4). Pottery and cloth made at Wari and at the Bolivian site at Tiahuanaco spread throughout much of the Central Andes at this time. Wari was a conquest state and may have introduced many administrative systems adopted later by the Incas.[15]

The Ayacucho Valley thus provided several key advantages for human populations and played a critical role in the history and prehistory of Peru. It was not just significant as a productive climate for maize cultivation, but it also was a critical location for pre-Hispanic, early Spanish, and colonial populations as well.

Our plane burst out of the clouds, and we had a spectacular view of the valley. As we saw major sections of its expanse for the first time, one of my colleagues shouted from the other side of the plane, "Wow! We're flying over a gigantic archaeological site! I wonder if it's Wari."

It was. An immense ruin, it lay in the middle of the valley. I could not see it from my side of the plane, but my view revealed other features of the Andean landscape. I could see some circular depressions that looked like they were internally terraced and noted the rich irrigated land in the flood plain in the bottom of the valley.

As we descended farther, I watched the lush river valley below get closer. The rainy season had swollen the river and filled it with the soil from erosion at higher elevations, tracing a web of different paths as it flooded the valley bottom with its creamy chocolate color. It would eventually reach the tropical forest in eastern Peru where it joined the Amazon, providing rich, fertile silt as it spilled over its banks and rejuvenated the fields of those living along its course. Ultimately, it would empty into the Atlantic Ocean some four thousand miles away.

We were still flying above the valley, and I glanced away for a moment— only to be greeted with a bump indicating that the plane had landed. The end of the airport runway in Ayacucho begins at the top of a cliff that rises several hundred feet above the valley floor, and for the unwary, sudden contact with *tierra firme*, still seemingly far below, was unnerving.

The plane taxied up to a small terminal building, and we descended the stairs to the barren ground that served as the tarmac. As we walked to the terminal, one of my colleagues yelled, "Hey, look at these sherds! We've landed on an archeological site!"

Doing an archaeological reconnaissance between the plane and the terminal seemed rather "over the top," something that only an archaeologist would do. But it was true! The dirt below our feet was littered with potsherds. It could only happen in places such as Peru where civilization had developed more than a millennium before, leaving massive traces of its ancient greatness. As I learned later, the Ayacucho airport was built on the only flat terrain nearby, and it happened to be an archaeological site that dated to the time of the early development of the Wari civilization.

Our professor, Dr. Zuidema, met us inside the terminal. We remarked about our experience flying over the valley and finding sherds on the tarmac. He told us that the immense site that we saw earlier was indeed Wari. Because learning about Peru, the Andes, and the Ayacucho region was our goal of working with Dr. Zuidema, he told us that we would be visiting Wari in a few days.

A JOURNEY INTO CULTURAL CONTRASTS

Doing fieldwork as participant-observer in the Andes is more than a review of Peruvian prehistory or living in a prehistorically significant location. It is more than visiting archaeological sites and seeing the stunning landscape of Peru. It involves engaging the local inhabitants of a place, their cultural heritage of foods, animals, and plants, and living in the high altitude in which the Incas and their predecessors lived. Whereas my flight to Ayacucho introduced me to the land, history, and prehistory of Peru, my first experience living there challenged my mind, my values, and my body. Learning to adjust to those challenges was an indispensable part of my journey into and through the Andes, and was also a journey into my cultural self.

Ayacucho was a relatively small and quiet urban center in 1967. The architecture of the place was stunning, and except for a few cars and trucks, its colonial heritage appeared to be unchanged for centuries.

Like most departmental capitals in Peru, Ayacucho had a tourist hotel, but it was too expensive for poor graduate students. So, we settled into another hotel near the central plaza. It had no obvious lobby on the street—only a narrow hall that led to the registration desk. The price was reasonable, and it served as our home for those first days until we could get settled.

Since we left Lima too early for breakfast, we were hungry, so we went down to the hotel's café. As with many hotels, its eating establishment was in front of the hotel and was open to the street. We sat at a table next to the street and watched the street life, noticing the waiters chasing away the beggars and stray dogs. Unlike their use as pets in North America, dogs in Peru were used principally for household security and garbage disposal. They had a different personality in Peru than back home and seemed to be more subservient and sheepish—mostly as the result of their owners' neglect. They were not fed but scavenged for whatever food they could find in the household and in the street. It was unclear whether the dogs had homes or not, but soon we learned that they were a problem. So, as we sat and ate, dogs would come by, whine, and pathetically beg for food. As they returned to the street, we watched one of them sniff again for food, but then collapse and die.

After watching this rather distressing event twice, we asked the waiters what was happening. They told us that the city fathers decided that there were too many dogs in the street, and they had instructed the street sweepers to put out poisoned food to dispose of them. Subsequently, we watched a street cleaner pick up one of the carcasses and put it in his cart, but hours passed before another was removed.

Some of these dogs may have been rabid. Fortunately, a physician at the University of Illinois Health Service had vaccinated me with an experimental rabies vaccine that had been restricted to students in the College of Veterinary Medicine who were at risk of contracting the disease. After learning that rabies was a health problem in Peru at the time, he strongly suggested that I should receive the vaccine to protect myself, and I consented.[16]

The dog situation, however, did not dampen my excitement about being in Ayacucho. I began to appreciate the charm of the place with its many churches, colonial buildings, and the drably dressed *campesinos* darting across its streets and plazas.

I spent a few days walking around Ayacucho enjoying its colonial past and its spacious central plaza. After the Spanish moved their settlement from Quinua to its present location across the valley, they laid out their new city in a grid pattern with a central plaza consisting of a park bordered by a cathedral and university on one side, and the municipal offices and a police post on another (fig. 2.5). The offices of the prefect (governor) for the Department of Ayacucho fronted the other side of the plaza with almost all of the buildings opening into a covered arcade that surrounded it.

FIGURE 2.5. The central plaza of Ayacucho in 1967. The front portion of the statue of General Sucre on his horse is partially obscured behind the palm tree on the right. The University of Huamanga occupies the building to the right of the cathedral.

In the center of the plaza, the city officials had erected a statue of General Sucre who was Simón Bolivar's general and led his troops to defeat those of the Spanish viceroy in 1824 in a decisive battle that forever broke the power of Spain in South America. Up to that point, the city of Ayacucho had been called Huamanga, its ancient name, but the conflict had occurred at a location across the valley where the Inca army had defeated the "ancient inhabitants of this part of the country called Pocras" about four hundred years before.[17] That battle left so many dead that the site was called the "corner of the dead," or "Ayacucho" in Quechua, and also gave its name to the battle fought there in 1824. Thereafter, the city changed its name to Ayacucho to commemorate the event. Nevertheless, many Peruvians simply refer to the city by its previous name, Huamanga.

Ayacucho's main plaza lies 9,000 feet above sea level. So, new arrivals from sea level may suffer the effects of altitude sickness, one of the physical challenges of living and working in highland Peru. Also known as hypoxia, altitude sickness results from the lesser amount of oxygen available at high altitudes. Although the symptoms are more intense at higher elevations, one still feels its effects in Ayacucho.

The main local antidote for this condition is *coca* tea.[18] Peruvians call it *mate de coca*, an infusion of the leaves of the coca plant in hot water. Used to make cocaine, a dangerous and addictive drug, the amount of the drug in one leaf is minuscule; a dried coca leaf contains 0.5–1.0 percent cocaine.[19] So, a leaf weighing 1.0 g would contain 0.005–0.01 g of cocaine. An infusion with a few leaves is sufficient to relieve a tourist's nausea and pounding headache.

Andeans have used coca leaves for millennia. Chewing it with slaked lime (calcium hydroxide) releases more of its active ingredients to produce a mild stimulant and anesthetic. These effects serve the highland natives well because it dulls their sense of tiredness and hunger as they trek along mountain trails.

The therapeutic value of coca tea for altitude sickness was one of the first things I learned in Ayacucho. Its taste was quite bitter, and not pleasant to drink. It was not a drink taken for pleasure or taste, but once ingested, the effect of the drug was immediate, settling the stomach and quelling a pounding headache.

Years later, when my wife and I lived in the Inca capital of Cusco, coca tea was a critical part of our medicinal arsenal. There was a time when I could not keep food or medicine down because of a splitting sinus headache. Coca tea alleviated the pain and allowed me to ingest both medicine and food without adverse consequences. On another occasion, I awoke in the middle of the night with a headache, a raw throat, and general malaise that interfered with sleeping. After five successive cups of coca tea with fresh leaves in each new cup, I returned to my bed and slept peacefully.

Only a few leaves are required for the therapeutic effect of the drug, and a small amount lasts a long time. It was also very inexpensive. At the beginning of my stay in Cusco five years later, I bought a handful of coca leaves at the market for about twenty U.S. cents, and nine months later, I still had a substantial amount that I gave away. The medicinal relief that I, my wife, and my father and mother (who had visited us) had received more than compensated for the small cost I had paid for the leaves.

Adapting to the culture of Ayacucho within a graduate student's budgetary limits brought other challenges. Staying in a cheap hotel gave me a new appreciation for the term "flea bag hotel." My first night in the hotel was troubled and sleepless. My body itched often, waking me with the impulse to scratch. At breakfast, I shared my ordeal with my roommate, Tom Myers, another graduate student from Illinois. He replied that the bed probably harbored fleas. Mattresses were made of wool, and fleas infested the wool either from the sheep themselves, from the people who processed the wool, or from those who had previously slept on my mattress. Tom suggested that I should complain to the management and get the mattress switched. I did, and two men showed up at our room to remove the mattress. Since Tom doubted that it would actually be changed, he suggested that I accompany the men downstairs to be sure that they actually replaced it with another rather than bring the same one back. I watched as they took another mattress from the storeroom and brought it to our room. They made the bed, and I looked forward to a pleasant sleep that night. Instead, I experienced a reprise of the night before—more itching and interrupted rest.

Conferring with Tom the next day, we decided that fleas probably infested all of the mattresses in the storeroom so that changing the mattress repeatedly was futile. Instead, he suggested another approach.

He had tangled with fleas himself on a previous trip to Peru, and suggested that I should buy a small metal container of the very potent insecticide DDT, punch two holes in the side, and squeeze it to expel the dust. I did as he said and rubbed down my entire body with the powder before I turned in for the night.

It was now the third night in our hotel, and I had already endured two miserable, sleep-deprived nights. Fortunately, that night I slept peacefully and woke up the next morning refreshed and eager to meet the new day. As I rolled out of bed, I pulled the covers back, and noticed the white power of the pesticide in the crumpled sheets. As I smoothed out the sheets, I was astounded by the number of tiny black specks sprinkled throughout the powder. Upon closer examination, I realized that they were dead fleas, hundreds of them—embedded in the powder hidden in the folds of the bed linen.

After that, I was always on the lookout for the pests, but fortunately, they never invaded my sleeping bag with its wool liner. If they did, I was ready for them. But, throughout my entire six-month stay in Peru, they never bothered me again, and I ended up giving away the remaining DDT in my small personal container.

At the time, I was unaware of the long-term effects of DDT on the environment, and its adverse effects on the food chain, even though five years earlier, Rachel Carson had exposed its dangers in her path-breaking book, *The Silent Spring*, in which she described the occurrence of the pesticide in human blood and on vegetables in supermarkets.[20] DDT was eventually banned in the United States and, with some exceptions, in most of the world.[21] Its persistence on my unbathed body and my sleeping bag was perhaps more responsible for keeping fleas off of me throughout my Andean journey than I thought.

Another challenge to my cultural values awaited me in the streets of the city. I had never thought much about the American value of privacy associated with one of humans' most basic activities. I frequently walked down side streets in Ayacucho and came upon peasant women squatting with their layers of skirts spread out around them. This behavior seemed rather strange because I had seen women squatting in Yucatán to tend the hearth, feed a child, or simply relax, but never saw them squatting on the street in this particular fashion. Before squatting to perform their daily tasks around the house, Maya women reached between their legs taking the bottom rear of their mid-calf-length white *huipil*, pulling it up between their legs, and tucking it into the waistband in the front. The result was almost a full-length white covering of their upper legs, but it kept their *huipil* clean.

The squatting Ayacucho *campesinas*, however, were different. Their full skirts were usually brown, dark blue, or black, and as they squatted, their skirts touched the ground around them. Not only did it seem unusual to me, but it exposed the skirt to the dirt on the street. I wondered why.

The explanation was not long in coming. As I walked along a street and casually approached a squatting woman, she rose to her feet and moved on. Curiosity prompted me to look at the spot where she had positioned herself, and I noticed that she had left behind something that had not been there previously. I never did get used to this behavior, but I eventually understood it because there were no public toilets in Andean communities.

A GREAT PRE-INCA CITY

The Incas are lauded for their great accomplishments in the early fifteenth century with their pan-Andean empire. However, many of these accomplishments were achieved more than five hundred years earlier during the Wari Empire. An immense archaeological site called Wari in the middle of the Ayacucho Valley is believed to be the remains of its capital (figs. 2.3 and 2.4).

Wari was a critical site for understanding Peruvian prehistory, but, more important for me, it was the source of a number of polychrome pottery styles that were widely distributed in the Andes during Wari dominance. Some

of these styles were unique to Wari, but others had emerged in other locations in the valley prior to Wari political and economic dominance. Some
revealed the influence of Nazca pottery from the south coast of Peru. One
of my research questions concerned whether the polychrome styles made in
the modern community of Quinua on the slopes of the valley above the
ancient city had developed from Wari pottery. Could the makers of modern
Quinua pottery be descendants of Wari potters? Could some of the Wari
styles have been made up the slope nearer to Quinua? A visit to the ancient
city of Wari was critical for my research. So, several days after we arrived in
Ayacucho, Professor Zuidema took us to see its ruins. It was relatively close
to Ayacucho, and we could visit the site and return easily within one day.

We left Ayacucho and descended into the river valley that we saw on
our incoming flight, and observed firsthand the detail of the dryness of
the bottom of the valley. The only vegetation was various species of cactus
and *molle* trees, a native species that thrives in these dry valleys. Its tiny red
fruits can be made into an alcoholic beer called *chicha*. When the fruits
mature and dry, they are ground to make Peruvian yellow pepper—a use
that accounts for the tree's common name, the pepper tree.

When we finally reached the level of the river at the absolute bottom
of the valley, we could see the chocolate-colored water with suspended
clays and soils eroded from land on the slopes of the valley. The rains were
heavy that year and the roads were partially washed out in places. To get
to Wari, we needed to cross the river, but the bridge across it seemed precarious because the swift current had eroded the soil around its abutments.
We crossed the bridge anyway, and on the other side, the road ascended
with curves and zigzags until we reached a relatively flat area near a hamlet
called Muruncancha (fig. 2.3).

At the time, there was no road into the ruins of Wari. So, Dr. Zuidema
turned onto a dirt track on the uphill side of Muruncancha and drove as
far as he could. He parked there and we walked west toward a large rock
outcrop. On the other side, the city center of Wari stretched out on a plateau that sloped gently toward the river in the valley below.

Wari was a giant city during its dominance from AD 650–1050. Estimates of its size vary, but some archaeologists believe that as many as fifteen
to thirty thousand people lived there (a small number by today's standards,
but a major population center during its time). Archaeological surveys of
the city and its environs reveal occupation that stretched far beyond the
city's core visible today.[22] Located at the approximate geographic center of
the valley, it was surrounded by excellent agricultural land in the flood plain

below and on the gentle slopes of the upper portion of the valley. Water was probably supplied to the city by a large canal filled from smaller canals diverted from streams at higher elevations.

Wari also was the center of an empire that included much of the central and southern parts of Peru. Evidence of its influence comes from the distribution of its pottery styles[23] and well-planned and organized sites located hundreds of miles away, such as Pikillacta near Cusco in southern Peru and Viracocha Pampa near Cajamarca in northern Peru (fig. 2.1).[24] The fortunes of Wari, however, appeared to have shifted with abrupt changes in climate. As the southern Andes became wetter than it is today and then drier again, decreasing amounts of productive agricultural land and reduced food security may have contributed to Wari's demise because of its inability to adapt to changing climate.[25]

No city is located on or near Wari today, and some of the factors that contributed to its greatness in prehistory are no longer present. Nevertheless, its position in the Ayacucho Valley was critical. So, although there is no occupation on the site today, its modern counterpart is the city of Ayacucho. The co-occurrence of a center of a great pre-Inca capital, the location of the first Spanish settlement in Peru after Lima and Cusco, the site of the Battle of Ayacucho, and the modern city of Ayacucho further affirms that the valley lies in a critical location in the south-central Andes.

Although I did not know it at the time, the road from the city of Ayacucho to its namesake battlefield would be relocated later and go through the center of Wari. Traveling on this road eleven years later, I could see steep sides around the plateau on which Wari sits. This topography protected the city from attack from the valley below, and a wall protected its uphill side separating its main core from a suburban occupation farther up the slope.

Wari was vast, and even though this was the rainy season, it was very hot. Above us, on the higher slopes of the valley, we could see the horizontal zones of vegetation that corresponded to changing elevations (fig. 2.6). Higher zones receive more rainfall but are colder. As the elevation decreases, rainfall decreases as well, but the temperature and the amount of sunshine increases. The bottoms of the valleys are warmer and drier because they lie in the rain shadow from the moisture-laden clouds coming from the east during the rainy season.

All of these factors influence agricultural potential. Wari was near the bottom of the valley, but above the river and its flood plain. During the rainy season, it thus receives little rain, and it is often sunny. It is too dry to grow maize and most other crops there, but some locals plant some wheat and

FIGURE 2.6. View of the Quinua area from the pre-Inca site of Wari. In 1967, almost all potters in Quinua lived in a dispersed settlement pattern in the area below the dark vegetation on the lower slope of the mountains, from approximately the upper center of the image upward and on the right side of the deep canyon visible here.

the Andean grain *quinoa* there during the rainy season. In the flood plain below, however, the alluvial soil, warmer temperatures, and irrigation water from the river created excellent agricultural potential, especially for maize.

Even though Wari lies near the bottom of the valley, the elevation of the city ranges from 8,500 to 9,500 feet above sea level. At that elevation, humans are exposed to the direct rays of the sun unfiltered by the thinner atmosphere above.

We had purchased felt hats to protect us from the sun. Hats, however, were part of the ethnic markers of the indigenous Quechua-speaking peasants. The people of the Andes, like those in some other parts of Latin America, mix the categories of race and class. Those who speak Indian languages and dress in an ethnic indigenous style with hats are often derided as peasants (*campesinos*) or Indians (*indios*). In the Peruvian Andes, the ethnic markers of clothing and language are also class symbols, and those who wear them are regarded as lower class. We initially wore hats, but locals told us that we looked like lower-class peasants. So, we only used our hats when we were exploring archaeological sites.

After we wandered around Wari, we got hungry and very thirsty. Unfortunately, we did not think ahead to bring food or drink, but noticed that nopal cactus covered the site, and its orange-red fruit was ripe. If we could get close enough to detach it without being impaled on the spines of the stems and leaves, and then remove the skin, we were rewarded with a delicious, succulent, and refreshing snack that tasted a bit like papaya. The trick was to remove the tiny spines, but the only way to do that was to peel the fruit. Unfortunately, only one of us had a pocketknife.

Our appetite tempted us to bite into the fruit after rubbing off the spines on our clothes before the skin was removed. Such impatience brought uncomfortable consequences because we were unable to remove all of the spines using that technique, and some of them always lodged on our tongues. They did not hurt, but they were annoying. Normal eating and chewing were the only way to eliminate them, and eventually they wore away and disappeared. In the meantime, eating with tiny spines in your tongue was a nuisance we had to endure.

Broken potsherds littered the surface of Wari with the fragments of pottery styles that were presumably made there during the hundreds of years of its occupation. Like the many potsherds that we observed on the tarmac at the Ayacucho airport, the inhabitants of Wari used pottery extensively. Just as archaeologist Dorothy Menzel found years earlier,[26] examining some of the Wari pottery in the storerooms of the Department of Archaeology in the University in Ayacucho revealed the complexity of the styles and their abundance. Why was pottery making so productive in Wari, and what happened to the craft after Wari's demise? These questions ultimately ended up stimulating some of my research in the valley to which I was able to provide some answers.

The trip to Wari was awe inspiring, even though there was not a lot to see. Its extent was astounding and required more than half a day even to begin to explore it. Even with our limited trek around it, I was left with a great appreciation of its vast geographic extent, its large population, and its strategic location.

AN UNEXPECTED TURN OF EVENTS

Wari didn't develop in isolation but appears to have resulted from the consolidation of populations of several earlier ancient settlements, a few of which lay on the outskirts of the city of Ayacucho. So, early in my stay in Ayacucho, Tom Myers and I decided to visit some of them.

One, Acuchimay, lies on a hill south of the city (fig. 2.3). Walking to the edge of the city, we climbed up the streets, and where they ended we struck out on our own and proceeded to the top of the hill. At that time, Acuchimay had a large cross on its summit, and when we got there we had a stunning view of the city. Unfortunately, little remained of the archaeological site except for some pottery that dated to the period right before the rise of the great city of Wari.

Since we had read the few archaeological reports about the Ayacucho area, we knew that there were two other archaeological sites beyond Acuchimay to the east of the city. One of these, Conchopata, lay under the airport, but we decided it was not wise to go poking around on the periphery of the airport because we would probably raise suspicion of the police and the military. Instead, we decided to trek beyond it to the site of Ñawim Pukyu, a site located on the slope of a hill that faced the city of Ayacucho (fig. 2.3).

On our way there, we came to a large house of a landed estate (a *hacienda*). As we approached the gate, we were invited inside to what seemed to be a party. We entered and stood around not really knowing what to do. In one room, several potters were making pottery. In the patio, a local musical group played music in an Andean style called the *huayno*, and soon the dancing started. Someone encouraged us to dance, and we did. Trying to learn how to dance the huayno at the elevation of Ayacucho, however, was exhausting and challenging to those of us who were new arrivals to the city.

All of those present were Peruvians, but some were dressed in a way that indicated that they were from the middle and upper classes. Soon, we were served some appetizers and drinks, and then were ushered into a room for a sit-down dinner.

Shortly thereafter, we heard great commotion and arguing in the next room. We had already sat down and started to eat when someone came and asked us who we were and why we were there. We explained that we had been invited into the hacienda as we were walking to the nearby site of Ñawim Pukyu.

We then discovered that we had come upon an event that the owner had put together for Peruvian tourists, and each had paid a hefty fee to eat, dance, and see potters at work at a hacienda in a rural setting. When they realized that two of their paying guests had been excluded from the meal when the places at the table had been carefully counted and set, the paying guests complained, and began to argue with the host.

This experience was another example of cultural misperception. We thought that the people of the hacienda were being hospitable, but they thought we were rich. How was it that we seemingly appeared "out of nowhere" if we had not come with the tour group? There was seemingly no other way to get to the hacienda except in a vehicle, and for tourists, it was too far from Ayacucho to walk there. Since we were obviously North Americans, they probably thought it unlikely that we would have walked there. So, they reasoned, we must have arrived with the tour group.

When they discovered who we were, they asked us to pay or leave. So, we left the hacienda, decided not to go to the archaeological site of Ñawim Pukyu, and instead walked back to Ayacucho talking about the cross-cultural misunderstanding.

CHAPTER 3

The Challenges of Rural Life

ONE OF THE INEVITABLE CHALLENGES of field research is the need to modify one's research design and goals given the realities of the local context. No matter how carefully one's proposal is prepared, making it work in the actual field context usually requires changes. Sometimes, these changes may result from simple logistics such as finding a place to live and obtaining food, to say nothing of evaluating the feasibility of the research in the actual field situation. Such challenges were the realities of my field-work in the Ayacucho Valley.

After a week in Ayacucho, Dr. Zuidema deemed that it was time to take us to our field sites and begin our research. I had already changed my proposal from exploring the different cultural and demographic influences found in the pottery of the valley to comparing actual pottery production among different communities. I knew that several communities made pottery and I wanted to study and compare them, analyze their raw materials, and determine whether it was possible to identify the pottery from those communities by the shape and style of the finished vessels and by the raw materials they used. Early in my stay, however, I visited a section of the city of Ayacucho that reportedly made pottery, but none was being made at the time, and when it was, few vessels were produced. Although I did obtain some data by interview, the results were disappointing and discouraging.

Dr. Zuidema, however, thought that the study of pottery making in the community of Quinua merited its own intensive study and should be my focus. Quinua pottery was so complex and distinct from that made in other communities in the valley that he believed I should just study the craft in Quinua.

Studying Quinua pottery was important for another reason. Quinua was only two miles up the slope from the ancient site of Wari that we had recently visited (fig. 2.6). Wari was the center of a great pre-Inca state that dominated the central and southern parts of Peru between AD 650 and AD 1050. It is an enormous urban complex consisting of an urban core of 250 hectares with extensive occupational debris covering an area of 15–18 km^2 (9.3–11.2 square miles). Population estimates of the city vary from a low of 10,000 to 20,000 to a high of 35,000 to 70,000. Ceramics reached a high point of development during this time when the valley was the source of a number of complex, unique, and highly specialized ceramic styles that utilized a wide repertoire of shapes, slips, and paints. Many of these styles presumably were produced in Wari and were associated with extensive state-constructed administrative facilities that included temples, storehouses, barrack-like quarters, and community kitchens.[1]

Wari also exported central planning and monumental architecture to planned centers in widely separated parts of Peru, indicating that it had developed a centralized administration for the collection and distribution of goods. For about four hundred years, it was the economic, political, and religious center of a vast Andean state that conquered territory, conducted trade, and probably extracted tribute from widespread regions of highland and coastal Peru.[2]

By the close of the first part (Epoch I, about AD 750) of Wari domination, settlement patterns in the Ayacucho Valley had shifted. Settlements in the northern, central, and southern parts of the valley were either abandoned or significantly depopulated, with much of the population concentrated in Wari, located in a vast area two to four miles down the slope from present-day Quinua (fig. 2.6).[3]

Later, the city of Wari was remodeled and immense walls were constructed to enclose architectural complexes. Trapezoids and elongated triangles seem to have been the preferred building shapes. In one instance, a large wall was erected across the site as an isolated unit.[4]

The distribution of Wari pottery reached its greatest extent during this time, and planned administrative facilities were constructed at Azángaro,[5] a site in the northern part of the valley that we visited with Professor Zuidema. During the early portion of this period, Wari-influenced pottery styles developed elsewhere in Peru, suggesting more cosmopolitan and diverse population centers that reflected the integration of diverse constituencies. One of these centers emerged at Pachacamac and produced pottery that diluted the Wari stylistic influence on the central coast, while a separate center and associated pottery style (the Atarco style) developed in the Nazca Valley on the South Coast.[6]

About AD 1050, the city of Wari was abandoned and large urban settlements in the Ayacucho Valley ended. No large amounts of fancy pottery were made in the valley thereafter, and centralized political power believed to be responsible for producing and distributing it disappeared along with the large, dense populations. No large cities arose in the valley again until the emergence of the city of Huamanga (Ayacucho) during the Spanish colonial period.[7]

Although the central portion of Wari lies three miles down the slope from the village of Quinua, many potters live much closer to the ancient urban complex than to Quinua itself. Most inhabit the rural area below the village center, and Dr. Zuidema suspected that the complex pottery made in modern Quinua somehow might be linked historically to ceramic production in ancient Wari. Some potters resided less than a mile from the urban core with only a large ravine separating them from the architectural center of the city (see fig. 2.6). Given the great size of the Wari archaeological zone, it is quite possible that some modern potters now live on what was once the edge of the ancient city.

Since ceramic production, like all technology, is socially embedded and transmitted, the geographical proximity of modern potters to the ancient city of Wari made a historical connection seem likely. Nevertheless, it was not possible to find the link between the pottery of modern Quinua and that of Wari without intensive survey and excavation in the areas between them.

Early in my research it became clear that Quinua pottery was unique in the Ayacucho Valley primarily because it was elaborately decorated. Observation revealed that vessels were painted in three different decorative schemes. Some of these vessels were placed on the tops of houses (fig. 3.1) as a tradition, potters said, and others were used in the celebration of local rituals, as well as for storing, carrying, and serving food, water, and other liquids (such as maize beer [chicha]).

Ultimately, the possible link between potters in Quinua and those in ancient Wari was less interesting to me than more general questions: Why was Quinua pottery so complex and unique? Why did elaborate pottery production evolve here and not elsewhere in Peru? Why was such elaborate pottery made in ancient Wari *and* in modern Quinua? Although the

FIGURE 3.1. A rural Quinua potter (Isak Sanchez) in front of his house. A ceramic figure is placed on the top of the roof.

answers to these questions were certainly relevant to Peruvian prehistory, they transcended cultural historical explanations that were limited to the Central Andes.

Another reason for studying pottery making in Quinua was more practical. Dr. Zuidema said that another anthropologist (William P. Mitchell) was working there on a very different project, and he thought I might be able to stay with him during my research there.

So, Dr. Zuidema took me to Quinua to see Mitchell, who occupied the second floor of a house there. During our conversation, Mitchell kindly offered me space to put my sleeping bag. The prospect of having my need for shelter met so easily was too good to refuse.

So, after my return to Ayacucho, I assembled my gear and hitched a ride on the back of a truck that delivered me up the eastern side of the valley to the Plaza of Quinua (fig. 3.2). Bill graciously welcomed me, and I inflated my air mattress, unrolled my sleeping bag in a corner near the door, and settled into my new abode. Thus, Quinua became my research site, and a corner of one of Bill's rooms became my home away from home.

With my research site and research topic radically changed, I set about studying pottery production in Quinua. Basic description seemed like a good place to begin, but much to my frustration, I soon discovered that most, if not all, potters were not presently making pottery. I had arrived in

FIGURE 3.2. The plaza of the village of Quinua in 1967.

the midst of the rainy season. Travel was difficult because of the rain and mud. Rain fell almost every day, turning streets into seas of mud that stuck to my boots like glue and made walking along narrow mountain paths an experience comparable only to mud wrestling. Slipping and sliding my way through the community was a frustrating experience. There was little sunshine; fog and mist often blanketed the area during the day, making my treks through the community depressing. The rain also caused frequent landslides, cutting Quinua off from bus and truck traffic to and from the city of Ayacucho and frustrating my attempts to obtain supplies and mail.

It was not the amount or the intensity of the rainfall that was important, but rather the number of days with rain, cool temperatures, and fog. The moisture from fog and rainfall drove the relative humidity so high that raw clay, the fuel for firing, and the newly formed vessels could not dry. The lack of the radiant energy from the sun further hindered drying because of overcast skies. Any pottery that was made during the rainy season risked damage from leaking roofs, and from very restricted indoor space that may compete with activities of household members and careless children and adults. The weather in Quinua thus made pottery production extremely difficult, if not impossible, and few, if any, vessels were made during the rainy season. Those that *were* made could not be fired.

It seemed that it rained almost every day during the first two months of my stay in Quinua, and this perception was borne out by the meteorological data from the weather station in Ayacucho across the valley to southwest. Ayacucho is lower in altitude and drier than Quinua, and during both February and March 1967, the rainfall data from the city of Ayacucho showed that there were only two days without rain.[8]

I took some comfort from the fact that the Spanish conquerors had also found the rainy season miserable. After founding the first settlement in the valley on or near the present site of Quinua in January 1539, they decided to abandon it fifteen months later, moving it to a lower and warmer location across the valley, citing the disagreeable climate as a reason.

Fortunately, Mitchell's principal informant, Mamerto, was a potter. Unlike most potters who were also agriculturalists and made pots only in the dry season, Mamerto worked most of the year as a potter-teacher in the local, government-run Artisan School, a facility that provided hands-on training for young people who wanted to learn how to make pottery. During the summer vacation (the rainy season of January–March), however, he made pottery in a large empty room in his house in order to make extra money. He was not able to make very much, and even though the large room could accommodate many vessels that were drying, he still had to wait until April to completely dry and fire them. Since there were times that Mamerto was otherwise unoccupied, Bill suggested I could observe Mamerto making pottery.

Visits to households of other potters in the community during this time did not yield much data until late March and early April and even then, few potters were practicing their craft. Furthermore, most potters were also peasant farmers and needed to work in the fields during the rainy season, a period of heavy labor demand. Most did not begin making pottery until the harvest was completed in late June which was just before I was scheduled to leave the field. Nevertheless, Mamerto, with income as a teacher, was less dependent on farming and was able to take me to visit a few potters, even though they were not making pottery, and visit some of the sources of raw materials.

The early part of my research in Quinua thus was a time of great frustration because the weather and climate radically affected my strategy for researching ceramic production. Few observations of pottery making were made and, to put it mildly, I was very disappointed. For years afterward I felt that my research in Quinua was a failure because of my inability to gather abundant data on pottery manufacture.

The frustration with the climate in Quinua and the relative dearth of production data collected in the early weeks of my fieldwork led me away from focusing on the actual production of pottery. Instead, I went to the stores and markets in Quinua and Ayacucho to see if pottery was being offered for sale, and I inventoried the vessels there, photographing them or copying their designs.

Even so, the daily rains and fog were isolating, forcing Bill and me to remain in our room for much of the day. As a consequence, life was dull, particularly in the evenings. Hardly anyone ventured out after dark. It was cold and wet outside, and dark inside. Bill had purchased several candles and kerosene lamps, but they gave only rudimentary light. The town did have electricity, but only for three hours in the evening. The wall switch was always left in the "on" position, so that at six o'clock, the single bulb in the ceiling of the room began to glow faintly as the generator began to feed power into the line, reaching peak illumination anywhere from thirty to forty-five minutes later. At nine o'clock, the light would gradually dim and then cease altogether.

The dim glow of the single, bare bulb provided little comfort from the cold and rain outside, and there was little to occupy ourselves at night.

Bill owned a battery-operated short-wave radio and kept a supply of Peruvian brandy, called *Pisco*, on hand. Drinking a little Pisco and listening to the BBC were our most exciting evening activities. I found the Pisco too strong and did not find the experience pleasurable, so I had to satisfy myself with the BBC.

Bill had developed a good relationship with his principal informant, Mamerto, who lived downstairs, and almost every evening we would hear his feet on the concrete stairs with a subsequent knock on the door. Bill always graciously invited him inside for some Pisco and conversation that provided interesting information about Quinua. Bill already knew some Quechua, and Mamerto knew some Spanish, so he provided a distraction and a diversion from otherwise lifeless evenings. Unlike my experience in Yucatán, where I had learned some Yucatec Maya, I had no knowledge of Quechua, and Mamerto's limited Spanish proved frustrating to me. Nevertheless, he was well intentioned and interesting, and Bill appreciated and welcomed his presence.

My interactions with Mamerto stimulated my desire to learn some Quechua. Early in my stay, my student colleagues and I realized that we needed to learn Quechua. I had successfully learned enough Spanish and enough Yucatec Maya in Mexico to describe the pottery-making process, but learning those languages was based upon social interaction. In Quinua, however, I had limited contact with potters except for my principal informant, Mamerto, and most others would not even respond to my queries: "How do you say?" in Spanish. Even so, I realized that learning Quechua would be important for my study of pottery making in Quinua.

So, my Illinois colleagues and I hired a tutor who was the informant for a pedagogical grammar called "Spoken Quechua" compiled by a local missionary. The tutorials were infrequent, but I didn't have the day-to-day exposure to Quechua in order to really learn the language. Further, Quechua uses a lot of infixes between the suffixes attached to the end of lexical items and this feature made learning the language difficult. I traveled to Ayacucho for the tutorials, but eventually, the tutorials ended, and I did not learn much Quechua, preferring to work in Spanish instead.

ENCOUNTERING THE LOCAL CULTURE

When we think about the Incas and other Andean civilizations in our culture's popular imagination, we marvel at their technical and organizational accomplishments, but seldom consider the ordinary activities of the common people that lived under their domination. Reading about them in our comfortable offices and living rooms, we rarely think about the daily activities of cooking, eating, washing, and toilet habits. How did they go to the toilet? Dispose of human waste? In rural communities like Quinua, many of these everyday activities have changed little from the time of the Incas and their predecessors. Women, for example, still cook food in pots, often ceramic, balanced over three stones encircling a small fire. In entering into their lives as participant-observers, we thus face a reality that readers of Inca life can never experience from the comfort of their own culture. Entering into the local culture experientially challenged my values and preconceptions about food, cleanliness, illness, and basic bodily functions in often unpleasant ways.

For those of us who are used to hot and cold running water, and generally gleaming restroom facilities, we seldom, if ever, think that many people in the world live without them. Rather, the excitement of foreign travel, often fostered by travel brochures, can entice us with the illusion that a strange land doesn't lack the amenities of a clean bed, attractive and pleasant food, and clean restrooms provisioned with toilet paper and hot and cold running water. This manufactured allure can be so compelling that we don't think about the interrelated issues of local food and health except perhaps as a result of an occasional bout with Montezuma's Revenge.

Dealing with illness is always annoying but growing up in the American Midwest in the mid-twentieth century, before the internet and other global sources of information, I didn't think at all of the serious and often foodborne illnesses common in the poor areas of the world. I dreamed mostly of the exotic beauty of other lands. Living in Quinua, however, I was soon forced to face the reality of sometimes debilitating illnesses, often caused by poor sanitation.

Although travelers are usually wary about drinking local water, they are often unprepared for the lack of running water and the absence of what most people in the United States consider basic bathing and toilet facilities. Living in rural South Dakota, my grandmother had an outhouse until I was nearly a teenager, and water was delivered to her kitchen in a bucket from a hand pump. So, even though I had nearly forgotten my experiences with my grandmother's outhouse (and its dual-purpose Sear's catalogues), limited toilet facilities and lack of running water were not strange or unusual to me.

Living and working in another society obviously involves different foods, but our perceptions of them usually are hopelessly tainted by our home experiences of the sanitized local ethnic restaurants found throughout the United States—exotic and different, but clean and regularly inspected by local health departments.

I had already done some anthropological research as a participant-observer in Mexico and faced some of the challenges of disease, but I ate fruit from the market for breakfast and often was invited to my Maya informants' houses for lunch. The local cuisine was delicious, and the fare varied. The table and setting were sometimes outside where stains, mess, and flies were common, but the dishes were clean and the food fresh and well cooked. I never got sick from eating in such circumstances.

At other times when I did not eat with my Maya informants, I ate at a restaurant in the center of town, however, the impact on my health sometimes left much to be desired even though the restaurant appeared to be clean, tidy, and took my American Express Card. Being infected with roundworms, even though easy to cure, was an unanticipated consequence of eating there. Once I stopped eating in the restaurant, and ate lunch only with my informants, my health improved. Appearances of cleanliness, or the lack thereof, can be deceptive.

I was used to dirt and less-than-desirable eating contexts. Growing up, I had regularly worked for my entrepreneur father who, among other activities, sold bedding plants, gardened, and repaired his buildings—painting, tarring roofs, pouring cement, and laying cement blocks. I tore down an old house next door board-by-board with decades of dust and dirt so that he could build a greenhouse with the salvaged lumber. Dirt was a constant presence, as it was when I worked on a construction crew one summer. Lunch was often eaten on the job site, and often in dirty surroundings that were less than pleasant, but it was what the job required.

In Mexico, studying pottery making as a participant-observer involved constant exposure to dirt, sweat, and excessive heat. Visiting sources of clay and temper involved crawling inside mines that left imprints on my clothes and body. Learning to fire pottery was exhausting, with exposure to one-thousand-degree heat of a kiln combined with the humidity and heat of the day. Not included were the carbon and slivers from the wood that impaled themselves in my hands and the clay from pots and ashes from inside and outside the kiln that soiled my body and clothing.

Living in a village in highland Peru was different from my experiences in Mexico, and I soon realized that among its greatest challenges was obtaining basic necessities such as food and staying healthy. Although Quinua was on the main road between Ayacucho and the tropical forest to the east, there was no daily market in the late 1960s, and no restaurant. Obtaining food was a problem.

Lodging arrangements in Bill's large room were quite comfortable with my sleeping bag on his floor, but other details of living were a challenge. I still needed to eat. So, I bought a primus stove fueled by kerosene and tried to cook my own food. Fortunately, I had the foresight to bring a pressure cooker from home knowing that I would be living far above sea level. Water boils at a lower temperature at high altitudes, and in places like the Andes, it is possible to heat the food without fully cooking it and boil the water without purifying it.

One doesn't usually think about the consequences of high altitudes on cooking, but one must be aware of them if you want to prepare your own food. Such a reality was brought home to me again several years later when my wife and I lived in Cusco, the ancient Inca capital. She tried to replicate a delicious coffee cake from a recipe that she mastered when we lived in Pennsylvania. She did not adjust the amount of baking powder for the 11,000-foot elevation of the city, so rather than baking, the batter boiled over in our small oven. She eventually learned how much to reduce the baking powder in order to compensate for the altitude.

I could not buy fresh food in Quinua except in the Sunday market, and even then, many foods were unavailable. Even ordinary Andean tubers were not present. Because everyone grew them, each family had its own supply, and no one sold them in the local market. There were one or two stores in Quinua where I could purchase crackers, cookies, and even Australian canned butter. Predictably, the shelves were also filled with tins of tuna and sardines from the Peruvian fishing industry that harvested the riches of the Peru-Humboldt Current off the coast. But the crackers, tuna, sardines, and butter were not attractive fare for me, and the inventory of the stores was not diverse or complete enough to sustain me over the length of my stay. So, I decided to cook for myself. If I wanted to cook and wanted diversity in my diet, I needed to travel to Ayacucho to buy my food, and my cheapest choices were local crops.

In addition to plants that the Spanish imported from Europe, such as wheat, barley, oats, and fava beans, Andeans grow a variety of other crops that have sustained them for millennia. Potatoes, for example, have an Andean origin in spite of their association with Idaho and Ireland. Introduced into Europe by the Spanish, the potato became an important crop in northern Europe where the cool and wet climate approximated that of the Andes, and where grains, such as wheat, barley, and oats, with their origin in the Middle East, did not always mature because of the damp, cold, and cloudy climate.

The potato, however, is not the only native root crop grown in the Andes. A variety of other tubers, such as *oca*, *añu/mashwa*, and *ullucu* (*papas lisas*), are also grown and are delicious fare, but they are unknown outside of the Andes.

Whether one uses scientific or folk classifications, the potato has hundreds of wild and domestic varieties that vary from region to region within Peru. Such great varietal heterogeneity indicates that the Andes was where it was first cultivated because of the amount of time required for it to evolve into its many wild and domesticated relatives. These criteria are generally true for every domesticated plant, and were first noted by cultural geographer Carl Sauer many decades ago.

Wild potatoes were everywhere, and when I later lived in Cusco, I spotted a wild variety growing as a weed in a university flowerbed. On an excursion above the city on another occasion, I saw tiny plants of wild potatoes growing next to a field of a cultivated variety, creating the potential for endless evolutionary variation because of cross-pollination. Such accidental hybridization in antiquity, and subsequent selection by humans, meant that the potato is probably one of the most dynamic, and the most adaptive, of all Andean crops growing in a wide range of environments.

Whereas I came to realize the extensive variety of potatoes of different sizes, colors, and shapes, I failed to realize that these varieties also possess varying qualities for cooking. Unlike North America, where the two common varieties of potatoes ("red" and "white") are interchangeable, Andean varieties are not. At home, a red potato can be substituted for a white variety without adverse consequences, but not in the Andes.

The complications of such a seemingly endless smorgasbord of varieties became evident when I tried to cook them on my small kerosene stove. I needed to travel to Ayacucho to buy fresh food, and potatoes seemed like an obvious choice. When I went to the potato section of the market there, I was not just confronted with the red and white varieties that I knew from supermarkets in the United States at that time, but at least sixty different varieties lay before me—each in a bin two feet squared juxtaposed on each of four long tables. Such an assortment made choosing a type for cooking confusing and difficult. I did not know how to select the appropriate kind.

Rather than asking someone which variety might be best, I chose one that seemed to be a reasonable size. In retrospect, however, even if I had asked, sellers were usually monolingual in Quechua, the indigenous language of this part of the Andes, and they probably did not have enough facility in Spanish to explain the preferred types to me. It did not matter to me at the time because I naively thought that all potatoes were the same, but that bigger ones were better than small ones. Nevertheless, I obtained enough potatoes and other produce for a week, returned to Quinua, and looked forward to cooking some of my purchases for lunch the next day.

Before midday, I put the tubers into my pressure cooker and covered them with water, firmly seated and sealed its cover, and then ignited the stove. In North America, potatoes take at least fifteen minutes to cook, and as I waited, I anticipated sinking my teeth into one of those succulent gems. As the pressure release valve rattled, I thought of the luscious potatoes that my mother prepared. I got more and more hungry as my stomach rumbled envisioning a savory meal.

Finally, the cooking time came to an end and I removed the cover of the pressure cooker. I had placed the stove on a table, and because of its height, I could not see into it. Anxious to sink my teeth into a succulent tuber as soon as possible, I jabbed a fork into the pot hoping to spear one. Instead, the fork hit the bottom of the cooker with a metallic thud.

"I missed," I thought.

So, I tried again. No luck. Again, a thud indicated no potato.

"I must have missed again."

A bit frustrated, I tried a third time but was again greeted with the sound of the fork hitting the bottom of the pot.

By this time, I was really frustrated and removed the cooker from the stove and looked inside. All that remained were potato skins and a thin mush of what looked like watery potato puree.

"Whaaaat the . . . ! What happened?"

I had chosen the wrong kind of potato. When I was in the market, I selected the kind that looked the best to me. That kind, as was now obvious, was not the variety that should be boiled for a long period, and *not* in a pressure cooker. I ate my thin potato soup in silence trying to remember what kind of potato I had chosen and wondering what kind I should buy next time. A potato by any other name is still a potato, but their flavors and mealiness are very different, and each variety must be prepared properly!

Making soups seemed like a simple and easy way to prepare a meal using my pressure cooker, and I created several different kinds using

FIGURE 3.3. Woman removing grains of quinoa from their stalks. The stalks are then burned, and the ash chewed with the *coca* leaf (see chapter 2).

quinoa (an Andean grain, fig. 3.3), carrots, and several other vegetables. I didn't worry much about dirt because the heat and pressure in my cooker would undoubtedly kill anything and everything undesirable during the cooking process.

Cooking my own food also resulted in other unanticipated consequences. Preparing my own meals not only required time to buy the food, and the time to cook it, but I also had to prepare the food and then, after the meal, take the dishes down to the water spigot in the patio below and wash them. In short, most of my time was consumed with cooking and associated activities just to sustain myself. I was getting very little work done, and I did not have much time available for research after cooking and washing the pressure cooker and all my dishes. I was very exasperated.

Unlike my attempts to cook for myself, Bill ate with his informant's family in their kitchen on the first floor, and after my time-intensive cooking fiasco, he suggested that I might be able to eat with them also. So, he asked his host, Mamerto, if I could join them. He said yes, and in gratefulness, I paid him weekly for his gracious hospitality. I was very appreciative for the provision of food, particularly after my failed and time-consuming attempt at preparing my own meals.

Eating in Mamerto's kitchen was a different experience than eating in North America or with a Maya family in Mexico as I had done two years earlier. Unlike eating in an open, well-lighted thatched house in Mexico, Mamerto's kitchen was relatively dark with limited light. Stranger still was sharing the kitchen with about twenty guinea pigs that lived under and around the raised hearth.

Guinea pigs are native Andean domestic animals. Kitchens may have as many as ten or more that scavenge for food scraps dropped on the floor. When Mamerto's wife placed grass on the floor to feed them, they scurried from their lair and gobbled it up.

During the meal, we did not eat the potato skins or the skins of *fava* beans, but just threw them on the hard-packed dirt floor. Spying our discards, the furry little critters rushed from their den squealing *"cui, cui, cui"* and ravenously consumed the morsels like they were famished. Because of the noise they make scurrying around, Quechua speakers use the word *cui* to refer to them.

Besides being scavengers, the guinea pigs are eaten for ritual meals such as birthdays. Because they are a fast-breeding rodent (the phrase "breed like rabbits" is *apropos* here), they soon replenish themselves.

After settling into living in Bill's large upstairs room and eating in his informant's kitchen below, the owner of the house celebrated his birthday, and true to form, guinea pigs were offered as part of the meal. My portion was a hind leg served over some rice, but the thought of eating the lovable little critters was so memorable that I could not tell you what else was served. The meat appeared to be roasted or pan fried, but was very greasy. The skin was tough, and after taking it in my hands and biting through it, I found very little meat between the skin and the bone. The meat was tasty enough, but it certainly was not much of a protein source.

ANSWERING THE CALL

I had already encountered a shockingly different cultural view toward one of humans' most basic functions when I saw women squatting on the streets of Ayacucho, but further challenges awaited me in Quinua. Answering the call of nature was both an ordeal and a challenge. Houses did not have indoor plumbing and there were no public toilets. Unlike the United States, there appeared to be no laws against urinating and defecating in public. If there were, they were not enforced. Not comfortable performing either activity in a such a context, I tried to answer the call of nature in as relatively private a location as possible.

Behind our house, a series of walls backed up against the rear of the houses along the street parallel to ours, and a path behind them led to a dilapidated door on an adjacent cross street; it was the only access to our house because our front door was usually locked. So, we always entered our room from the path around the back of the house which went around a half-built adobe structure that was our latrine. Urination was not a problem except at night when I had to rise, put on my clothes, exit into the chilly Andean air, find the adobe structure, and perform the necessary function. Sometimes rain and the darkness of night necessitated a shorter visit outside with a discharge off the second-floor balcony onto the tile roof of the house next door.

Defecation posed a more complicated problem. I shared the adobe structure that served as a latrine with three other people in the household, so I had to find a location within the structure where no one could see me. I was in no mood to make myself a public spectacle. Further, I also needed to find a spot that no one else had used before (for obvious reasons). The longer I stayed in Quinua, the more challenging this task became.

On one occasion someone had placed a pig in this half-built structure, and I had to chase the pig away from the spot I had selected for my personal activity. Once I had finished, I stood up, pulled up my pants, and fastened my belt. As I left the spot, the pig squealed, rushed to what I had left behind, and gobbled it up.

I stood there stunned. I came from a rural community and had been around farm animals and knew their fare, but this consequence of "free-range pork" in an Andean context was shocking if not laughable. Pigs transformed human offal into edible protein!

Needless to say, I lost my appetite for eating pork! I understood in a new way at least one of the reasons why some Middle Eastern cultures prohibit the consumption of pork! If human excrement was ritually "unclean," then the animal that consumed it would also be unclean.

LIFE WITHOUT A BATH

With few bathing opportunities in Quinua, personal hygiene was a challenge. So, my grooming and personal cleanliness became more relaxed. There was no running water except for a single spigot in the interior patio area that each member of the household could access. Water was drawn for cooking and, if one wanted, for bathing. There was no private room devoted to personal hygiene with white, gleaming porcelain fixtures for bathing, washing, and answering the call of nature.

Bathing also created challenges unique to high altitude. At the elevation of Quinua (10,786 feet above sea level), the air is less dense and has less oxygen pressure, so it doesn't hold heat. The radiant energy from the sun creates a feeling of warmth during the day when it hits you directly, but moving into the shade brings the chill of the air's true temperature. Because the air doesn't hold the sun's heat, a great temperature difference exists between day and night, but during the dry season, temperature variability is exacerbated, and nighttime temperatures often drop below freezing even when the day has been quite warm.

I made one attempt in Quinua to bathe using a small wash basin on the cement portion of the patio area next to the tap, and it was an unforgettable experience. There was no hot water, and the water drawn from the tap was ice-cold. Mornings and evenings were too cold to shed one's clothes and wash. The only comfortable time of day to bathe was midday, but if I wanted privacy, I had to be sure that no one was else was around. Ultimately, the unpleasantness and anxiety of the experience overwhelmed me so much that I no longer cared about my personal cleanliness. Consequently, I bathed little, sharing this characteristic with Bill and most native Quechua speakers in the community.

RAPPORT AND SELF-DECEPTION

Almost all of the potters in Quinua lived in the rural portions of the community below the elevation of the village. The rainy weather, the preoccupation of my informant Mamerto with his own work, and my own hesitation prevented me from launching out on my own to visit potters in the community. I was anxious to expand my observations beyond Mamerto's practice of the craft and develop rapport with other potters.

Bill had already developed a great deal of rapport in Quinua and I was able to ride on his coattails for some of my engagement with the community. One day he informed me that he had been invited to a birthday party, and he asked me to come along. Since the party would take place below the village where some of the potters lived, I jumped at the chance to attend. Hopefully, I would meet some potters.

Because trekking along Andean paths after dark was treacherous, we walked down the slope in the early evening so that we could find the party before night fell. Soon, we arrived at a house perched on a spot overlooking the valley to the south. We ate and talked with the partygoers, and soon the evening turned into night. At first, the night was moonless, but with just enough light from the starlit sky to outline the front of the house. In the distance, the lights of Ayacucho twinkled and, no doubt, beckoned many potential migrants from their perch on this side of the valley, drawing them away from the problems of insufficient agricultural land and lack of economic opportunity. The lights seemed closer than the eighteen miles that separated us, but since Ayacucho lies at an elevation two thousand feet lower than Quinua, the lights created the illusion that the city below me was nearer to us than it actually was.

Kerosene lamps lit up the inside of the house, and a battery-operated radio blared local huayno music from one of the Ayacucho stations. By the time night fell, the crowd was animated and lubricated with substantial amounts of alcohol. The lamps illuminated the upper part of the room with an eerie glow that traced irregular moving shadows of the partygoers against the mud brick wall.

I did not realize it at the time, but drinking alcoholic beverages was a deeply entrenched Andean practice that goes back to the time of the Incas and beyond—at least to the time of the Wari Empire. The Incas used a maize beer for libations and religious offerings, and modern Andean peasants also made offerings of alcohol to the Mountain God (*Tayta Urqu*), their supreme deity. Equally, if not more important, however, is that drinking alcohol in Quinua took place in social contexts that followed a ritual pattern.

Bill went to a table near the front of the house, and I sat down at a table with a group of men at the back of the house. They offered me a glass of beer from a two-liter bottle, and since the glass was small, I accepted. As I drank, however, the glass was refilled and I found myself placing the glass on the bench beside me in the darkness, emptying a generous portion of its contents onto the dirt floor below. Every time I delayed raising the glass to my lips, my companions insisted that I drink, and every time I reduced its contents—either into my stomach or onto the floor—it was promptly refilled.

With no obvious effects of the alcohol, even at this altitude, I was feeling confident that somehow I had survived the pressure of frequent demands to lift my glass and drink because I had emptied substantial amounts of it on the floor hidden by the shadows of the dim light. My smugness, however, turned out to be my own self-deception as I allowed myself to be pulled into multiple rounds of what I learned later was ritual drinking, where each person in the group toasts his neighbor with the utterance of the word *salud* (health), and takes a drink. Then, the toasting and drinking moves person-by-person around the table with great obligatory social pressure to imbibe. Later, I learned from Bill that no member of the group is allowed to break the chain by saying "no" to a drink. Disposing of a drink on the floor was acceptable, but if discovered, Bill said, the miscreant is fined by having to take two drinks.

Since I thought I had mastered the art of deception by appearing to drink and pouring my beer on the floor in the shadows of the kerosene lamps, I thought my companions were too plastered to notice what was happening to the contents of my glass. On that count, I was correct, as no one ever suspected the final destination of most of the beer poured into my glass.

Even drinking modestly left me with a need to answer the call of nature, however. I rose from the table, explained my need, and apologized for having to take a break. As I did so, and headed for the door of the house, I realized that, in addition to deceiving my companions, I also had deceived myself about my tolerance for alcohol, and found myself dizzy with less than my normal faculties. I carefully exited the house, groping along its side to steady my movement into the shadows at the rear of the house, and relieved myself there.

By this time, the moon had risen and the front of the house and the valley below were bathed in its light. Realizing that I had deluded myself about my ability to handle alcohol at this elevation, I decided to sit down in the moonlight beside the house and just wait. I knew I was in trouble because no matter when I decided to leave the party, I still had to climb up the slope to the village where my sleeping bag and its wool liner awaited me. I was frightened that the alcohol would impede my safe return to my room in the village.

A bit of a chill filled the Andean night, and I shivered while I sat in the moonlight. Soon, my drinking companions came looking for me, and asked me to return inside and continue. I just told them I needed to rest.

As time passed, I inched my way little by little out of the moonlight and into the deep shadows of the back of the house, away from the inter-rupted play of the amber light from the door produced by guests entering or leaving the party. Once in the darkness of the shadows, I paused, got up, and walked up to my room in the village in the moonlight alone.

The desire to form relationships and develop rapport always accompanies research in the field; it is an appropriate goal of the anthropologist. Sometimes, however, one's enthusiasm for "fitting in" results in adverse consequences that are unanticipated. I was raised a teetotaler. My first exposure to alcohol occurred in grad school, and I never drank much of it. So, I did not respect it, nor did I understand or appreciate its potential effects on me.

My participation in the birthday fiesta, and my decision to get involved with a drinking ritual, was my first encounter with alcohol in the Andes; it was also my first experience with a ritual that was so much a part of Andean culture. As a budding anthropologist, I had wanted to "fit in" to the culture as a participant-observer and build rapport to do my research. For the first time, I understood the pressure of drinking in such a context, and I realized my own naivete and overconfidence. I thought that I could deceive my hosts about my own consumption of alcohol and avoid its effects, but that decision was, most of all, ignorance of its power and my own self-deception. I was a slow learner and had to repeat experiences like this one before I became more cautious about getting involved with Andean drinking rituals.

Fortunately, I seldom ran into these rituals again because they occurred on special occasions such as birthdays. With Mamerto's assistance, I was able to visit a few potters in the community and didn't need to worry about participating in drinking rituals during most of my time in Quinua.

ENCOUNTERING ANDEAN ANIMALS

The high altitude of the Andes, its greatly variegated climate, and the geographical isolation of South America from the rest of the world until about ten to fifteen million years ago resulted in a vast array of plants and animals that were different from the rest of the world and, more important, different from those in North America. Living in a rural community in the Andes provided another opportunity to learn firsthand about the animals of this unusual place.

One of these animals that the Andeans domesticated was the llama, a critical component of the economics of ancient Peru (fig. 3.4). During much of Andean prehistory and especially during the time of the Incas, llamas were pack animals that provided transport for food for conquering armies and for tribute that was returned to the Inca capital. In 1967, llamas were also important for interregional exchange.

FIGURE 3.4. Llamas laden with bags secured on their backs with wool ropes to provide transport for crops over mountain trails. The trucks in the upper left and upper right transport rural inhabitants and their produce to and from remote areas.

One afternoon, I descended from my room to find the small area between the walls along the path filled with llamas. One of the peasants from the high-altitude grasslands (the *puna*) above the village had temporarily quartered his llamas there while he attended to other business in the village.

The animals were white, brown, and black, and emulated that detached, aloof look that only a camelid can manage. All were branded with red yarn pulled through holes pierced in the cartilage along the edges of their ears, but in unique positions for each owner of the animals. I had never been so close to llamas before, so I wandered in and among the animals, admiring them and taking pictures. Eventually, I came upon one that was wearing a large bib-like cloth hanging from the base of his neck to a position about ten inches from the ground with a detailed image of Peru's coat of arms embroidered on it. No other beast in the herd wore anything like this around its neck, and Mamerto said that this bib-like affair marked the animal as the leader of the pack.

The llamas are direct descendants of ancient camel-like creatures that populated much of the earth during the Ice Age. Llamas and alpacas, along with their wild cousins, *guanacos* and *vicuñas*, are the only four survivors of the ancient camelid population in the Americas and are found only in the Andes. Some remnant populations of guanacos survive in the Patagonia region of Argentina, and vicuñas, known for their fine, high-quality wool, are protected and found only in the national parks and remote highland regions of Peru and Bolivia.

Being the only camelids easily encountered in Peru, llamas and alpacas are easily confused. Alpacas are distinguished from llamas by the tufts of wool on their mutton chops, their low squat appearance compared to llamas, and the long strings of wool that often hang from their unshorn bodies.

Most important, llamas and alpacas provide one way for human populations to adapt to the challenges of the high-altitude Andean environment. Both provide wool for clothing, but alpaca wool is more valued. Although llama wool may also be used for weaving, llamas are more important as beasts of burden, and Andean peasants used them to move their produce to market, each bearing about eighty pounds in one bag loose enough to be distributed in equal portions on each side of its back. This feature of llamas was another reason why the animals were domesticated by the ancient Andeans, and herds of llamas provided the means of transporting goods along mountainous roads and trails (fig. 3.4).

Not only did llamas provide transportation for root crops from isolated rural hamlets to larger communities, but they linked different regions of the Andes even in the late 1960s. In Quinua, they may have carried pottery from producers to communities in the puna and other distant locations where vessels were exchanged for their volume of maize or root crops.

When I arose the next morning and descended to our latrine in the half-built adobe structure, the llamas were gone. They were already on their way up to the settlements high in the mountains above us.

CHAPTER 4

Engaging a Changed Research Design

BY EARLY APRIL, the rainy season was ending and my informant, Mamerto, decided to prepare to fire the pottery he had made. Up to this time, he had been making pottery in a large, vacant room in his house that had the space to dry it sufficiently and to shelter it from the fog, rains, and cooler temperatures outside. Firing his pots, however, was a different matter because he had to obtain fuel and then dry it in the sun. Using undried fuel would damage the vessels, extend firing duration, and increase fuel costs. Further, firing required dry weather so that rainfall would not damage the pottery during the process. Quinua potters used a small Spanish-derived updraft kiln with an open top, and rain entering the top of the kiln would irreparably damage, if not destroy, the pottery inside it.

Firing required a unique kind of bush called *chamizo* that was quick-burning and relatively smokeless, but it only grew on the high slopes above the village and required a trip up into the mountains to obtain it. It was not possible for one man to carry enough for a firing episode; only draft animals could transport a sufficient amount.

Bill had been adopted by a local family, and they owned some mules. So, Mamerto approached Bill about asking his adoptive parents to borrow their mules to make the trip. They consented and we prepared to depart the next day.

Since chamizo is easier to cut in the early morning before the sun comes over the mountain and it gets too hot, we left at five a.m. and started up into the mountains with Bill, his visiting younger brother, Charles, Mamerto, and three mules. Mamerto drove the mules ahead of us up the narrow, rocky trail behind the village. About an hour later, we arrived at the temporary camp of Bill's adoptive parents. Rural Andean agriculturalists often establish such camps when their fields are located away from their primary residences in order to prevent theft of their crops at harvest time. The camp consisted of a small, beehive-shaped grass hut (fig. 4.1) and a small enclosure with several pigs that Bill's adoptive family had built on a relatively flat area in a tiny valley. Nearby they had planted wheat, fava beans, quinoa, and chickpeas together in the same field. All except the quinoa were Old World crops, but all were tolerant of the cold and high altitude.

Bill's adoptive mother was delighted to see us and wanted to feed us. She disappeared into the hut and soon emerged with soup in a porcelain-covered metal bowl in each hand. In a gesture of gracious hospitality, she gave them to us, but they reeked with such a vile smell that it seemed like the food was rotten. Repulsed by the odor, we speculated about its cause and finally identified the meat as the problem. When meat is dried outside to make *charqui* (the origin of the English word *jerky*), it may not dry enough before some of it spoils, and flies lay their eggs in it.

FIGURE 4.1. This hut, called a *choza*, is built near fields that are distant from the household to protect the ripening harvest from theft. This particular "home away from home" was Bill Mitchell's adopted parents' field house that we visited to obtain fuel (*chamizo*) for firing pottery.

We knew that we should accept our hostess's hospitality and eat the soup so as not to offend her. But we were in a quandary. How could we do that without ingesting the vile-smelling meat? Our American culinary values were challenged, but this dilemma was more than just a value conflict. Our health could also suffer from ingesting the meat.

We debated about what we should do, and decided that if we just discarded the meat, we could eat the soup. So, as our hostess disappeared into the hut to retrieve the bowl for the last of us, Bill's brother and I fished out the foul-smelling meat, and threw it over the fence to the hogs. They squealed with delight as they finished off the morsels. Meanwhile, we found that the soup no longer smelled so vile, and with no spoons available, each of us lifted our bowl to our mouth and consumed its contents.

It seemed better to close my eyes to drink the soup, but ultimately I opened them only to see a tiny dirty rag plugging a hole in the bottom of the bowl. Deeming it better not to see any more questionable additions to my bowl as I drank, I closed my eyes again. To avoid further assaults on my visual and olfactory senses, I raised the bowl to my mouth and emptied its contents as quickly as I could.

Soon, our hostess emerged from the hut again and, noticing that no soup remained in our bowls, she asked:

"Would you like more?"

Apparently, she did not notice that there were no bones in our bowls, and thankfully she did not ask about them.

"No, thank you," we replied.

Meanwhile, Bill had decided that he would not acquiesce to our choice to throw out the meat, and he consumed both the meat and the broth. Needless to say, he got sick the next day and was confined to his bed for four days. His brother and I, however, suffered no ill effects from eating the broth without the meat.

This experience highlighted a common problem that one faces in another culture. Food is a widespread expression of hospitality and acceptance of a guest, and to refuse it implies rejection of that hospitality, the giver, and indeed the giver's culture. It is one thing to accept an unknown food or drink, whether you think you will like it or not, but it is a struggle to accept food that was given in a gracious expression of hospitality that you also know will probably threaten your health. Long-term residents who are familiar with a culture often have culturally acceptable ways of refusing food without offending the host, but I did not know how to do that in Quinua, and neither did Bill.

After we finished our visit and meal, we found a place to cut the chamizo. Mamerto cut the plants close to the ground and loaded them on the mules. Then we descended the trail back to the village. We crossed the Ayacucho battlefield and then followed the path into the village, unloading the fuel and placing it on the ground in our backyard where it would dry sufficiently to be used for firing.

THE VIEW FROM THE *PAMPA*

After the rainy season passed, the heavy overcast clouds cleared and each day was bright and sunny with a rich blue sky. On many of those days I would exit the door of my second-floor room and stand on the balcony at the top of the stairs. I looked up the valley to the northwest, marveling at the pristine beauty of the mountains with the dark green tinge of brush covering their lower slopes. Higher up, the yellowish tan of the high puna grassland marked their crests. I could not see very far up the valley, but because the village sat on a ridge, I could see the rich green color of trees and fields of maize that filled the nearby *pampa* (flat area) just below the village (fig. 4.2).

Maize is the most valued of Andean crops. Both today and in the remote past, the fields that I saw from my balcony probably had been cultivated continuously from before the time of the Wari Empire.

On Sundays, I left my room and went to the local market. During the rainy season, no pottery was being sold there, but after the rainy season passed, vendors peddled decorated bowls, water-carrying jars, and storage containers. I memorized the shapes and designs after seeing each vendor, then briefly retired to my room to reproduce the shapes and their painted design before returning to the market again for more observations.

I discovered that the potters of Quinua made three painted styles—each associated with different shapes. One style was made in Muya, a hamlet located between Quinua and the village of Huamanguilla, and another was produced below the village in several of the hamlets of Lurinsayuq toward Wari below the village. A third style came from the area between the village of Quinua and Muya called Patampampa. Sometimes I observed water-carrying jars from one part of the community were sloppily painted with the design structure of another style. Mamerto recognized the creator of this unusual pattern as coming from a potter farther down the slope in Lurinsayuq.

FIGURE 4.2. The view of the rural area of Quinua from the balcony outside of my room. The image shows the intensively irrigated area northwest of the village of Quinua. The dark area on the lower slopes of the mountains is the montane forest along the eastern side of the valley; the lighter area above is the high *puna* grassland.

After visiting the market, I usually climbed up to another pampa above the village, where the Battle of Ayacucho was fought in 1824, decisively breaking Spanish power in South America and freeing the continent from Spanish colonial domination. It was here that the leader of Simon Bolivar's troops, General Sucre, met the forces of the Spanish viceroy and defeated them. The surrender papers are reputed to have been signed in a small adobe structure on the plaza of Quinua where a framed drawing illustrated the event.

The battlefield had been cleared of agricultural fields and houses because of its historical significance, but one adobe house still remained. The roof tiles and the rafters were gone, and some of the walls had collapsed. On those beautiful Sunday mornings, I climbed to the top of one of the walls and sat there meditating, praying, and generally relishing the incredible view that my perch offered.

It was no accident that the viceroy's troops chose this location for their battle. The terrain was one of the few perceptibly flat areas in the valley, and the steep rise of the mountains behind the battlefield protected them from an attack from the rear. Overall, their position provided a defensible and commanding view of the valley (see fig. 2.4). Ultimately, however, the viceroy's army failed to hold their position, and General Sucre's troops defeated them.

Up the valley to the northwest, the green fields of maize and the maturing fields of wheat and barley created an image that mimicked Picasso's cubism, with quadrangular fields of yellow and green marked by lines of trees and eroded gullies slicing diagonally through the landscape as if it were a canvas. To the south, hues of pink, yellow, and white of the eroded beds of clay and volcanic ash dominated the drier central portion of the valley. Beyond, on its far side, lay the city of Ayacucho, some eighteen miles away, with its airport runway pointed directly toward me (see fig. 2.4).

Along the uphill edge of the battlefield, the mountains rose abruptly with their steep slopes disappearing into the sky. Covered with low shrubs, they provided a dark green contrast to both the sky and the lighter grasses of the battlefield around me. Immediately below, the buildings of the village of Quinua peeked above the trees planted along the base of the slope.

The peacefulness and the quietness of the place called forth tranquility within me. Occasionally, a truck broke the silence as it rattled along the road that followed the base of the pampa. On its way to the valley on the other side of the mountains, it briefly interrupted my meditation only to disappear into the silence of the landscape before me.

To the southeast, the valley ended as the terrain rose to the high puna grasslands, then dropped into the Pampas River Valley out of sight. Again, I could see why the Spanish Conquistadores had chosen Quinua for their first settlement between Lima and Cusco. Its position was strategic because one could see approaching enemies long before they arrived.

Far below me lay the ruins of Wari, now an abandoned archaeological site with its remains covering a vast area. I had visited Wari two months earlier, but I had not seen it from this perspective. Again, I noted its critical position in the center of the valley, and I wondered what it was like more than a millennium ago when Wari was a large urban center and the capital of a great Andean empire. Much of the city and its environs needed to be investigated further, but it appeared that the agricultural land that I could see below me was fed by the local irrigation systems that had their roots in the period of Wari domination that preceded the Incas by at least four hundred years. Without such a system of intensive agriculture between the ancient city and around Quinua, it probably was not possible to sustain the zenith of Wari population.

THE THREAT OF JAIL

Because my observations of pottery making during the rainy season were limited, part of my revised research design was to observe as many vessels of pottery as I could. I had already visited the Sunday market in Quinua for several weeks. Although little pottery was offered for sale there, I was able to record some information about it. I also went to Ayacucho occasionally to observe the pottery sold in the market there.

Subsequently, I learned about other markets, one of which was held in the nearby village of Huamanguilla. On the map, Huamanguilla was less than four miles away, and I could see it perched on a ridge on the upper edge of the valley to the northwest.

So, one Sunday morning I decided to walk to Huamanguilla and observe the market. The path was rocky and narrow, and I soon learned that the four-mile distance on the map was misleading because the path crossed two deep ravines, zigzagging into their depths and then up the other side. Higher ground had obscured them from my vantage point in Quinua. So, what appeared to be a simple four-mile walk took more than two hours.

My first descent into one the ravines revealed that it was an erosion channel that had cut through a thick layer of what I discovered later was volcanic ash. Along the way down into the bottom, several large holes were dug into the walls of the ravine that apparently served as sources of temper for the potters who lived nearby in Muya.

When I reached Huamanguilla, I noticed that people were bringing crosses to the church. It was the Feast of the Holy Spirit, and the priest would be blessing the crosses. Some pilgrims also came dressed as jungle Indians called *chunchus*. With feather headdresses and long, flowing cotton garments, chunchus symbolized the economic link between the Andes and the tropical forest to the east. Some local inhabitants did not have access to sufficient agricultural land, so they traveled to the tropical forest to cultivate fields, bringing their crops back to the highlands to supplement their subsistence.

I found the market in the central plaza. It was small, but a couple of the women were selling pottery that looked like it came from Muya, a political subsection of Quinua that is only slightly closer to Quinua than it is to Huamanguilla. I watched and recorded the transactions, keeping track of the cost of the pottery, its shape, and its designs.

I had spent only a few minutes in the market, and had just begun my observations when a corporal of the *Guardia Civil* (the police force in these rural areas) came up to me and said:

"The commandant wants to see you."

Not knowing what to expect, I complied with his request and followed him across the market toward the police station that occupied the uphill side of the plaza. A long series of wooden steps led up to its position on the slope.

With some apprehension, I ascended the steps and walked into the building. Inside, the commandant sat behind a massive desk. The corporal motioned me to approach the desk and face his commanding officer.

"What are you doing here?" he asked in a gruff voice.

"I am studying pottery making in Quinua, and I live there. I came to Huamanguilla to see the market and observe the pots being sold."

"Who are you and where do you come from?"

I explained that I was a student from the United States and was a pupil of Professor Zuidema at the University of Huamanga in Ayacucho.

"How do I know that you are who you say you are?"

At this point, I realized that I had neglected to bring my passport and my letter of introduction from the *Casa de la Cultura* (a government organization and museum for Peruvian crafts) in Lima introducing me as a student researcher under the supervision of Professor Zuidema. I never dreamed that they would be necessary for my trip to Huamanguilla. I explained my work, but realizing that the only link of communication of any speed between these villages was the telegraph and that I might be in deep trouble, I replied:

"You can telegraph the police in Quinua, and they will tell you that I live there with Guillermo (Bill) Mitchell, another North American who is studying there."

"Let's see your bag," the commandant ordered.

Because I wanted to take some pictures of my visit, I had placed my camera in a small shoulder bag. It also included candy and a pack of cheap cigarettes to give to informants as a thank-you for their help, no matter how brief. I am not sure why I thought that a gift of a cigarette would be a thank-you except for the advice of Bill, but I had them nevertheless.

The commandant opened the bag, took out the camera and the cigarettes, and then demanded:

"Empty your pockets!"

I had only brought enough cash for a bottle of soda and perhaps something to eat. It was not very much, but I laid it on the desk.

"Is that all?" he questioned.

"Sí, comandante."

He then turned to the corporal who brought me to the station and asked, "Is there a cell ready?"

"Yes!" The corporal replied. "It was just vacated this morning."

A long pause ensued, and I pondered what it would be like to be jailed in Huamanguilla.

Guerrilla activity had occurred in the jungle to the east of Huamanguilla with occasional ongoing skirmishes. Guerrillas had already fought government troops in the eastern part of Bolivia, and newspapers reported that Ché Guevara, an Argentine activist and revolutionary, was leading the movement there. Ché rose to prominence in Castro's revolution in Cuba, and presumably was leading the guerrilla activity in the jungle in eastern Peru.

These events might have set the stage for the commander's suspicions about the unusual stranger who stood before him. Could he be a spy? Later that year, news reports confirmed that Ché was indeed behind the fighting in Bolivia, but he was captured and summarily executed in October.

Some years later during the peak of the "Shining Path" guerrilla movement in Peru, I recalled that another American anthropologist was arrested in the rural areas of the Andes and suspected of being a revolutionary. Fortunately, I was young enough and naive enough in 1967 not to know much about being incarcerated in Peru. Nevertheless, I still experienced great anxiety about being thrown into jail.

I raised the stakes that hopefully might lead to my release.

"You can telegraph Dr. Zuidema at the University of Huamanga in Ayacucho and he will vouch for me . . . that I am who I say I am."

I hoped that if there was a question about the truthfulness of my story, and Professor Zuidema was available, he could confirm my identity.

The comandante deliberated with another subordinate about telegraphing the police in Quinua to verify my claims, but after questioning me further and forbidding me to take photographs, he said I could leave. As I slowly descended the steps of the police station to the market, I thought, "Who would care about pictures of women selling pots in little, insignificant Huamanguilla?"

I suspect the absence of automatic weapons in my camera bag and the lack of hand grenades in my pockets were the most convincing evidence that I was not a guerrilla, but I will never forget the lesson I learned: always carry some identification and letters of introduction with you when doing fieldwork in an area where you are not known, and then check with the local authorities before proceeding.

After my return to Quinua, I told Bill about my experiences with the police in Huamanguilla. He suggested that my temporary detention by the police was likely an attempt at trying to extort money from me. By threatening me with jail, the police hoped that I would grease their palms with Peruvian currency, even though there was no real reason to charge or hold me.

This discussion with Bill was perhaps the first challenge to my cultural assumption that my encounter with the Huamanguilla police was something other than what it appeared to be—a suspicion of being a guerrilla. I have since learned that in many parts of the world, including parts of Latin America, the police are poorly paid because it is expected that they will extort money from those they encounter whether they have broken the law or not. North Americans, tourists, and the wealthy may be targeted simply because they are assumed to be rich. That the police anywhere would do anything except enforcing the law was rather shocking to me, and since then, I have heard many stories from friends, colleagues, and students of being a target of the police simply because it was thought that they would be able to pay a bribe.

After reflecting on this incident many years later, it seemed like a frightening portent of future events because the "Shining Path" guerrilla movement of the 1980s had its beginning at the University of Huamanga in Ayacucho. Abamiel Guzmán, the notorious head of the movement, was already a member of the philosophy faculty at the university in 1967, but I did not know him personally, nor knew he existed. Since I often interacted with university students there, I wondered whether any of the students and faculty that I met were members of that infamous terrorist group. I did learn, however, that there were at least six types of communists at the university: Marxists (purists), Maoists, Trotskyites, Leninists, Stalinists, and Castroites. The differences between these groups were unclear except for their names, but each group's adherents appeared to be united against "Yankee" imperialism. Clearly, 1967 was a year in which revolutionary fervor was already percolating at the university. The cautious acts of the Huamanguilla police thus were understandable, if not prophetic of things to come.

Some years later, memories of my detention by the police in Huamanguilla were rekindled. During the ascendance of the Shining Path

guerrillas, armed men ushered the males out of a church service near
Huanta, lined them up against a wall, and then shot them all. This strategy
was typical for these guerrillas, and many hamlets were decimated. The
military also allegedly practiced such brutal atrocities in the remote areas
of the Andes. Those people that survived fled to the safety of the highland
cities (like Ayacucho) and larger provincial capitals like Huanta, emptying
out many of the rural hamlets.

About a year after my encounter with the police in Huamanguilla,
the Peruvian military staged a coup and took over the country, national-
izing some critical industries and instituting strong currency restrictions.
General Juan Velasco became president and imposed strict controls on
the movement of people across Peru. His government used two popular
icons of the revolution: Ché Guevara and Tupac Amaru, an Indian rebel
who resisted the conquest of the Spanish in the late sixteenth century
and who, like Ché, was eventually captured and executed. Posters erected
during the military regime showed Tupac Amaru with his finger pointed
to the observer with the words "Peru needs you" (*Perú te necesita*).

Ironically, the Peruvian government changed from fighting and
killing revolutionaries during the democratic Belaúnde administration
to embracing them as symbols of the new order—the resistance of the
native Peruvians against the Spanish (Tupac Amaru) and against transnational capitalism (Ché Guevara). Ché might not have become the symbol
of Peru's revolutionary struggle against status quo capitalism if the Bolivian army had not executed him in 1967. My detention by the police in
Huamanguilla as a suspected guerrilla in 1967 thus took on new meaning
of even greater irony for me, even if it was a pretext for extortion.

The antagonism to U.S. foreign policies, however, was not just idle
prattle, but reflected deep frustration with my country's foreign policy
and its perceived attitudes toward Peru. It seemed out of touch with the
realities of the Peruvian economy and social structure, and often appeared
to be in collusion with exploitative policies of multinational corporations,
as well as linked to policies that were poorly thought through. The impor-
tation of U.S. wheat into Peru, for example, although providing a subsidy
for farmers in the United States, reduced the price that poor Peruvian
peasants could charge to sell their own—so much so that they could not
afford to plant it. The corruption and a class structure with deep economic disparities were other sources of frustration, and both Peruvian
internal politics and the foreign policy of my government seemed to favor
the wealthy Peruvian upper class as a thinly veiled American self-interest.

I was disillusioned by my government's policies toward Peru, and at the time, I lost a lot of respect for our administration, the State Department, and our foreign policy.

In spite of all this, many Peruvians liked us even though they despised the actions of my government and the power of multinational corporations. This difference was reflected again and again in my experiences in Latin America. At a professional meeting of archaeologists in La Paz, Bolivia, in 1973, one Peruvian archaeologist rose to his feet during a discussion and ranted and raved about American and European archaeologists exploiting the cultural patrimony of Peru and exporting it to fill the museums of Europe and North America. He was seated directly behind me, so when the discussion was over, I stood, turned, and introduced myself. He smiled and gave me a copy of his latest book. He knew I was a North American, and he had been humiliated during transit through my country by being taken through an airport in chains because he was a known Marxist. Nevertheless, he did not hold it against me personally. Most Peruvians did not hold me responsible for the policies of my government.

The lack of congruity between the on-the-ground realities in Peru and U.S. policy again was highlighted five years later. I had been awarded a Fulbright lectureship to teach at the University of Cusco, and my wife and I were invited to Washington for an orientation for all the Fulbright grantees who would be working in Latin America. We attended lectures about Latin American culture and foreign policy at the Foreign Service Institute and participated in events that focused on our individual countries. One of these was a cocktail party at the Peruvian Embassy where we met the ambassador and his staff, and mixed with the other Fulbrighters going to Peru.

Before that event, all of us went to the State Department on Foggy Bottom for a series of welcome speeches. After the speeches were finished, a State Department employee took each of us to the desk officer of the country to which we were assigned. We took the elevator to an upper floor of the building and found the appropriate office of the Peru desk. It was a very small room with few chairs. Peruvian newspapers and magazines were stacked everywhere. The ceiling of the room was low with a single window that overlooked the lower end of the Mall.

Since I already had spent six months in Peru five years earlier, we discussed what was happening there more recently. In 1968, the military coup of General Juan Velasco had wrought great changes. After a lengthy discussion, there was a pause in our conversation and I asked:

"You seem to know a great deal about Peru, its government, and its problems. Why then, doesn't American foreign policy toward Peru reflect the economic, political, and social realities on-the-ground there—those that we just discussed?"

There was a long pause, and the desk officer leaned back on his swivel chair and, without turning around, extended one arm backward glancing over his shoulder toward the window.

"Up the hill."

"You mean Congress?"

"Yes," he said.

"You mean that even though you may suggest a policy based upon the realities in a country like Peru, Congress can overrule State Department's recommendations?"

"That's right!"

I left the office stunned, and I never forgot the encounter. After it, I gained tremendous respect for the State Department. But, I feared that a failure to take the knowledge of any country into account would inevitably doom American foreign relations, and that vested interests, whatever they might be, would inevitably cause unnecessary harm to my country and to its foreign policy. I naively thought that Congress represented the will of the people in a democracy, but I have since wondered how Congress (and the people they represent) could ever have the extensive and deep on-the-ground knowledge to modify foreign policy possessed by foreign service officers in the State Department. Even spending only six months living in Peru provided me with a perspective that I could have never gained by just living in my own country and reading about Peru.

Since then, I have asked several diplomats about the problem. Knowing that the departments in the president's cabinet are professional information collectors, and then having that information countermanded by congressional partisanship, bias, innuendo, and ignorance (in some cases) frightens me that decisions about my country's future are not being made with respect for the best information available. I especially thought about how difficult it would be to implement a policy toward any country abroad that did not take into account the vital information about it. One diplomat replied that the embassy press offices abroad were especially in a difficult position because they had to "sell" American foreign policy regardless of the realities of the country in question.

All of this emphasized the need for Americans, and especially for those of us who teach, to understand the perspectives of other cultures—economically, politically, historically, and socially. Passing this knowledge and experience to our students was critical for the well-being of our society and for our country's responsible participation on the world's stage. In this sense, the goals of my National Defense Foreign Language Fellowship were fulfilled during my forty-three years of teaching anthropology.

SELF-DECEPTION: TAKE TWO

Having recovered from my brush with the law in Huamanguilla, I finished my observations in the market and started my trek back to Quinua. By this time, it was midday, and during my return I encountered a man who had brought a cross to the village church for blessing by the priest. He was going to Muya, a pottery-making hamlet between Huamanguilla and Quinua. As we walked, we conversed and I asked him many questions about Muya and about the pottery made there.

The potters in Muya made different shapes than the rest of the potters in Quinua and painted them with an unusual style: usually alternating red and black lines over a zone of white paint. I had seen some of these vessels in Huamanguilla, but I couldn't photograph them because the local police forbade me to do it.

We descended into the large ravine between Huamanguilla and Quinua, and as we reached the top of the ravine on the Quinua side of the gorge, he stopped, saying that he lived there, and invited me to eat the noon meal with him. Surprised, but hungry, I accepted his invitation, and was deeply grateful for his gracious hospitality.

As we ate, we sat in the doorway of his house, and I admired the view down the ridge that was the lower part of Muya. The rainy season had ended and the landscape was flush with the green of abundantly watered fields and rows of agave cactus marking the field boundaries along the edge of the public path. As we finished eating, he asked me if I wanted to go to a birthday fiesta for one of his relatives.

"Where is it?" I asked.

"Down there," he said as he pointed.

My eyes followed his arm and finger toward the houses below. The terrain outside of his house sloped downward along a narrow ridge. Near the end of the ridge close to where it dropped off steeply on three sides, I saw a small house that he said was the location of the fiesta.

I was apprehensive because my own cultural assumptions told me that the invitation should come from the host, not one of the invited guests. But I was perhaps too awed by the prospect of participating in the life of another Andean household, and the opportunity for building rapport with its members and friends, to reject the invitation. So, I consented to go with him.

We walked the half-mile down the ridge along a rocky, well-worn trail. Near the end, we turned off the path to the house. At the door, the host greeted us warmly and asked us to come in. We sat in two empty chairs facing the door in a circle of men that extended around the perimeter of the room.

I should have known what awaited me, but again my naivete prevented me from properly understanding the meaning of the seating organization with an all-male cast. Soon, *chicha*, a homemade alcoholic beer made from germinated corn, was passed around. Another beer, called *chicha de molle*, is produced from the fruits of the pepper tree, but this brew was not served. Although safer to drink than water from an irrigation ditch, both types can pack a punch if consistently imbibed. (A third type, *chicha morada*, is not alcoholic and is made from purple corn.)

"Salud!" One shouted as he filled his glass, raised it to his neighbor, and then drank.

He then filled his neighbor's glass, who did the same and drank. The ritual continued with the man next to him repeating the exhortation, filling his glass, and then drinking.

The brew made its rounds, and in a desire to fit in, I dutifully allowed my glass to be filled, and then drank.

"Fine," I thought. "This brew is just chicha. I can do this!"

Chicha was not so bad. It quenched my thirst from the hot day and refreshed me from the exhaustion of my trek from Huamanguilla. With chicha, I thought, I could hold my own and survive with a limited alcohol intake with no serious consequences.

I was wrong again! No more than half an hour into the drinking ritual, the brew was supplanted by *aguardiente*, a distilled product whose taste indicated that its percentage of alcohol approached several exponential powers of concentration higher than the chicha. When this switch happened, I knew I was in trouble and realized I needed to leave the party as soon as possible.

In my excitement of walking down the ridge to the fiesta, I was not paying attention to where I was, and I had descended a thousand feet or more along a ridge that increased both the horizontal and vertical distance from my room in Quinua. By now it was after dark, and in order to return to the village, I had to descend into a large ravine, ascend the other side, and then climb a vertical distance of about two thousand feet to reach my house.

I excused myself saying that I had to relieve myself—an acceptable but temporary reason to leave a party. Again, rising from my chair, I prepared to leave, and as I left the house, I discovered that I had lost some of my faculties. After answering the call of nature, I paused.

Rather than go back inside to say goodbye, I explained to my companion that I had drunk too much and should return to Quinua. If I was to follow the trail down into the gorge, trek up the other side, and reach my room without suffering serious injury during my climb, then I must leave the party. I could also fall to my death into the steep canyon. He apparently noticed my alcohol-induced state and walked with me to the edge of the gorge, watching me as I descended the trail to the bottom. He remained standing there as I ascended the other side, and I noticed that he was still there until the topography obscured my view of him after I reached the top of the steep slope on the canyon's far side.

The remainder of my trek was uphill and out of sight of my companion, but I managed my climb without incident. I ultimately reached the plaza of the village, walking across it to access the passageway behind our house. I ascended the stairs to my room, opened the door, and collapsed into my warm sleeping bag on my air mattress, grateful that I had returned safely.

The next day Bill reiterated the critical role of drinking rituals in the Andes, and I realized that my desire to identify with the people led me to make a poor decision. Identifying with the people and participating in their life was essential for showing respect for them and developing rapport with them. This goal not only would provide a more enjoyable field experience but ease the acquisition of information for one's research.

But, as Casagrande pointed out, anthropologists cannot go native if they are to have a relatively objective perspective of the people they study. Understanding another culture is a perspective situated somewhere beyond the myopia of one's own personal and cultural perspective, and lies between the totally culturally relative view of someone within that culture and that of the antiseptic view of an outsider.

Again, I realized that my participation in the drinking ritual created a slippery slope. Thinking that I could handle the alcohol and still engage the locals in conversation revealed a self-deception about my ability to imbibe at such a high altitude and still retain my faculties. Even though my initial accounts with drinking a couple of months before involved an attempt to deceive my new companions in order to continue my participation without drinking too much, that approach ultimately failed. I needed to learn that other means must exist to develop rapport, and I had to learn the hard way to avoid such attempts. Nevertheless, with little experience in drinking, I learned again to respect alcohol and its effect on me, especially at high altitude.

Unfortunately, long after I made the trek to the house in Muya with the drinking ritual, I discovered that the source of black paint used by Muya potters was located nearby. If I had known about that source at the time, I could have asked to see it. That distraction could have kept me from an unpleasant experience, and I could have obtained a sample of the paint and information about the source. Unfortunately, I never returned to that area.

IRRIGATION AND THE MYSTERIOUS PUNA

Being a participant-observer in a new and different culture means that one has to be open to new opportunities to learn about local life. I had already discovered that one of the sources of the red paint used on Quinua pottery was reportedly mined in a location in the puna above the village. I had also learned from Bill that irrigation was important in the community and the sources of its water lay in the puna above.

It was obvious that irrigation was critical for agriculture on the dry Peruvian coast where no rain fell during most years, and I had seen the role of water used for irrigation drawn from coastal rivers during my initial flight across the Andes to Ayacucho. What I didn't know until much later was the importance of irrigation for agriculture at high altitude, its importance in Andean prehistory, and its relationship to social and political organization—a role that Mitchell discovered in Quinua.[1] Again, an unusual opportunity presented itself to learn about it.

Irrigation was critical for the development of complex society on the Peruvian coast and in the Andes, but as Mitchell later discovered from reading the work of Karl Wittfogel and Julian Steward, irrigation itself was not the critical variable that led to complex society, but rather the way that it was organized.[2] The Incas used it, but it probably was an ancient pattern dating at least to the time of the Wari state. Feeding the population of Wari could be enhanced by irrigation on the slopes above the city to intensify agricultural productivity. Since Quinua is directly above Wari, and Wari lies nears the end of the modern irrigation system, information about the irrigation system in Quinua might be able to contribute information for understanding the ancient irrigation system around Wari. Only much later did I learn about the role of irrigation and how its contribution to agriculture in Quinua related to pottery production. Potters lived on land that was marginal for agriculture because of its dryness near the bottom of the valley, and the lack of accessibility to irrigation water. Pottery production (and that of other crafts) turned out be a way to supplement subsistence activities for those who lived on land with limited agricultural productivity, or who had no tillable land at all.

Irrigation water was critical for agriculture in Quinua because it expanded the amount of arable land, particularly for maize cultivation.[3] Maize is a critical crop for the Andean peoples, and is consumed in a variety of forms prepared by boiling (ears and kernels), toasting (kernels), and fermenting (chicha). Although it was grown in many parts of Quinua, the elevation around the village was too high for its cultivation because maize is a tropical grass, and unlike potatoes and other Andean root crops, it is sensitive to frost. Maize also requires abundant moisture at critical times, particularly when the grains on the cob are filling out. Sufficient rain falls during the rainy season but occurs largely during four months (from December through March). The rains taper off in April, and when June arrives, frosts threaten the immature crop. The six-month period from the beginning of the rainy season to the advent of frost is too short for maize to mature because the cold at the altitude of Quinua slows its growth. If one wants to plant maize at the elevation around the village, the crop needs nine months of maturation time with abundant moisture before the frost kills the plants. To give the maize more time to mature, irrigation extends its growing season backward into the dry season before it rains regularly and consistently. This strategy supplements the availability of water when the rains are irregular and insufficient for growing crops, allowing maize enough time to mature before the onset of frost, particularly at the altitude of the village of Quinua.[4]

Using irrigation water for agriculture also requires an understanding of the local topography. Quinua sits on a ridge between two drainage systems, each feeding into a different stream that descends from the mountains above. To adapt to this drainage pattern, the community utilizes two irrigation systems, each of which flows down the slopes into a separate drainage pattern divided by the ridge on which the village sits. Each system is fed by a different source high in the mountains above, and each follows the natural drainage pattern on its side of the village.[5]

Each irrigation system defines a major political subdivision of Quinua. One irrigation and political subdivision is called *Lurin* and uses water from a source high in the mountains northwest of the community. That water ultimately drains into a large ravine west of Quinua that flows along the northwest edge of the Wari center, and eventually into the river in the bottom of the Ayacucho Valley.[6]

The other major political subdivision corresponds to the other drainage system, called *Hanan*, which has its source high in the mountains above in a valley roughly parallel to that of the source of the Lurin system. It flows into a ravine that defines the eastern boundary of Quinua, and reaches the river in the bottom of the valley far to the east of Wari.[7] In each system, a large canal draws off water high in the mountains and channels it into a pattern of smaller canals that drain into these two separate ravines. The Lurin system, however, irrigates a much larger area than the Hanan system, and has chronically insufficient water.[8]

All of the potters live in the Lurin section of the community with its insufficient irrigation water. This section also has highly eroded land with steep gullies and great changes in elevation that make some of it impossible for the irrigation water to reach it. In retrospect, the poor quality of this land for agriculture favored those families who practiced both agriculture and nonagricultural activities such as pottery making and other crafts. This land could not support those who practiced agriculture alone; others had to migrate to the cities. This land was also highly eroded and exposed a number of ceramic resources such as clay, volcanic ash (used for temper), white and black paint, and consolidated volcanic ash that was shaped into a circular platform upon which pottery was made.[9]

The link between maize cultivation, irrigation, and the amount of land devoted to agriculture was of concern to the Peruvian government, and it initiated a development project to increase the amount of irrigated land. One day, an agricultural engineer from the ruling *Acción Popular* party showed up to help the community obtain more irrigation water which was normally in short supply.

The engineer talked with the town officials, and the officials wanted to take him to the source of one of the irrigation systems (Little Black Lake, see fig. 2.3) above the community showing him what they thought would fix the problem. Little Black Lake was created by a dam that had been built there to impound the water, and community officials wanted the engineer to assess whether a larger dam could supply a more reliable source of water during the dry season for those portions of the community where rainfall was insufficient.

Unfortunately, this strategy exclusively favored that part of the community (Hanan) and its irrigation system that needed water the least. That system was controlled by the town officials (including the mayor) of the village of Quinua, and when the engineer arrived, it is likely that he only talked to those officials, and they directed him to Little Black Lake. Apparently, he did not talk to the more rural administrators of the other irrigation system (Lurin). Nevertheless, the mayor tried to get all of the people in the community to help build the dam, but those served by the other irrigation system (Lurin) understandably refused to work on the project because it would not benefit them.[10]

I happened to be in front of the mayor's store at the time the engineer arrived, and the mayor asked me if I wanted to join them for their excursion to Little Black Lake. I saw it as a great opportunity to see the high grassland and tundra (called the *puna*) above the village and visit the sources of the irrigation systems. Since I was studying pottery making, potters said that their red paint came from a location above the village, and I realized that a trip to Little Black Lake would provide an opportunity for me to try and find the source of that paint.

As the engineer drove up the winding road that went north and east over the mountains, we talked about the project. Along the way we saw plowed potato fields—quadrangular black patches on an otherwise green landscape. These fields were not level but were cultivated on a slope of more than 60 degrees. Impossible to be plowed with the Mediterranean scratch plow that used draft animals, peasants used the Andean foot plow (the *chaqui taclla*), a spade-like device with a handle near the top for one hand, and another handle at the bottom for one foot. It requires the effort of two people, one to use the device to cut and raise the sod and the other to turn it over.

The irrigation system in Quinua consisted of earthen and rock canals, and the engineer thought that the gravity-fed system was inefficient because the canals lost a considerable amount of water over their length of many miles. Rather, he argued, drip irrigation uses water more efficiently. That observation was of course, true, but he didn't understand that, unlike the current irrigation infrastructure in Quinua that required only labor for its construction and maintenance, drip irrigation required intensive capital investment for pipes—something that Andean peasants did not possess.

Finally, we reached a pass where the road descended into the valley to the east. The engineer parked the truck and we started walking along a narrow path that led up over a high ridge that separated the sources of the two irrigation systems.

We passed a dam with a small reservoir that I learned later was the source of the other irrigation system (Lurin) in Quinua. That system irrigated most of the rural area in Quinua, and chronically provided insufficient water for those who irrigate their lands below. Ironically, this portion of the irrigation system was not the one that the engineer wanted to improve with a greater supply of water. The source of the other irrigation system was called "Little Black Lake," our ultimate destination, and lay beyond a ridge to the east (fig. 2.3).

We had arrived at the high altitude *puna*, a mystical and mysteriously quiet place that serves as a great resource for peasant and potter alike. On the lower portion of the slopes above the village, several kinds of brush grow. One kind, called *chamizo*, is a unique quick burning fuel used for firing pottery. Above this zone, the brush thins and merges into grass in the montane prairie, and both zones include scattered fields of frost-resistant crops such as Andean tubers and *quinoa*, a uniquely Andean grain in the genus of *Chenopodium*. The prairie continues upward until one reaches the high alpine tundra about 14,000 feet above sea level.

Beginning our climb on the other side of the reservoir, we zigzagged up the trail to the ridge separating the drainage of the two ravines that define the territory of each irrigation system. Soon, we passed grazing llamas on the slope below tended by a young girl.

Further on our upward trek, I noticed a bundle of gelatinous tubers tied up in plastic perched on a rock beside the trail. Apparently, the herders had gathered them while they watched their llamas below us and had placed their trove on a rock along the path. These tubers were wild varieties of the potato and perhaps those of other wild plants that provided hybrid vigor to the domestic varieties already growing here.

I paused to take a photo of the tubers and then turned to look down into the valley (fig. 4.3). There, at the base of the steep slopes of the mountains, three stone houses with thatched roofs occupied a narrow ribbon of relatively flat land with irregularly shaped stone corrals surrounding them. All were empty of animals, but several had crops planted within them. Inhabitants rotated their fields among their corrals to utilize the fertilizer

FIGURE 4.3. A rural hamlet in the *puna* above Quinua showing the irregularly shaped rock corrals that alternatively sheltered llamas and then served as fields for root crops. Those fields in the lower center and lower left of the image currently grow root crops, whereas the corrals in the center left and upper left of the image are used to shelter llamas.

from the dung of the llamas that were returned to the empty corrals every night. Eventually, a corral was cordoned off and cultivated, the animals were turned into another corral empty of crops, and the cycle would be repeated, alternating corrals for protecting llamas with fields for growing crops fertilized by the llama dung.

By this time, we had climbed to almost 14,000 feet above sea level. Fortunately, living in Quinua below at 11,000 feet, I was well adjusted to high altitude, but I still had to pause to rest and catch my breath. I had not realized how high we would ascend to get to the "Little Black Lake."

As we moved higher and higher, the vegetation changed from grasses of the high prairie to tundra plants with a lower profile; many looked soft and spongy. Curious, I wanted to see if they were indeed soft. So, I placed my hand on one of them only to be pricked by a set of tiny spines unseen on the top of the plant. I had unknowingly touched a low, and very small tundra cactus.

Eventually, we passed over the mountain ridge between the two drainage patterns at 14,117 feet and started down the slope to the lake located at 13,796 feet in a deep depression at the head of a valley. After we arrived above the lake and inspected the dam, I decided that I did not want to walk back up the trail over the ridge to return to our vehicle. Instead, I chose to take the trail down to the village.

As I descended, the Valley below was visible only as a wedge-shaped slit between the mountains. As I neared the end of the ravine, the trail broke out of the mountains, and I had stunning views of Quinua, the Ayacucho battlefield, and much of the Ayacucho Valley (fig. 2.4). I paused to take a picture and then moved along the mountainside to the northwest to have better views of Muya and the other rural portions of the community.

I arrived back in Quinua about an hour later thinking that the engineer and the mayor must have returned to the village before me, but they did not show up for several hours. My walk down the mountain was not only more interesting, but it was easier and quicker than climbing back up over a 14,000 ft mountain ridge. By the time that my companions had made that ascent, followed the trail back to the truck, and then drove down to Quinua, I had already returned to the village.

Was the government able to implement the irrigation program even though it would not benefit the entire community? In May 2013, I looked up the location of Little Black Lake on Google Earth. To my surprise, the image of the lake dated July 5, 2005, revealed a dam that measured 150 yards long. In early 1967, however, the dam only extended one tenth of that distance. So, even with the lack of cooperation from many members of the community that would not benefit from the dam, it was still built and served that part of the community that needed the water the least. Bill said that the project managers ended up paying the workers to build the dam rather than using the *faena*, the Andean version of the labor tax for public projects.[11]

ENCOUNTERING THE POTTERS' LANDSCAPE

I wanted to visit as many sources of the raw materials used for making pottery as I could so that I could collect samples for analysis. One source of clay appeared to be on public land and was located along the path down the slope from the cemetery, but others were located in privately owned fields below the community. During visits to these latter sources, Mamerto frequently cautioned me to be careful and hurry with my sample collection so that the owner of the land would not discover us.

One of my trips with Mamerto followed a trail through the fields where I collected some clay samples from fields of his relatives. At one point we peered over the edge of an eroded gorge to see a massive bed of volcanic ash approximately one hundred feet thick that had eroded to form a small flat valley near its base. We followed the path to the other side of the gorge and went down the path into the valley. Above a talus of chunks of ash, potters had dug a mine horizontally into the deposit to extract their temper, and the mine was apparently a source used by all the potters in this portion of the community.

On another occasion, Mamerto told me that he would take me to the source for the white paint because he wanted to obtain some for his own use. He insisted that we must leave early in the morning for our trek, and I wondered why. At first, I thought he wanted to finish the task before he started work at the Artisan School for the day. I was mistaken.

We left early the next morning, and as we walked down the slope, Mamerto was suspicious almost to the point of paranoia that we would be discovered. At one point, we walked past the location that I realized later was actually the source of the paint, only to double back from below so as not to arouse suspicion. It was not clear to me why a clandestine visit was important, but I suspected that the owner would either forbid him from removing the raw material from the field or make him pay for it.

Eventually, we ended up in a stubble field on a rather steep slope. Mamerto helped himself to a sizable amount of clay, testing it on the handle of his pick to be sure that it dried to a white color. Meanwhile, I collected a very small sample to take back to the University of Illinois for analysis. In retrospect, the field was on a slope of more than 45 degrees, and removing any clay would accelerate its erosion. Regrettably, I learned later that field owners considered surreptitious removal of clay as theft, probably wanted compensation, and apparently did not want clay and paint exploitation to contribute to the erosion of their fields.

The field was located across a narrow ravine from a small promontory of consolidated volcanic ash called *chaqta parada*, "the place where the eagle sits." At the time, this name did not mean anything to me, but as I was to discover later, its significance was deeply rooted in the local religion.

The promontory was a source of *qiqatu*, the material for the rotating platform on which pottery was formed. We climbed up to the promontory, and I collected a sample of the ash, but there was no evidence of quarrying the layers from this deposit. Since the deposit continued across much of the rural portion of the community at this elevation, potters could have mined the materials for their platforms in any number of locations.

I had forgotten about this trip until Bill told me later that Mamerto had described a frightening dream to him in which he had traveled to the jungle with his wife and his young son. Upon entering a cave, an earthquake caused it to partially collapse, and Mamerto rushed to escape. On his way out, he discovered that he was covered with blood, and encountered a bearded man. The man told him that he had eaten his wife and his young son, but that he would allow him to escape.

Mamerto believed that the bearded man was the Mountain God (who is always bearded) and had sent him the dream because he had not made an offering of alcohol and coca leaves when he dug the white paint several days earlier. Why? As it turned out, the promontory was a sacred location of the Mountain God, and the white clay source was a part of his territory. Removing anything from a sacred location requires an offering to propitiate the deity.

All of this puzzled me until I reflected on this series of events, and I realized that my informant and I had committed theft, stealing samples of clay, temper, and paint from sources on private land. I pondered why I was unaware of this at the time, but I realized that besides trust in my informant's integrity, my seemingly cavalier view of stealing was rooted both in my previous experience in collecting raw materials in Ticul, Yucatán, Mexico, and in my own cultural biases.

In Ticul, many of the clay and temper samples I collected came from *ejido* lands that were publicly owned but privately worked, and anyone could go and mine there. When I did a systematic survey of potters using structured observations, I offered to purchase a small amount of clay and temper from each potter. I was delighted to pay what was an outrageous amount (one peso, or eight U.S. cents) for about an ounce of temper, when eighty-eight pounds cost eight pesos (or sixty-four U.S. cents) at the time. When I collected samples at the sources, however, informants knew what I wanted and would secure permission to enter house lots for me to collect samples from marl mines there. In Quinua, I suppose I assumed that my informant simply knew what he was doing and had usufruct rights. In retrospect, it appears that in some instances, at least, stealing clay was standard procedure for some potters, and even though households were somewhat removed from fields, I realized that I was still an accessory to theft by stealing raw material.

A second reason for lack of reflection about my behavior at the time was my own cultural bias. I assumed that because clay was essentially dirt and abundant, it had no value. Coming from a farming community in the Midwest, it would seem that taking a few chunks of dirt from the edge of a plowed field may seem strange, but not likely regarded as theft. But clay, in this case, was valuable, and the people were poor, and besides not showing respect for them and their land, taking clay without permission was certainly stealing a valuable commodity even if it was only a small amount. Even so, the cumulative impact of numerous potters surreptitiously stealing clay would significantly degrade agricultural land.

Sometimes, one doesn't realize that the meaning of an action in one cultural context can be very different than in one's own culture. In retrospect, propitiation of the Mountain God reinforced the value of not stealing.

UNCOMFORTABLE AND DANGEROUS TRAVEL

Challenges to living in Peru came in many forms. All created great learning opportunities, and often involved challenges to comfort. One of them was simply getting from place to place. I regularly traveled back and forth over the approximately thirty-mile road between Quinua and Ayacucho to see what pottery was being sold in the Ayacucho market, and to get my mail from Dr. Zuidema. The trip, in itself, was an adventure because, even though there was a bus to Quinua, I usually rode on the back of a truck. Although the trucks passed through the village on an irregular basis, they were more frequent than the bus, and the ride was cheaper. Just showing up in the village plaza when I wanted to leave often coincided with the passing of a truck that could take me down the mountain to Ayacucho. This kind of transportation, however, meant that I shared space with peasants and their freight whether it was potatoes or other tubers, or animals such as guinea pigs, chickens, or pigs. It was also dangerous because trucks would occasionally go off narrow mountain roads and roll down the steep slopes, killing or seriously injuring the passengers riding in the cargo area. In order to avert such accidents on narrow roads, traffic moved in each direction on alternate days.

Even the mundane can pose physical challenges and provide learning opportunities. On one occasion, I left Ayacucho on a truck to go to Quinua, but it dropped me at a fork in the road called Muruncancha (see fig. 2.3). One road went up to Quinua and the other road went to Acos Vinchos, another small village about the same elevation as Quinua but further down the valley to the southeast. Muruncancha was about halfway up the slope, and I thought I could easily walk the remaining three miles up to Quinua. Whereas the road twists and turns as it climbs the slope, the trail followed a straight line up to village.

Shortly after I started my trek, I passed a house with a woman outside feeding her child with a spoon from a metal bowl. It was a touching scene and I thought I would take a picture of the two. I put down my backpack and pulled out my camera. I cannot remember whether I asked her or not, but she was very concerned about my attempt. She asked me what I was going to do with the photo, and whether I was going to take it to my *tierra*—my country. Her reaction to my request puzzled me and she may have thought that I would be making money on the photo. Eventually, I was able to take a nice photo of her that belied her unhappiness with me.

In retrospect, I would never do this again. In all of my subsequent fieldwork, I would always ask informants if I could take a picture of them and respected their wishes. Most informants in Yucatán hadn't cared and were delighted to have their picture taken. Perhaps that experience influenced my decision to take the photo over the woman's query.

As I continued my walk upward, I passed through some gently sloping land that had been left fallow. The sparse vegetation had not inhibited sheet erosion leaving many isolated rocks on the surface. The soil appeared to be clay, and I discovered later that this location (called *Uqurumi*) served as a clay source for making cooking pottery and large brewing and storage vessels that required no temper. Even so, I did not see any obvious excavation resulting from digging clay in this location.

As I neared the village, it started to rain. I donned my poncho, but as I approached the village, people asked me if I was in the *ejército*. I was puzzled and somewhat troubled by the question since I didn't know what the word *ejército* meant. Although I was rather fluent in Spanish, having learned it from my informants in Yucatán, I had never been in a context where the word *ejército* was used, nor was it relevant to any of my experiences in Mexico.

Later, Bill explained that the word meant the "army." Before I left for Peru, I had gone down to the army surplus store in Champaign, Illinois, and bought a cheap backpack and a rain poncho. In the United States, military gear from army surplus stores was common. But this was not the case in Peru. Because I wore army gear, informants thought I was in the army. Even something that seems benign to an American may have a different and even sinister meaning to someone in a different cultural context.

My choice of an army surplus backpack for traveling in Peru had no serious consequences for me, but it sensitized me to the fact that those in another culture may not see my possessions the same way I did. After that experience, I learned that I should not go into the field with army surplus gear or anything khaki if I want to avoid being branded as a military person, and subjected to unwanted scrutiny and harassment.

CHAPTER 5

Engaging an Andean City

ALTHOUGH QUINUA was my research site and my basic needs of shelter and food were met, life there was frustrating and, at first, relatively unproductive. The rainfall and cloudiness made trekking along mountain trails difficult. Potters did not make pottery during the rainy season because of the rainfall, cold, and agricultural responsibilities, and it looked like my study of Quinua pottery making was going to be a failure.

One way to salvage my research was to visit the market in Ayacucho repeatedly and observe, photograph, and document the pottery sold there. Hopefully, such observations would provide sufficient data about pottery made in different communities in the valley. Unlike Quinua, the market there was open daily.

Furthermore, unlike Quinua, where much of the undercurrent of pre-Hispanic Andean culture still remains, Ayacucho became the focal point of Spanish influence in the valley, and I had wondered whether Spanish influence might exist in Quinua pottery and in its production technology. I had already discovered that pottery made in the barrio of Santa Ana in Ayacucho did not seem to have Spanish influence in its shapes and technology, but visits to the market should at least show me whether other potters in the valley made Spanish vessels for a local population, and whether it was made with a Spanish technology.

Visits to the Ayacucho market revealed that pottery sold there was not made with Spanish technology. Rather, traditional pottery was made in the village of Huayhuas between Quinua and Huanta, and cooking pottery was produced in the village of Ticllas northwest of Ayacucho.

Occasionally, merchants brought cooking pottery from the region around Huancayo.

LIFESTYLE CHALLENGES

Even with a modified research design implemented in a large city, a graduate student with limited funds faced challenges in meeting the everyday requirements of living such as sleeping, eating, bathing, and staying healthy. Those challenges were mitigated somewhat by receiving mail, especially from my new girlfriend in Urbana.

During most of those visits to Ayacucho, I either slept in the vacant maid's quarters under a staircase that opened onto a patio at the rear of Professor Zuidema's house, or stayed across town in a rent-free, half-built kitchen across from the prison. The kitchen was dark and cold, but it had enough room for my air mattress and sleeping bag with sufficient space for dressing and laying out my backpack.

Bathing in Ayacucho was also a challenge. Behind the kitchen, a large open courtyard served as a common area shared by several houses. Someone had built a small cubicle in the center of the patio that served as a shower. A tank above supplied water, but for most of the day, it was icy cold. After several attempts at trying to shower in the morning, I came to realize that it never would be pleasant. With near-freezing nighttime temperatures, it was coldest right before dawn. Even later in the morning, the rays from the sun did not sufficiently warm the water in the tank. Only by showering in the early afternoon when the water was warmer could I be assured of a tolerable bathing experience. As a consequence, I only bathed during my visits to Ayacucho when I could use the shower in the courtyard.

Illness provides an inevitable but unpredictable challenge to doing fieldwork, but it is one of the realities of living in a culture with different standards of health and cuisine. Even in the more Hispanic culture of Ayacucho, and its role as department capital and university city, life could still be a challenge health-wise. I went there frequently, sometimes attending Professor Zuidema's seminars at the University of Huamanga. I often wore an old sport coat because it kept me warm in the cold of the rainy season and the approaching winter. The coat also provided abundant pockets to stow money and possessions. The pockets turned out to be a critical asset during my next challenge—a health crisis that was one of the most difficult in my career of working in the field.

As the Andean rainy season waned and moved into the beginning of the dry season, I got extremely sick with a severe upper respiratory disorder and rampant diarrhea losing complete control of my bowels. I was too sick to do any work, but I thought I could stick it out and that my malady would pass in due time. So, I went to the central plaza and sat in the intermittent but frequent sunshine. To prepare myself, my sport coat's abundant pockets held those necessities that my illness demanded. One side pocket held a roll of toilet paper (which was necessary whether or not I was ill) while the other concealed a pair of clean underwear. As I sat there in the sunshine, I waited until nature called and then hurried across the plaza to the toilet in the university. Then, I would walk to a little café on the opposite side of the plaza to hydrate myself and replenish my strength. When my arrival at the toilet failed to coincide with the movement of my lower digestive tract, I would change my underwear, rinse them, wring them out, wrap them in toilet paper, and put them in my pocket. Then, I would return to the bench on the plaza or to the café on the other side to drink some tea.

After I soiled my extra set of underwear, I returned to my room on the east end of town and changed my clothes, replacing the soiled underwear in the pocket with a clean pair. On the return trip to the plaza, I replenished my supply of toilet paper at a local store.

Eventually, the toilet paper failed me. Peruvian *papel higénico* (literally "hygienic paper") available at the time possessed a texture somewhere between the coarseness of the craft paper of a grocery sack and fine sandpaper. Needless to say, the repeated use of this not-so-gentle product could not be sustained without injury!

After I went through my second set of underwear and had to revisit my room, it finally dawned on me that I had a problem and was, in fact, very sick. Waiting out my problem with tea, changes in underwear, and toilet paper was really a very stupid choice. I found a doctor in a building near the plaza, and after talking to him about my condition, I discovered that I had bacillary dysentery! He gave me an injection for the upper respiratory infection and a prescription for a sulfa drug to cure the dysentery. I filled the prescription at a local pharmacy and quickly recovered.

RACE AND CLASS

My visits to the market in Ayacucho created unique opportunities for learning about Peruvian society. During those visits, I frequently passed a dry goods store on a corner of the central plaza on my way to and from the market, and became acquainted with two young women, Angela and Julia, who worked there. Their father owned the establishment, and I had purchased a felt hat there to protect me from the harsh Andean sun and the greater ultraviolet radiation that occurs at high altitudes. Subsequently, I engaged them in conversation during my errands, and during frequent visits to the central market to document the pottery for sale there. I was lonely, wanted companionship, and enjoyed their company.

As we became better acquainted, they asked me over to their house for tea. After finding their house near the central plaza and knocking at the door, they ushered me into a two-story colonial structure. Spanish colonial houses mirror the structure of the city with a patio in the center, and rooms built around the perimeter of the lot. Similarly, the city of Ayacucho was built around the central plaza with a covered arcade in front of the buildings facing it with the exception of the portion occupied by the cathedral. Just as this arcade provided access to the buildings around the city's plaza, so a covered portico built around the perimeter of the household patio provided access to the rooms of colonial houses.

The parlor was one of the rooms adjoining the portico, but it was a stark, cold, and windowless room except for a window toward the patio. The chairs were upholstered with red cloth covered by clear plastic. At the far end of the room, a large radio/record player dominated the wall. Above it was a large picture of an Andean peasant couple dressed in their ethnic finery. The picture caught my attention because my new friends were not part of a peasant family, and it seemed a strange accouterment for a house of upper-class Ayacuchanos in the most central and most prestigious part of the city. My new friends did not dress as ethnic peasants and spoke flawless Spanish. Their clothing reflected a contemporary style with skirts and sweaters, and their father wore a suit with a white shirt and tie. All wore shoes and not the sandals made from vehicle tires worn by the Quechua-speaking peasants.

I subsequently discovered that the couple in the picture were the young women's grandparents. This seeming incongruity between the picture and the family that I knew illustrated the cultural nature of the difference between Andean Indian peasants and *mestizos*, defined as "mixed-race" individuals. People may appear to be "Indian" in appearance, but if they learn to read and write Spanish, and change their clothing to reflect more of the national style, they become mestizos, or *cholos*, an intermediate position between peasant and mestizo. They may ultimately become upper-class Peruvians.

Unlike the United States, race in much of Latin America is more fluid and characterized more by cultural and class attributes. Most Peruvians have some indigenous genetic roots, but the issue is not the genetic heritage, rather social class and its symbols. Those who can read and write Spanish and dress like Westerners are upper-class, whereas those who know only Quechua (the indigenous language), are illiterate, and dress like peasants are considered lower-class. These observations fit a pattern elsewhere in Latin America where there are substantial indigenous populations with interrelated patterns of race and class.

A PUZZLING RITUAL

Unlike Quinua, where Catholic beliefs overlay a dominant pre-Christian religion such as belief in the Mountain God, Ayacucho had stronger roots in Roman Catholicism brought over by the Spanish during the Colonial period. This religious tradition is evidenced by the many churches found in the oldest portion of the city. Many of them are small, but they reflect a time when Roman Catholicism dominated the lives of the inhabitants. Unlike northern Europe, which experienced the beginning of the Protestant Reformation twenty-seven years after Columbus arrived in the New World, the dominance of the Catholic Church continued in Spain without the Reformation, and the Spanish brought medieval Catholicism to their American colonies.

Congruent with its deep colonial roots in Roman Catholic Spain, Ayacuchanos celebrate Holy Week (*Semana Santa*) with an intensity that draws many tourists. With great pride, they believe that their celebrations were the most elaborate and extensive outside of the Spanish city of Sevilla.

I was there for Holy Week, which began on Palm Sunday with a crowd gathering outside the convent of Santa Teresa. Many carried palm branches. At the appointed time, the doors to the convent opened and four priests in colorful satin robes emerged carrying a chair with an image of Christ seated on it. Taking the image out of the chair and placing it on a donkey, the brightly dressed priests held it in place as they walked alongside, leading the donkey down the streets to the central plaza about a half a mile way. As the image moved through the streets, a crowd followed behind waving palm branches. At the central plaza, the priests guided the donkey to the door of the cathedral, dismounted the image, and then took it inside.

The daily processions of Holy Week, and the dramatic visual expression of faith challenged my protestant sensibilities where my faith was a response to verbal symbols, not visual ones. Images were never a part of my experience with Christianity, but they provided learning experiences about Hispanic Peru and about Roman Catholicism.

One personally challenging experience during Holy Week was what one Ayacuchano called a "black mass" (*misa negra*), an event that would take place in the cathedral on Good Friday afternoon. Protestants usually have a service to commemorate the death of Christ on Good Friday—usually between noon and three in the afternoon—the time corresponding to the period of darkness between the sixth and ninth hours that Christ spent on the cross according to the New Testament books of Matthew, Mark, and Luke. While Roman Catholics and Anglo-Catholics may celebrate the Stations of the Cross on Good Friday, their focus is more on the Last Supper on Maundy Thursday as the most important event between Palm Sunday and Easter Vigil on Saturday night. For them, the Maundy Thursday event is critical because it is the archetype for the Eucharist—the focus of their worship services. Non-Anglican Protestants, however, may not celebrate Maundy Thursday at all.

Even so, a "black mass" on Good Friday seemed strange. I had heard of it, but I had never seen it, and I was curious as to what it was. When I asked someone about it, they corrected me saying that it was not a "black mass" at all, but a different kind of rite called a *reseña*. Nevertheless, I wanted to see it.

At the appointed time on Friday afternoon, I entered the cathedral and found a seat near the front on the center aisle. Below the steps leading to the altar, acolytes had placed a row of black pillows along each side of the aisle. Soon, priests covered with long, black flowing robes and large black hoods hiding their faces entered from the rear and walked slowly down the center aisle. They knelt on the pillows and prostrated themselves facing the altar at various times during the ritual.

Another priest walked up the aisle carrying a large, square black flag with a large red "X" sewn on it from corner to corner. He stood at the base of the steps to the altar and waved the flag back and forth thirty-three times, symbolic of the number of years Christ lived. At least in this way, it was indeed a reseña, a ritual summary of the life of Christ.

During the service, the organ played music in a key and genre that was not characteristic of the Western church music I had known—either Catholic or Protestant. It created an eerie atmosphere that made me very uncomfortable.

Now, I realize that my discomfort came from the deeply entrenched structure of Western music within me. My father was a high school band director (among other professions) and I learned to play the cornet at an age of eight or nine. I played in the high school band from age ten through high school, participating in every instrumental and vocal group that was open to me. (It was a small high school with only about 120 students.) I learned to tune my own instrument and recognize even small deviations from the standard tone intervals. The seven-tone scale of Western music and its five half-tones in between became an unseen part of my musical understanding and affected the way I understood music.

So now, after many years, I realize that my discomfort with the music in the Ayacucho cathedral that Good Friday afternoon resulted from the ways the musical scale, tonal pattern, and tonal sequence were different from music familiar to me, and appeared to be a result of the Moorish influence from southern Spain. The Moors were Muslims from North Africa, and during their almost eight hundred years of domination of Andalusia, their culture left an indelible mark. Even today, cities such as Sevilla, Cordoba, and Granada exhibit Moorish influences in the art, architecture, and other aspects of culture. Since much of the migration to the New World during the Colonial period came from Andalusia, those same Moorish influences came with the Spanish, including the high value and importance of interpersonal relationships (as opposed to the value of "time" among North Americans), not "losing face," and parts of the humoral system of medicine, particularly the "hot-cold syndrome" for diagnosing and treating disease.

In retrospect, the Good Friday "black mass" in Ayacucho was not really a mass at all because there was no Eucharist and no distribution of the consecrated Host to the congregants. In the Roman Catholic (and Anglican) ritual, the consecrated Host is removed from the altar on Maundy Thursday and not returned until Easter Sunday. Since the Host is the central focus of the mass, there was no possibility of celebrating the mass between Maundy Thursday and Easter, unless the priest had con-secrated the Host previously. If Catholics observe the Veneration of the Cross on Good Friday with a mass, the priest distributes a Host that was consecrated before Maundy Thursday. In this case, however, there was no mass. Rather, the Good Friday ceremony in Ayacucho was a different kind of ritual observance of the life and death of Jesus heavily influenced by Moorish culture, commemorating his life during the period of his Crucifixion. The ceremony was filled with symbols and behaviors that were strange to me, and I never forgot it. I have never heard of, or seen, anything like it since 1967—even after repeated research and queries of catholic priests.

As was true in medieval Europe, economic life is also tied up with the ritual calendar in both colonial and modern Latin America. So, on the next day, Holy Saturday, a large market was held on the slopes of a hill called Acuchimay located just outside the city—the location of an important archaeological site in the valley that dated to the period just prior to the zenith of the city of Wari, located across the valley. Hundreds of people came to buy and sell produce, food, coca leaves, cooking utensils, and gourds (fig. 5.1). I visited the market hoping to see pottery for sale, but there was none.

FIGURE 5.1. The Easter Saturday market on the hill of Acuchimay. Located southwest of the center of Ayacucho, the hill also harbors an important archaeological site that dates prior to the development of the Wari Empire. The cross marks the summit, but it is not necessarily a Christian symbol. It may also be a symbol of the Mountain God, the most important deity in indigenous religion. According to Google Earth, the site is now covered by urban sprawl.

Although tied to the yearly cycle of the church calendar, the Acuchimay market has a unique sense of place in the history and prehistory of the Ayacucho region. Historically, the market was known for its buying, selling, and trading of cattle, horses, and mules, presumably associated with the adjacent barrio of Carmen Alto, the home of muleteers, who, in recent history, used their animals to transport products back and forth to the Nazca drainage on the south coast (fig. 5.2). Indeed, Bill's adoptive father in Quinua was a muleteer who regularly went to Nazca. Contact with Nazca has a long history dating back at least to the last half of the first millennium AD when pottery from Nazca and that from the Ayacucho Valley showed stylistic similarities. Nazca stylistic influence reached its apogee during the development of the city of Wari when it was emerging as the center of a great pre-Inca empire.

That evening I ran into my women friends whose father owned the store on the plaza, and they invited me over to their house for a meal. They told

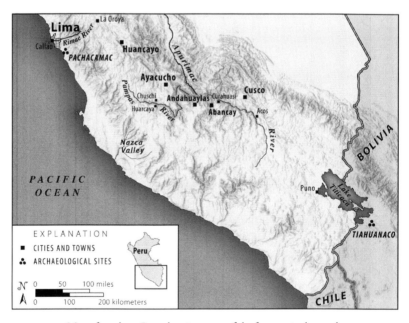

FIGURE 5.2. Map of southern Peru showing some of the features in the southern part of the Department of Ayacucho, and some of the cities and towns encountered during the trip from Ayacucho to Cusco. The map also shows the spatial relationship between the Valley of Ayacucho and the Nazca drainage on the south coast of Peru. (Map by Chelsea M. Feeney)

me that at dawn the next day (Easter), a large float would emerge from the cathedral, and they invited me to stay up all night with them to witness the event. Our little group stayed in their house as long as we could, and then went down the street to the central plaza to wait for dawn. To pass the time, one woman brought a guitar, and my friends wanted to learn American folk songs. So, I tried to teach them "Home on the Range," "Old Susanna," "She'll be Comin' Round the Mountain," and other traditional tunes.

As I came to realize many years later, this waiting was a part of what Roman and Anglo Catholics call "Easter Vigil," during which congregants ritually commemorate waiting in the darkness of night in anticipation of the dawning of a new era marked by Christ's Resurrection. This activity in Ayacucho, however, did not take place in the cathedral, but outside in the plaza which could accommodate many more people and, as I came to appreciate much later, celebrate in a way that was impossible in the cathedral itself.

Easter was early that year, and the latter part of the wet season had been rainy and cold. So, singing and playing music was not only a distraction while we waited for dawn, but it kept our mind off the chill of the Andean night as we anticipated the first light of morning.

During the previous day, large piles of the quick-burning chamizo brush were placed on the streets around the plaza in roughly fifty-foot intervals—the same brush as that used for firing pottery in Quinua. Interspersed less frequently were large wooden frames containing fireworks.

Finally, as dawn neared, the large wooden doors of the cathedral opened slowly and an immense rectangular float emerged. In the shape of a tiered wedding cake, it was carried on the shoulders of approximately fifty men positioned unseen underneath it. As it moved around the plaza, the statue of Christ was raised and lowered through its top to provide a visual metaphor to commemorate his Resurrection. As the float approached each pile of chamizo, the brush was set alight. It burned with vigor illuminating the float's pathway in the dim light of the early morning symbolizing the light that marks the beginning of a new era marked by Christ's Resurrection. As it reached each wooden frame, the fireworks were ignited in celebration, letting others in the city know nonverbally that the image had emerged from the cathedral, and was moving around the plaza. The procession advanced slowly, but eventually returned to the cathedral.

The leadership in the cathedral thus organized a ritual for the people of Ayacucho to celebrate the centerpiece of the Christian faith in a dramatic way. With the visual metaphor of the statue of Christ coming out of the float, the Resurrection message of Easter was nonverbally reenacted, symbolized, celebrated, and commemorated. Burning the pyres of chamizo and igniting the fireworks as the procession approached them visually illustrated two prominent metaphors used in the New Testament: fire and light.

Being raised a non-Anglican protestant, I had no appreciation for images—even Christian ones. Most Protestantism is built upon responses to verbal symbols—not responses to visual symbols as among Orthodox, Catholic, and some Anglican believers. But, in Ayacucho I began to see the benefit of images to remind the faithful nonverbally about the basis of their faith. Images of Christ and the saints are not idols as some Protestants believe, but rather are physical reminders that visually reinforce the stories of the Bible and the saints in a material way. Unlike reading, listening, and preaching, images can call out a person's faith in ways that may seem heretical to some Protestants, but they aid in socially reproducing that faith generation after generation.

A JOURNEY TO LURICOCHA

Not all religious beliefs and rituals in the Andes have their origin in the Roman Catholicism that the Spanish brought with them after the conquest. When one gets away from the big cities, Catholic symbols such as the cross and images of the saints are still evident, but their meaning may be syncretistic, fusing Catholic beliefs with those coming from the pre-Hispanic period. The cross, for example, although appearing to be a Christian symbol, is in reality a symbol of the Mountain God, the most powerful and most revered deity in the Andes.

I had learned about this symbol in Quinua where the cross was sometimes incorporated into the modeled ceramics. Such syncretism also manifested itself in the fabrication of ceramic churches which, like ceramic crosses, were placed on the top of newly constructed houses (see fig. 3.1). Some of these churches modeled the twin bell towers of the Ayacucho cathedral with their clocks showing different times. Unfortunately, I could never obtain what I thought was a definitive explanation for the placement of objects on tops of houses beyond that it was their traditional practice to do so.

Professor Zuidema was convinced that the study of the beliefs and practices in rural communities in the Ayacucho Valley might reveal

FIGURE 5.3. Inhabitants in and around Luricocha bringing their crosses to the village church to be blessed by the priest on the Day of the Crosses.

patterns that shed light on ancient prehistoric beliefs, especially those of the Inca period. He thought, for example, that the "Feast of the Crosses," a fiesta in the town of Luricocha in the northern end of the valley, might illustrate the survival of those beliefs (see fig. 2.3). Each household and hamlet around Luricocha had a cross associated with it, and these crosses were brought to the church for blessing by the priest (fig. 5.3). The pattern of the location of these crosses relative to the church in the village, Zuidema believed, might emulate the Inca structure of lines linking center and peripheral ritual places around Cusco called the *Ceque* System that he had studied for his PhD dissertation.[1] So, on May 3, about six weeks after Easter, he took us to Luricocha for the festivities.

I was not as interested in the crosses and their spatial pattern across the landscape as I was in learning about pottery production. When we stopped in Huanta, I observed the pottery for sale in the market there (fig. 5.4). After we arrived in Luricocha, I observed pottery in the market there and asked if pottery was made in the area. I soon learned that inhabitants of a remote hamlet northwest of Luricocha called Pampay made pottery, and I wanted to visit that community to learn what I could about the craft. So, I told Professor Zuidema that I was going to walk there, and

FIGURE 5.4. Selling pottery in the Huanta market. The vessels in the center of the image are used for carrying water or *chicha* (maize beer). The vessel held by the woman on the right is a common form of cooking pot made in the Ayacucho Valley and some other localities as well. Buyers of pottery usually carefully inspect the vessels they intend to purchase, and then test their integrity with a single-finger knock to its rim.

that he should not wait for me to return. I would walk back to Luricocha and then to Huanta and catch a ride on a truck to Ayacucho at the end of the day.

I found someone from Pampay and we walked the two and one-half miles to the hamlet. We enquired about pottery making there, and discovered that, like the potters in Quinua, they only made pots during the dry season, obtaining their clay in the mountains above the community to the north and producing only cooking pottery and some storage vessels with limited plastic decoration. The best I could do was to photograph some vessels from a household inventory that were reportedly produced in the hamlet, and elicit the name of the source location of the clay used to make them.

I walked back to Luricocha and then made the two-and-a-half-mile trek to Huanta. On my way into town, a North American woman called to me in English from her house. She and her husband were missionaries, and they invited me inside for a piece of American apple pie. I was grateful for the food because I had eaten very little that day and was very hungry. Their hospitality to an unknown stranger was deeply appreciated and never forgotten.

Soon, I had to leave and get transportation back to Ayacucho. It was too far to walk, but I was able to catch a ride on a truck. After being dropped off near the edge of the city, I walked to my cold, unheated kitchen across from the prison and arrived exhausted.

When I talked with Professor Zuidema later, he said he was disappointed with our visit to Luricocha and was unable to gather sufficient data to support his hypothesis about the relationship of the modern "Feast of the Crosses" in Luricocha with pre-Hispanic patterns of the central places and rural religious sites.

A BIRD'S EYE VIEW OF THE PAST

My experiences with Professor Zuidema had already revealed that the Ayacucho Valley was rich in archaeological sites and again reinforced its crucial role in the history and prehistory of the Peruvian Andes. Many figured critically into the cultural history of the valley that related to my original, but now secondary, goal of trying to understand if the pottery of Quinua was historically related to Wari. We had already visited many of these sites, but there were many more that indicated the valley's critical importance in the ancient past.

When the weather improved in the dry season, Professor Zuidema took us on an excursion to visit another important archaeological site on the southwestern edge of the valley that he believed was related to the fall of Wari. The site was located on the highest mountain, called Quehuahuilca, that lay on a long ridge with a low peak in the center. I had noticed it from across the valley in Quinua, and during my descent from Little Black Lake (see fig. 2.4).

We left Ayacucho in Professor Zuidema's truck, and as he drove, the road rose into a cooler and wetter climate of the high mountains. Soon, we entered the high puna grassland with waist-high grasses on every side, and moved along a poorly maintained dirt road that followed the contour of the mountain about five hundred vertical feet below the south and west sides of the ridge that was part of Quehuahuilca. We drove to a point that paralleled the end of the ridge, found a place to park, and then walked up to the summit through the grasses. Still in the prairie zone and not high enough to be tundra like that on the mountain range across the valley, the ascent was still exhausting because its altitude exceeded 13,800 feet above sea level. Even with heavy cotton twill jeans, the grasses penetrated them like needles making my climb annoying if not painful. So, trekking through the grass was slow and tiring even though the slope was gradual.

At the top, we had a panoramic view of the entire Ayacucho Valley as it spread out before us to the north, east, and south (fig. 5.5). In the bottom of the central portion of the valley, we could see the ancient site of Wari perched in its strategic location on a plateau above the flood plain, protected on three sides with steep natural slopes. Above it lay Quinua and the eroded land below it, and along the lower portions of the other side of the valley.

Along the slopes on that side of the valley, we could see the horizontal bands of different zones of vegetation and land use that varied with the altitude and the amount of precipitation that each received. A broad, horizontal green strip just below the rise of the steep mountains marked the

FIGURE 5.5. The central portion of the Valley of Ayacucho as seen from the top of Quehuahuilca on the southwestern edge of the valley. The ancient site of Wari lies in the center of the image in the lower part of the valley. The image also shows the horizontal ecological zones on the slopes of the mountains on the far side of the valley. The lighter area at the tops of the mountains is the high *puna* grassland zone. Below it, the dark band is the area of low forest, and below that is the main agricultural zone. Quinua and its immediate environs lie at the base of the dark area on the lower slope of the mountain (slightly to the right of center). The elongated light area there is the Ayacucho battlefield.

agricultural land around the villages there, and above it lay a dark-green zone of low brush that I had visited in my trek to procure fuel for firing pottery. Above this zone, the tan grass of the high puna topped the mountains, with a few craggy peaks of black rock beyond them in the distance. Below all of these zones in the bottom of the valley, I could see the white of the eroding beds of volcanic ash, and the beige of dry vegetation that stood out as the consequence of rain shadow from the weather coming from the east.

We remarked that our vantage point was a strategic position to view Wari and to monitor activity in the center of the valley. Above Wari, we could see the unique position of Quinua, the site of the first Spanish settlement in the valley, and the Ayacucho battlefield above it. Again, I reflected on the strategic location of the Quinua area in Peruvian prehistory, the Spanish conquest, and the battle that liberated Peru from Spanish rule.

On the ridge behind us, a large archaeological site stretched out to the south (fig. 5.6). Following the ridge, we discovered that the site extended one-half to three-quarters of a mile to its highest point.

In exploring the site, we found some coca leaves and a glass drinking vessel on some rocks. Placed on the highest peak in the area (elevation 13,965 feet), these objects were probably offerings to the Mountain God (*Tayta Urqu*) or to the mountain spirits (the *Wamani*).

Besides being strategic and defensible locations, mountains have great meaning in Andean religion and are the dwelling places of the Mountain God (Tayta Urqu), and the mountain spirits (the Wamani), and such deities must be placated with offerings. Such rituals were, and are, a significant theme of the religion of the modern descendants of the pre-Hispanic peoples of the Andes.

Professor Zuidema thought that the archaeological site probably dated to the period after the Wari domination. Archaeological survey in this area and research elsewhere in the Andes have revealed that settlement patterns shifted to mountaintops after the demise of Wari. Although very visible, Wari still was a long distance away, but we speculated that the large size of the site on which we stood somehow might be related to the collapse of Wari and its empire, or was perhaps occupied by the Chankas whose homeland lay farther south in the Department of Apurimac.[2]

Examining the site using Google Earth almost fifty years later (image dated July 23, 2016) revealed a settlement on the summit at 13,965 feet surrounded by an oval wall that extending 400 feet along its longest

FIGURE 5.6. The archaeological site on top of Quehuahuilca looking southwest. The wall on the lower right is a portion of the defensive wall around the summit. Below the summit and the structures visible here are a series of walls that follow the contours of the slope around much of the perimeter of the mountain and might have been used for agriculture, fortification, or for corralling camelids.

dimension. Another settlement stretched along the ridge for half a mile southwest of it. The remains of many parallel walls, following the contour lines of the mountain, were spread along its northern and western slopes, and around the lower mountains to the south. Whatever their purpose, which appeared to be defensive, their construction revealed a massive amount of labor, and the existence of a sizable resident population.

As the sun continued its descent in the west, we walked down the slope to our vehicle and returned to Ayacucho discussing what we had seen. The site was consistent with the placement of other mountaintop settlements elsewhere in Peru after the Wari Empire collapsed but before the ascendancy of the Incas. Mountaintop sites farther south appear to coincide with the location of the ethnohistoric Chankas who dominated the area around Andahuaylas, even though this settlement pattern also occurs in many parts of southern Peru.[3] Whether Quehuahuilca was a refuge of the Chankas who might have conquered Wari (as Dr. Zuidema suggested at the time) was, of course, another question, but the size of the site, its location, and its apparent defensive walls on the slopes of the mountain also suggested that it might have provided a refuge of the inhabitants of Wari after its abandonment, and a defensive location *from* hostile groups such as the Chankas.

We now know that the fall of Wari and its empire was far more complicated and was, at least in part, related to the inability of the city to respond to two long droughts.[4] Inhabitants of the city probably moved to other areas as the amount of agricultural land decreased, leaving much of the population without an adequate subsistence base. The massive site that we had just visited, Quehuahuilca, might have been one of those locations to which some of the Wari population had migrated. If the site was a refuge from residents from Wari, the demand for the elaborate Wari polychrome styles disappeared as religious and economic institutions (such as interregional trade) collapsed without a large population of consumers, and left a massive expanse of an abandoned city. Some of the rural population that lived above the site in Quinua, however, may have continued practicing agriculture and making pottery using some of the same paints and colors as those found on Wari pottery.

A DANGEROUS ROAD

The influence of the Wari Empire and that of the Chankas who followed them extended far beyond the Ayacucho Valley. One area that would link the Ayacucho Valley to the Chanka homeland around Andahuaylas to the south was the Pampas River Valley (see fig. 5.2). Dr. Zuidema had placed three Illinois graduate students in the village of Chuschi in the valley to investigate both its archaeology and its contemporary culture. So, after the rainy season passed, Zuidema wanted to take us there to learn about their research, and to teach us more about the Andes and its people.

Chuschi was a remote village at the end of the road. Like many trips I took in the Andes, the trip required travel over a narrow, unpaved gravel road with only one lane.

There were more of us than could fit in the cab of his truck, so we took turns riding in the cargo area in the rear. My turn came as we entered the Pampas River drainage—a gorge so deeply cut with sides so steep that we never did see the river far below. The road was constructed midway up the side of the gorge where it widens into a more gradual slope. Covered with irregularly shaped terraces following the contours of the topography, many fields were planted with maize; its yellow tassels stood out in an

FIGURE 5.7. The village of Pomabamba and surrounding rural area in the Pampas Valley south of Ayacucho. This middle zone of the slope of the gorge is an ideal elevation for maize cultivation. Irregularly shaped terraces can be seen across the middle of the image.

irregular patchwork against the adjacent green fields of immature wheat and barley (fig. 5.7).

We traversed the road through the upper reaches of the valley, dotted with small valleys that extended back from the steepest gorge, sometimes nestled in between mountains on three sides. Settlements were concentrated in and around small villages with fields both above and below them just as they were on the eastern side of the Ayacucho Valley. We could see other villages on the other side of the gorge with green fields standing out against what appeared to be dry beige grasses—sharp color contrasts that indicated the communities practiced irrigation. In any event, both terracing and irrigation revealed a pattern of intensive agriculture.

Chuschi lay farther up the Pampas gorge in a side valley that lay deep below high mountains on its eastern side. It was almost midday when we arrived.

The only place to stay was a small hotel that consisted of a few contiguous single rooms at the back of a house. Each room opened onto the rear patio of the house, but they were tiny and spartan. Built for Andean peasants rather than *gringos*, the lintels of its doors were placed at a fraction of my height so that I had to duck to enter a room with a ceiling so low that I could not stand upright. After entering its cramped quarters, I had to move stooped over from one part of the room to the other. The bed was too short for me, and in order to lie on it, I had to position myself diagonally. A single thick blanket was my only protection from the cold of the Andean night. If I laid flat, the blanket covered me, but if I turned on my side to sleep, the blanket was too narrow, and my body lifted its edges above the bed exposing me to the frigid air that flowed down from the high puna during the nights of the Andean fall.

I arose the next morning after spending a cold, uncomfortable, and relatively sleepless night in the confines of my tiny room. Ducking to leave my cramped quarters to avoid colliding with the lintel of the door, I emerged into the chill of the early morning. The sky was bright blue, but the rising sun still remained behind the mountains to the east. Across the valley to the south, perched halfway up the slopes of the gorge, bright sunlight bathed the village of Huarcaya (see fig. 5.2) and its environs as a green island among the tan and brown rocks above and below it.

Chuschi, however, was still shrouded in deep shade from the morning sun. The Andean air sent a deep chill through my body as I made my way to the house of my graduate student colleagues thinking about how difficult it would be live in a community that did not see the sun until late morning.

We all chatted with Dr. Zuidema over breakfast, and he debriefed our visit to Chuschi. After he consulted with our colleagues about the progress of their research, we prepared to leave for our return to Ayacucho.

On the trip back, we met a large ten-ton truck on the road only slightly wider than one vehicle. The truck was no match for our professor's little Datsun pickup, and the encounter soon became a game of chicken. Both vehicles finally stopped, facing one another, and someone from each vehicle searched the road behind to find a wide spot so that the two vehicles could pass.

Like many Andean roads at the time, the road was not only narrow, but in some places was blasted out from the rocks against the vertical face of a mountain. Our side of the road sometimes dropped off steeply for hundreds of feet into the valley below. For this leg of the trip, I was seated on the passenger's side of the pickup, but I could not open the door and leave the truck because there was no space between the truck and the edge of the road. Any attempt to step outside would be my last. If I were still alive after that, I would find myself gravely injured hundreds of feet below.

Soon, the drivers calculated who had to back up and how far each had to move in order to allow the other to pass. Since our vehicle was much smaller, we had to back to a wider spot in the road. Finally, after negotiating about which vehicle would move, the truck crawled past us carefully on our left, but the clearance was so small that the truck tore off the left rearview mirror of Professor Zuidema's vehicle. Understandably angry, he managed to come to terms with the truck driver in resolving the ensuing conflict.

CHAPTER 6

Retracing Inca Steps

MY INTERMITTENT VISITS to the market in Ayacucho provided some knowledge of pottery made in the valley and that made outside of it, and helped compensate for the limited amount of data that I collected about the craft in Quinua. By mid-May, however, the rainy season ended and a few Quinua potters were beginning to make pottery. I had started to make some progress in my study when Professor Zuidema suggested that I should travel to the village of Acos south of Cusco. His reasoning was based on the historical documents related to the Inca conquest of the Ayacucho area more than five centuries before when the Incas resettled the people of Acos in the Quinua area. I resisted his suggestion because I saw great opportunities to observe the increased frequency of pottery production after the rainy season ended. The maize harvest had begun, and those potters who grew maize wanted to finish their harvest before they made any pottery. If I went to Acos, the length of the trip might mean that I would return shortly before I was scheduled to leave Peru, providing little opportunity to observe the craft in Quinua when most potters would begin production. Dr. Zuidema, however, explained the details of the Inca conquest of the Ayacucho area and why a trip to Acos might be important for my research. As a consequence, I might be able to solve the mystery of why Quinua pottery is so unique in the valley.

The Inca influence in the Quinua area began when the ninth supreme Inca, Pachacuti, rose to power in the early fifteenth century. He defeated the attacking Chankas in Cusco, and moved across the Apurimac River to the west, conquering them again in Andahuaylas (see fig. 5.2). He then turned his attention northwest to the Ayacucho area where several ethnic groups resisted his advances. He eventually defeated them and secured the area by replacing its inhabitants with pacified groups (called *mitimaes* in Spanish) from the area around the Inca capital.[1]

Two of these groups were resettled in the Quinua area. One group, from the village of Anta west of Cusco, was relocated around the village of Huamanguilla northwest of Quinua (see fig. 2.3).[2] A second group came from Acos, a small community located 33 miles southeast of Cusco. They were resettled in the Quinua area and their position was corroborated by a Spanish soldier named Pedro Cieza de Leon, who traveled throughout southern Peru in 1553 and wrote about his trip. He mentioned that there was a village called Acos along the Inca road north of the city. The Acos Indians, he said, lived in the rugged mountains to the east.[3] Their position is further verified by viceroy Francisco Toledo who traveled around Peru about twenty years later (1572), taking a census of the population for the Spanish crown. His report, called the *Visita* of Toledo, indicated that the section of the Province of Huamanga (the province around the city of Ayacucho) called Quinua (the *Repartimiento de Quinua*) was made up of Acos Indians.[4]

Other evidence corroborates the presence of the Acos Indians in Quinua. Two legal documents that Dr. Zuidema found in the Peruvian National Archives also revealed the historical link of Quinua with Acos. These seventeenth- and early eighteenth-century documents of land disputes indicated that the two major divisions of Quinua (called Hanansayuq and Lurinsayuq in 1967) were called "Hananacos" (Hanan Acos) and "Lurinacos" (Lurin Acos) in 1632 and 1702. They indicated that the territory of Hananacos extended to the small hamlet of Suso southeast of Quinua and hence to its border with the District of Acos Vinchos.[5] This extent revealed that the Acos resettlement encompassed the entire Quinua area, and because Acos Vinchos had "Acos" in its name, it presumably included Acos exiles as well (see fig. 2.3).

The Inca resettlement of the Acos Indians around Quinua raised a provocative research question. Did the tradition of pottery making in Quinua come from the relocated Acos population? Since pottery making in Quinua was elaborate and unique in the valley,[6] and none of the other pottery-making communities in the valley came from Acos, Professor Zuidema thought that they may have brought knowledge of pottery production with them.

Dr. Zuidema had never visited Acos. So, with his urging, I decided to travel overland to Acos to explore the possible relationship of ceramic production in Quinua with Acos. I wanted to find out if the people of Acos made pottery and, if so, whether the Acos pottery resembled that made in Quinua. Could the origin of Quinua ceramic production be found in Acos?

In retrospect, travel to Acos was a courageous journey. Traveling alone to a location 170 miles away over some of the highest and most rugged mountainous terrain on earth didn't seem to bother me, but the motivation to make such a trip was perhaps based less on courage than on Professor Zuidema's suggestions, my own curiosity, and a heavy dose of my own naivete; I had no idea what would happen to me during my journey. I didn't even consider it. The danger from the Shining Path guerrillas was still more than a decade in the future, and the thought of stopping in Cusco and seeing Machu Picchu enthralled me. In retrospect, the trip provided a deeper knowledge of the Andean landscape and culture, and resulted in more challenges to my body, mind, and spirit. And, it provided much more adventure that I could have ever imagined.

The only way I knew to get to Acos was to travel overland across the Andes, retracing the steps of the Incas as they expanded their empire from their capital in Cusco. Unlike the Incas, however, I would use modern transportation to make my trip, but not necessarily traveling along Inca roads and trails. I planned to stop in Cusco, but I was unsure where to go from there.

I asked about buses that went to Cusco, but I discovered that I would first need to travel to the city of Andahuaylas (see fig. 5.2). So, eager to begin my journey, I went to the office of the bus company and bought my ticket.

Early the following morning, I boarded the bus not knowing exactly how to get to Acos and not knowing when I was going to arrive there. Although the purpose of my journey was to visit to the village of the exiled Acos Indians, it also turned out to be a journey through Peruvian history, prehistory, culture, and geography.

The bus trundled out of Ayacucho, bumping along littered streets with playing children. After a few minutes, it passed the last houses on the city's outskirts and began to climb out of the valley.

Soon, the bus moved past the remains of the ancient site of Ñawim Pukyu, one of many archaeological sites that dot the valley. This site and many like it were occupied before the city of Wari and its vast pre-Inca empire emerged as a great power.

Beyond the site of Ñawim Pukyu, we passed the plain where the Battle of Chupas was fought in 1542 when the forces of the Spanish

crown defeated rebel soldiers led by a general who resisted the domination of Pizzaro and his brother. Two years previously (1540), the nascent
Spanish settlement had moved from its original foundation in what is
now the village of Quinua to its present location across the valley at what
is now Ayacucho. Shortly thereafter, a power struggle ensued between the
rebels and the forces of the Spanish crown, and in 1541 the rebels assassi-
nated Pizzaro. When the struggle continued and culminated in the Battle
of Chupas in 1542, royalists were firmly in control of the newly established
Spanish settlements in Peru.[7] To commemorate the victory, the name of
the newly relocated population from Quinua was changed from *San Juan
de la Frontera* (St. John of the Frontier)—the name given to the original
settlement in Quinua—to *San Juan de La Victoria de Huamanga* (St. John
of the Victory of Huamanga). It subsequently became known simply by
its Quechua name, Huamanga, and ultimately grew into the city known
as "Ayacucho" after the defeat of the Spanish viceroy's troops on the battlefield above Quinua in 1824.

As the road rose out of the lower slopes of the valley, it zigzagged
upward through the vegetation contrasts that reflected the different environments of changing elevation. At the base of the valley, little precipitation falls because it lies in rain shadow from the seasonal rains that come
from the east. Plants here largely consist of various kinds of cacti and other
drought-tolerant vegetation. As one moves out of the valley, however, the
temperature cools and rainfall increases.

Finally, we reached the puna, a grassland with a few fields and herds
of llamas dotting the landscape. Varying from ten inches to two feet high,
the hardiness of the grasses can pierce even a pair of heavy cotton trousers, touching the skin like needles, as I had discovered earlier when I
climbed Quehuahuilca above Ayacucho. With a relatively flat topography
compared to the Ayacucho Valley below, and reaching to the horizon, its
elevation, exceeding 13,000 feet above sea level, seemed deceptively lower
than it actually was.

Since the trip began in the late Andean fall, the diurnal temperature
changes at such high elevations vary greatly from the balmy sixties during
the day to well below freezing at night. This region is cold, and the tundra
above it is even colder. Precipitation in these zones often falls as snow,
and because winter was approaching, we passed through a blizzard at the
highest elevations of our trip with snow clinging to the *ichu* grasses like
frost. An hour before, we had passed through a dry, subtropical valley with
orange groves and bright warm sunshine.

The excitement of the first leg of my trip soon wore off, and I fell asleep as the bus rattled and bounced along the narrow road, climbing and descending through thousands of feet of elevation.

Some thirteen hours after leaving Ayacucho, the bus stopped. Moments before, I vaguely remembered multiple sensations of bounding along city streets with the noise of shouting children and impatient truck drivers who used their horn more than their brakes. As I slowly emerged into consciousness, I realized that it was dark outside! I had left Ayacucho in the early morning.

I glanced around the bus and noticed that others were stirring from their sleep. Earlier they had been talking and singing as the bus wound its way along the treacherous road. Fear gripped me once again as I recalled meeting another bus going in the opposite direction on a one-lane road that clung to the side of a cliff.

We had arrived in Andahuaylas, a sleepy Andean city quite distant from the national culture of Peru's capital, Lima. It was the end of the first leg of my trip to Acos. As my eyes focused on activity outside the bus, I realized that the driver was requesting permission to proceed from a police checkpoint.

Still half-asleep from my journey, I barely noticed when the door of the bus opened and a well-dressed man climbed aboard, shouting to the passengers in Spanish, "Is anyone going to Abancay?"

The words jolted me awake, dispelling much of my sleepiness as I realized that "Yes, *I* was going to Abancay!" Unable to speak and still groggy from my trip, all I could think of was the throbbing pain in my head. This was no ordinary headache, but a malady compounded by altitude sickness. And, although I had faced it earlier in Ayacucho, I drew little comfort from that knowledge. It was still annoying. Nevertheless, I was closer to my destination, but it was dark, and I still had a long trip ahead of me.

The three traveling companions in front of me gathered up their coats and parcels. The peasants in the back of the bus were exchanging goodbyes in Quechua.

Once again the words of the well-dressed intruder jogged me closer to full consciousness, and he repeated his question.

"Is anyone going to Abancay? My company will pay."

The thought of taking the next leg of my trip at no cost appealed to me, but my mind was too foggy to respond, and I was tired. Traveling along winding one-lane roads at night was not something to look forward to. Further, the Andean autumn was slipping into winter during the last month before the solstice, and even though it was pleasant during the day, the temperature dropped below freezing at night.

After a brief pause, I learned the reason for his persistence.

"There is no tourist hotel here, and I want to go on to Abancay," the stranger explained.

In other words, there were no first-class accommodations in Andahuaylas. It was just an ordinary Andean city without a warm room, a hot shower, or good food. The thought of sleeping in an unheated room during the late Andean fall made me shudder.

So, I motioned in the affirmative with a half-hearted response.

Again, the man reiterated his request. "I'm going to Abancay. There is a fine hotel there. Will you come along? I need some company."

Would I come along? Responding instinctively, I replied, "Well, er, no."

My throbbing head said no. Reflecting further, I knew without adequate hotel facilities I could not look forward to anything pleasant in Andahuaylas. The memory of the previous thirteen hours of frightening curves, and the cyclical sequences of snowstorms in the high tundra and the heat of the river valleys further convinced me that more discomfort would follow if I remained in Andahuaylas. Pressing forward into the unknown with a more pleasant destination seemed to be a preferable choice.

Contradicting myself, I replied again. "Yes," I said with more conviction, "I'll come with you."

I struggled to collect my belongings. The seat had been built for someone half my size, and extricating myself from it was no easy task. The lady who sat next to me on the aisle now awoke with a start as oranges from my package on the overhead racks began bombarding her.

As I emerged from my window seat, I stumbled and sprawled over her.

Embarrassed by my clumsiness, I apologized and said, "Perdón" (Excuse me).

I was glad to leave the bus—at least I would not have to bend forward and crane my neck to look out the window. With a flurry of polite apologies to nearby passengers, I made my exit.

Outside, still in a partial stupor of sleepiness, I stumbled to the side of the bus to collect my backpack. The driver had placed it on top of the bus, and he carelessly tossed it to me.

As I reeled under the impact, I realized that it was only half full. In the driver's haste to remove the tarp from the top of the bus and unload the baggage stowed there, he had grabbed my backpack and spilled its contents into the dusty street around me. Too sleepy and tired to protest, I collected my clothing, sleeping bag, and poncho. Even so, the driver's carelessness irritated me. Sensing my displeasure, he obliged by helping me pick up my clothes off the street. His selfless act sufficiently suppressed my irritation, and I walked silently toward the waiting vehicle of the well-dressed stranger.

My new traveling companion placed my backpack in the rear of his station wagon, and I climbed into the passenger's seat. As we started our journey, he introduced himself. He was the district manager of the National Cash Register Company in Peru, and was delivering some new machines to clients in Cusco; he had offered me a free ride because he wanted a traveling companion. He had driven his late-model station wagon all the way from Lima—filled with tools and an oxygen supply. He was ready for almost anything.

As we drove through the streets of Andahuaylas, I explained that I was a student of anthropology returning to the homeland of an ethnic group near Cusco that the Incas had relocated in the fifteenth century. I wanted to go to their village of origin and see if they made pottery there.

As the lights of Andahuaylas faded behind us, the road began to climb and we exchanged pleasantries, conversing on topics of mutual interest. He was an *Aprista*—a member of a large political party opposing the policies of the current president, Fernando Belaúnde Terry. He was concerned about what was happening throughout Peru, and the direction that Belaúnde was going.

"The American imperialists," he said, "are exploiting our natural resources."

I had heard this accusation before, and as an American, it didn't bother me. Peruvians had expressed anger that U.S. corporations exported raw materials cheaply, manufactured products abroad using them, and then imported those products back into Peru, selling them at what Peruvians perceived as greatly inflated prices.

His attitude toward President Belaúnde was equally negative. The Apristas were in control of the national assembly at the time and resisted Belaúnde's policies.

"One reason I took this trip," he said, "was to see what the President was doing in the countryside."

Belaúnde's party, called *Acción Popular* ("Popular Action"), was trying to enhance pottery production in Quinua by funding the Artisan School for potters. They had also tried, but so far had failed, to make irrigation water more accessible to peasant farmers there.

We soon tired of discussing Peruvian politics and talked about more pleasant and mundane topics.

"I have a son in the U.S.," he said. "He's going to college in Dayton, Ohio, and working for my company."

The headquarters of the National Cash Register Company was in Dayton.

Soon, my head began to throb again. My stomach churned endlessly as we sped around the hairpin curves. As we climbed higher and higher, I realized I was suffering from altitude sickness again. An occasional milepost marked the elevation of the road in meters which I converted to feet in my head. We passed one that was 10,000 feet above sea level, and soon another at 10,500 feet. At the 11,000-foot level, we were still going up, but finally we reached the highest point of our journey at 12,400 feet! Pilots breathe oxygen at 10,000 feet because most of the oxygen in the atmosphere lies below. Walking at high attitude is one matter, but someone behind the wheel of a motor vehicle at this elevation could pass out because of oxygen deprivation, and the consequences were frightening. Our journey was downhill after that, but I took little comfort—the mileposts showed that we were only halfway to Abancay.

It was a moonless night, but in the thin atmosphere at that altitude, a myriad of stars illuminated the sky with a low eerie light. It was so clear that one could make out the rough-hewn forms of the dark mountains against the dimly lit background in the distance.

CHALLENGES OF THE ANDEAN NIGH

At last, the lights of Abancay twinkled in the valley below (see fig. 5.2). Breathing a sigh of relief, I was convinced that we were nearing our destination. But, as I discovered in Quinua, line-of-site distances in the Andes can be deceptive, and the mile posts revealed that we still had thirty miles to go! Before we could reach Abancay, we had to descend the mountain and ascend still another.

Just as I settled back into semiconsciousness, I felt a thud from the bottom of our vehicle. In the driver's haste to get to Abancay, the station wagon hit a rock. Another clunk followed shortly thereafter, and then another.

After those encounters, we seemed to move uneventfully until my host exclaimed, "We're losing gasoline!"

Not knowing what to do, he paused as he considered his options. After a few moments, he came up with a plan of action.

"Help me find a place to pull off the road that will raise the rear of the car high enough to inspect the gas tank," he said anxiously.

His job was to drive, and my task was to search for a suitable location to view the undercarriage of the vehicle.

So, the search began for a gradual slope on the right side of the road to lift the rear of the station wagon sufficiently so that we could crawl underneath for an inspection. Soon, we found a spot that allowed him to pull off the road as much as possible and not face oncoming traffic. It sloped upward just enough to raise part of the vehicle's chassis off the ground with space for us to peer under it with ease.

My host found a flashlight in the glove compartment that I guided with his instructions while he inspected the underside of the gas tank. The cold numbed my hands, as it was certainly below freezing. After a detailed examination, he announced that gasoline was indeed leaking from the tank.

We climbed back into the station wagon, and my companion's first response to the crisis was to drive as fast as he could down the mountain in order to finish the trip before the gasoline ran out. Fortunately, there was no oncoming traffic. Everyone else had sense enough not to travel on this mountain road at night. I was unsure which was better, spending the night cold and alone on a frigid mountain during the late Andean fall with an empty gas tank, or rushing along the road only to tumble down thousands of feet in a station wagon filled with cash registers!

My host soon realized the folly of his speeding strategy because he could still see the falling level of the gauge, and he calculated that we were not traveling fast enough to finish the trip before the gas ran out.

He asked me if I had any chewing gum to plug the leak, but I didn't. I never used it, and never dreamed that it could be used for anything but its intended purpose. So, we brainstormed about what we could use to plug the hole. We had few options. I checked the glove compartment, and came up with a bar of soap. He decided that the soap was sufficient to fill the hole temporarily, and at least slow the flow of leaking gasoline.

We pulled off to the side of the road again, and he asked me to put my finger over the hole in the tank while he prepared to plug it with the soap.

After that, we moved forward to our destination at a much slower pace. My host had driven like a madman so far, and I was relieved that we were progressing at a much more reasonable speed.

We reached Abancay well after midnight and found the tourist hotel. A knock at the massive wooden doors aroused the desk clerk. He emerged through a narrow opening between them and let us in. Before we separated to go to our rooms, my host asked me if I would be interested in continuing with him on his journey to Cusco after the gas tank was fixed. I had few resources, and with little cash, I consented. A free trip to Cusco in a car rather than on a bus was a welcome perk for a poor graduate student, even if it meant delaying my journey and spending some of my money for two nights in a tourist hotel in Abancay.

Repairing the gas tank required most of the following day, but in the meantime, I walked around Abancay. Like most other Latin American cities established during the Colonial period, Abancay was organized around an attractive plaza with a church as its most prominent feature. Beyond the church and the small plaza, however, there was not much to see. Since I was studying pottery making, I went to the market and talked to the women selling pottery there, learning as much as I could about where it was made, and photographing the range of vessels for sale (fig. 6.1). They thought I

FIGURE 6.1. Woman selling pottery in the Abancay market. The two vessels upturned on the left are cooking pots.

was crazy when I asked permission to do so, but I was able to document the range of vessels made locally. Some of those vessels had maker's marks that were impressed on their bases when the bottom of the vessel was first formed.[8] They were mainly cooking vessels but these and other vessels sold showed no similarity to the decorative vessels made in Quinua.

AN UNUSUAL BREAKFAST

By the end of the day, the gas tank was repaired and we prepared to continue our trip. Cusco was still eight hours away by difficult mountain driving. So, my host decided to leave early the next morning.

In the meantime, he had acquired another traveling companion who occupied the front seat, and I was relegated to the seat behind the driver. Behind me were the cash registers, but with enough space in the rear to accommodate the additional luggage.

It was still dark with no sign of dawn when we pulled out of the parking lot of our hotel. I was hungry and was concerned about eating before we embarked on such a long trip. My host was sympathetic, but assured me that we would eat breakfast along the way; nothing was open at that hour of the morning anyway.

Soon we left the paved streets of Abancay and proceeded along an unpaved gravel road that was typical of the Andes at the time. During the dry season, driving along such roads created a trail of dust, and following too close behind another vehicle not only meant eating dust, but also reduced visibility—a dangerous condition on narrow roads that precariously clung to the sides of mountains. Driving in the early morning darkness further impeded the ability to see potential dangers along the road—particularly at the speed that he had driven from Andahuaylas to Abancay.

Dirt and dust are part of the unpleasantness that complicate the life of an anthropologist, but on this particular morning, the dust on the road created another problem that was unexpected, making the beginning of our trip even more uncomfortable. It wasn't long after leaving Abancay that I noticed an unusual amount of dust obscured my view of the front seat—a strange perception since the front seat was only two feet away. I coughed and complained that it was dusty in the back seat, and suggested that the rear window of the station wagon might be open. My host dismissed my complaint with some nonsensical explanation, but a short time later, the front seat was filled with so much dust that the driver and his companion were coughing. I reminded him that I had told him the window on the tailgate was open and that I had asked him to close it.

He stopped and closed the window, and the rest of us exited the station wagon to dust ourselves off. Returning to our seats, we were off again with cleaner air, and hopefully a more pleasant trip.

We arrived at the town of Curahuasi at dawn and ate breakfast at a poorly furnished local eatery (see fig. 5.2). After the meal, my companion asked the waiter for a cognac. In Peru, cognac was a colorless, anise-flavored beverage that came in small bottles of clear glass, enough for two or three shot glasses. Downing a cognac after breakfast seemed rather unusual. Not the least of my concerns was my host's sobriety because one drink in the Andes packs the punch of two or three depending on one's elevation above sea level. As my host poured his drink, I pondered the consequences of a driver less than stone-sober careening along a dangerous one-lane road seldom wide enough for two-way traffic. One wrong move would put us over the edge and down a precipice to certain death thousands of feet below.

Not wanting to drink alone, he offered me some of his cognac. I was not a drinker, and all of my preceding experiences with alcohol in the Andes were negative. I had already tried drinking Peruvian cognac but had hated its taste. But, he persisted. I eventually grew tired of his insistent badgering. Finally, I succumbed, and said "yes" to his increasingly importunate requests.

Silently, he filled a shot glass and carefully pushed it to me across the table. Not wanting to prolong the misery, I took the glass and downed it in one gulp. Visibly astonished, my host responded:

"Are you a whiskey man?"

"No!" I replied. "I don't like whiskey or cognac, I just wanted to get it over with, and keep you from pestering me."

"Would you like another?"

"No! I complied with your request. No more! Now, just leave me alone!"

That verbal joust ended the respite for breakfast, and soon we were back on the road again for the next leg of the journey down the mountain into the gorge in which the Apurimac River flowed.

The Apurimac River is one of the major rivers of the Andes and one of the major tributaries of the Amazon. Beginning high in the mountains in southern Peru, its source lies southwest of Cusco, and it flows through some of the most remote terrain on Earth. It joins the Ucayali River in the tropical forests of eastern Peru eventually reaching the Atlantic more than four thousand miles away.

The Apurimac was a major barrier to movement across the southern Andes. In some locations, it flows through narrow canyons with such roaring fury that crossing it is impossible. Elsewhere, it flows through relatively open valleys, but even then, crossing is difficult without a bridge.

In southern Peru especially, the Apurimac impeded travel between the Cusco region and most of the south-central Andes to the west of it. During the early years of the Inca state, it served as a natural barrier between the Incas of Cusco and the Chanka people to the west. This separation did not last long, however, because in the early fifteenth century during the reign of Inca Viracocha, the eighth Inca, the Chankas crossed the Apurimac and attacked Cusco with vengeance. This confrontation reportedly frightened the reigning Inca Viracocha so much that he fled Cusco with one of his sons (Inca Urcon) and retreated to his palace at Yucay in the nearby Sacred Valley, leaving his younger son, Cusi Yupanqui, to take charge of the defense of the capital.[9]

Yupanqui was also a general in the army, and he immediately strengthened the defenses of Cusco. One of these was a massive structure called Sacshayhuamán immediately above the city to the north. Yupanqui's response to the Chanka attack was so desperate that he reportedly called out to the stones to rise up and defeat the advancing troops. Ultimately, he repulsed the Chankas, successfully defended Cusco, and succeeded his father as the ninth Inca, calling himself, Pachacuti, or "transformer of the world"—an apt title given his reputed fierceness in battle with the Chankas.[10]

After his defeat of the invaders, Pachacuti began his conquest of the Andes, the first major expansion of territory that became the Inca Empire. At its zenith, it included much of the Andes from Ecuador to northwest Argentina and northern Chile over a distance of two thousand miles—a region that included some of the highest and most diverse terrain on earth. Called *Tawantinsuyu*, or "Land of the Four Corners," the empire was ruled from the city of Cusco, our destination.

One of the earliest conquests of Pachacuti was the Acos Indians, who inhabited the village to which I was headed. After conquering and killing most of them, he exiled the remaining population to the area around Quinua, the village in the Ayacucho Valley from which I had come for this trip.[11] This movement of people across the Andes was no easy task—Quinua was more than 170 miles from Acos over some of the most difficult terrain in the Andes.

Perhaps the conquest and exile of the Acos Indians were uniquely part of Pachacuti's strategic plan of dominating the Andes. The diverse topography of mountains, gorges, and rivers presented significant barriers to advancing armies. Bridges and roads were needed to connect distant regions with the capital, and they provided the infrastructure that was crucial for the smooth functioning of the Inca state, its military efforts, and the flow of tribute back to the capital. So, Pachacuti used two groups to help administer the empire's infrastructure. The Anta Indians, from the Plain (*pampa*) of Anta northwest of Cusco (through which we would pass), were given the task of building and maintaining the roads of the empire (fig. 6.2), and the Acos Indians were given the task of building and maintaining the bridges.[12] So, Acos, my ultimate destination, was not only the source of the population resettled in Quinua, but played an important role in the infrastructure of the Inca Empire.

Eventually we descended into the gorge of the Apurimac River (fig. 5.2). Our road crossed the river on a small iron bridge only a few meters above the water, but about AD 1350, the Incas built a suspension bridge far above, made of maguey fibers, and anchored it on each side of the gorge. The bridge endured into the nineteenth century, and traveler and explorer E. G. Squier wrote that the bridge was the only bridge across the Apurimac at the time and was 148 feet (48 meters) long and 118 feet (38 meters) above the water.[13] Those that maintained the bridge lived in Curahuasi, the village in which we just had breakfast.

Squier provides a vivid description of the bridge and its approaches:

> To the left of the huts, swinging high in a graceful curve, between the precipices on either side, looking wonderfully frail and gossamer-like, was the famed bridge of the Apurimac. A steep, narrow path, following for some distance a natural shelf, formed by the stratification of the rock, and for the rest of the way hewn in its face, led up, for a hundred feet, to a little platform, also cut in the rock, where were fastened the cables supporting the bridge. On the opposite bank was another and rather larger platform partly roofed by the rock, where was the windlass for making the cables taut, and where, perched like goats on some mountain shelf, lived the custodians of the bridge....[14]

It was a memorable incident in my traveling experiences, the crossing of this great swinging bridge of the Apurímac. I shall never forget it, even if it were not associated with a circumstance which, for the time, gave me much uneasiness and pain. The fame of the bridge over the Apurimac is coextensive with Peru, and everyone we met who had crossed it was full of frightful reminiscences of his passage: how the frail structure swayed at a dizzy height between gigantic cliffs over a dark abyss, filled with the deep, hoarse roar of the river, and how his eyes grew dim, his heart grew faint, and his feet unsteady as he struggled across it, not daring to cast a look on either hand.[15]

This graphic and harrowing account of crossing the bridge appears to have inspired Thornton Wilder's novel, *The Bridge of San Luis Rey*.[16]

About twenty-five years earlier (1852–1853), Sir Clement Markham also wrote about the bridge from the approach on the west side of the river. His description broadly corroborates Squier's description, but his brief narrative is not as dramatic.[17]

A FLAT TIRE WITHOUT A SPARE

We had crossed the Apurímac and were driving up the other side of its gorge when my host noticed that the dashboard warning light indicated that the radiator was overheating. As I realized in Quinua, water boils at a lower temperature at high altitudes and it can dissipate quickly. In this case, our travel at high altitude had greatly reduced the water level in the radiator and it was so low that it failed to cool the engine. With no gas station or settlement to obtain water, we stopped when we spotted water in a nearby irrigation ditch. Eager to fill the radiator and move on, my host looked for any container available to transfer water to the radiator. The best he could do was a plastic bag with holes in it.

I did not want a reprise of a car fire that I had experienced with my parents in Hawaii three years earlier when the driver of our touring car completely ignored the engine warning light. As a consequence, the engine caught fire and burned through the entire length of the vehicle.

So, I was relieved that no matter how much it delayed our trip, filling the radiator of the station wagon was the preferred alternative to no transportation, and being stranded between Abancay and Cusco. Fortunately, my host stopped well before the engine caught on fire.

In order to avoid cracking the engine block because of the shock of the cold water hitting the overheated radiator and cooling system, he left the engine running, and after he had removed the radiator cap, he filled the plastic bag with water from the irrigation ditch. Holding the bag of water, he asked me to help him position the flow from the bag's largest hole so that it went into the radiator's opening. The leakage from the other holes, however, hit the fan blade and sprayed us with water. So, the task of filling the radiator became a dance of holding the leaking plastic bag over the radiator at arm's length while directing the flow from the largest hole into the radiator itself, but trying to avoid the spray from the engine fan. Even so, the spray from the leaking bag still drenched us as it hit the fan blade. Eventually, he stopped the engine.

We managed to finally fill the radiator, and once again we were on our way to Cusco. Not one to delay, my host again drove at a hazardous speed, considering the condition of the road, which, like all those from Ayacucho, was unpaved, narrow, and full of pot holes. Apparently only driving on paved roads on the coast, he was either unaware, oblivious, or did not care about the effect of speed and potholes on the tires.

On a trip to Alaska several years before on the unpaved, thousand-mile Alcan (Alaska-Canada) Highway, my parents noted that those who sped past them ended up alongside the road changing a tire or doing repairs because of the beating their vehicle had endured at higher speeds along such a road. Although my parents took many spare parts with them and an extra spare tire, they found that by driving more slowly, they avoided problems, and had no flat tires or other repair issues.

As I expected, speeding over a gravel road with potholes soon resulted in a flat tire. There was no shoulder and no place to move out of the way of traffic. So, we changed the tire in the middle of the road.

Continuing on our journey and still unconcerned about the relationship between speed, the condition of the road, and the flat tire, my host still drove unrestrained along a road with many unrepaired potholes. Fortunately, the terrain for this part of the trip was flat and was relatively straight most of the time, with no cliffs or vertical drop-offs that would have meant certain death to three passengers tumbling down a mountain with a load of cash registers if the vehicle went off the road. Rather, fields of swamp-like terrain bordered the road on both sides, but this lack of drainage also compromised its integrity.

Unfortunately, my host continued to drive at top speed, and a short time later, our vehicle suffered another flat tire. With no service station to repair the previous flat, we were now in even more serious trouble because we had no spare tire.

After we disembarked from the station wagon, our first task was to determine what kind of a flat we had. Was it a puncture, or a flat resulting from the separation of a tubeless tire from the metal rim of the wheel? We did not know, but after feeling all around the tire to see if there was glass or a nail in it, we jacked up the wheel and carefully looked around the tire again to assess the damage.

Eventually, we found the puncture in the tire. But, if we were to continue on our journey, we had to repair the tire. The first task was to remove the tire from the rim, but with limited tools, we could not do that. In a stroke of insight (but not genius), my host decided that the only way to separate the tire from the rim was to drive over the tire with the naked wheel housing so that the rubber tire would separate from the metal rim. Since the car was now up on the jack, we needed to lower it carefully so that the wheel housing would rest precisely on the horizontally positioned tire and the driver could move the vehicle back and forth over it. So, there we were, a station wagon full of cash registers with one rear tire missing, moving back and forth across a detached tire in order to dislodge the rubber portion from its rim.

This solution did not work very well. The tire had to be positioned precisely under the wheel housing, and it was no easy task to keep it from being pushed away by the moving vehicle rather than putting pressure on the tire. Giving instructions to the driver when he could not see the consequences of his movement complicated the problem, but this ad hoc method finally unseated the rim. That success, however, was only part of the problem because we still needed to remove the rim from the rubber tire enough to repair the tire's interior.

About that time, a large truck approached us from behind and the driver, seeing our dilemma, stopped to offer his help. He had the appropriate tools to properly remove the tire from the wheel housing so that we could inspect its interior. Fortunately, he also had a rubber patch so that he could repair it.

With the repair complete, the tire then needed to be snapped back inside the steel rim. The trucker's tools aided in that task, but my host still had to back the vehicle over the tire to pop the tire back onto the rim. For this, he backed over it again and again using the other rear tire that was still on the vehicle.

Once the tire was seated properly, the next challenge was to fill it with compressed air to the appropriate pressure. Unfortunately, neither vehicle had an air pump, but my host and the truck driver figured out a way to attach a hose to the truck engine to inflate the tire. I thought he had attached the hose to the pressurized fuel system, a solution that seemed incredible to me because any leakage from the tire plus a random spark or cigarette would have been the end of us.

My knowledge of the Spanish vocabulary of truck and automotive engine parts was nonexistent, and for decades I wondered whether I had misunderstood and that the trucker instead had connected the hose to the vacuum line of the windshield wipers so that the pump attached to the motor somehow would fill the tire with air. I have since learned that large trucks use compressed air to power their brakes. Rather than using fluid as a means to transfer pressure from the brake pedal to the actual brake mechanism in the wheel, as in an automobile, large trucks use compressed air to transfer that pressure to the wheel. The compressed air is stored in a reservoir with a valve and a hose so that it also can be used to inflate the truck's tires. The source of the air used to fill the tire on our station wagon thus likely came from the compressed air tank that powered the truck's air brakes. In any event, the problem-solving ability and creativity of my host and the truck driver astounded me.

Eventually, the tire was inflated enough to drive, although nowhere near the appropriate level to safely support a moving vehicle. Further, there was no sealant between the tire and the steel rim. The amount of pressurized air in the tire was, however, adequate to travel.

One worry remained. Would the tire continue to deflate and lose enough air to cause another flat? If so, we would have to go through the entire procedure again because the spare was also flat. If we drove too long on a tire with too little air, we could easily ruin the tire. If it was ruined, we would not just lose the tire, but also damage the metal rim. Worse yet, a deformed rim would not fit tightly on a tubeless tire even if we could fix it, and it would not hold air. All of these scenarios would seriously delay the trip.

So, the repaired tire was moved to the right side of the rear of the vehicle so that I could safely hang out the window and watch it during the remainder of the journey to determine when it should be inflated again by the truck that was following us.

Much of the remainder of the trip was across the Plain of Anta (fig. 6.2), and I spent all of that time hanging out the window to watch

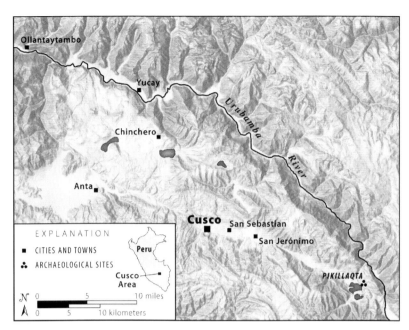

FIGURE 6.2. Map showing the region around Cusco, Peru. This portion of the Urubamba/Vilcanota River is called the Urubamba River, and is the "Sacred Valley of the Incas." (Map by Chelsea M. Feeney)

the tire. I remember little of the scenery or anything else about that leg of the trip.

My host had brought many tools and even a tank of oxygen for his trip from Lima. Presumably, he thought that he had brought everything he needed. None, however, were useful for the mechanical challenges of the journey, and the simplest of all, a tire patch, was not in his tool kit. He did not have an extra spare and, surprisingly, he did not even have the most basic tools of all—a water container to fill the radiator and an adhesive as simple as a stick of gum to plug a leaking gas tank.

Finally, we reached the far side of the Plain of Anta and the road gradually rose to go over a low pass. As we topped the pass, a large city stretched out in the valley below us. It was Cusco at last! Beyond it, a valley stretched some twenty miles into the distance.

The journey to the Inca capital was harrowing, and the extremes of altitude, climate, and topography were challenging. Even with modern transportation, traveling over dirt roads and moving through environmental extremes without the most basic of tools was not wise. Somehow, the Incas had managed to unite such a vast and diverse area into a single imperialistic state without the benefit of modern technology.

Although my arrival in Cusco was a milestone, I still had to get to Acos, and I was unsure about how to make that trip. A new set of adventures was about to begin.

CHAPTER 7

The Navel of the Inca World

I ARRIVED IN CUSCO exhausted and needed rest. It also was the end of my trip with my host in his station wagon full of cash registers. I had retraced Inca steps from Quinua to Cusco, and now it was time to retrace them throughout the Inca capital.

As we entered the city, he inquired about directions to the tourist hotel, and drove directly there. I was planning on staying somewhere cheaper, but at the last moment, I decided that I needed a good meal as well as a good night's sleep. I had spent most of the previous three hours hanging out of the rear window of the station wagon watching the right rear tire as we sped along the dusty road to Cusco. Dust still occupied the nooks and crannies of my clothes and body from the adventures of the day. So, most of all, I needed a good bath.

I spent one night at the tourist hotel, but I knew that I would have to find a room at a cheaper rate if the remainder of the $1,000 that I had brought from the United States would last the rest of my six months in Peru. Four and a half months had already passed, and my stash of travelers' checks was running low. For safekeeping, I had left some of my money in Ayacucho, so I had to be careful with my funds. Although I had arrived in the Inca capital, I still had to get to Acos, and I had no idea how much that portion of the trip would cost.

The next day, I found a hotel a few blocks from the center of town for $2.50 a night. The bed had thick wool blankets that were a welcome sight for keeping warm during the Andean winter nights, but my room was scarcely big enough for a single bed; there was no other furniture. Its size afforded sufficient space to change my clothes and store my backpack, but beyond that, there was little more. The digs were sparse, but they were very inexpensive and certainly adequate. The room did not lend itself to anything except sleeping, and I did not want to spend any more time there than was necessary.

ALTITUDE SICKNESS AND SUN WORSHIP

Because Cusco lies at an elevation of 11,200 feet above sea level, tourists that fly into the city from Lima are well advised to rest for at least half a day to acclimate themselves to the reduced oxygen and air pressure. Here, even more so than Ayacucho, the medicinal qualities of *coca* tea are needed to work their power on the headache and nausea that plague those who arrive from sea level.

Native residents of the high Andes do not experience the same problems with altitude sickness as the rest of us. They have been adapting to high altitude for millennia and have evolved a unique set of physiological mechanisms to thrive. Among them is a larger heart size, a larger lung capacity with a barrel-like chest, a higher concentration of oxygen-bearing red blood cells (hemoglobin), and a greater efficiency of the movement of oxygen to the cells because of higher arterial oxygen content. Non-Andeans, on the other hand, adapt to the paucity of oxygen by an increase in the concentration of red-blood cells (hemoglobin) over time, along with an increased heart rate, and a higher respiration rate. Even so, a month or more of residence at the altitude of Cusco is necessary to fully acclimate. Fortunately, coming from Quinua, my body had already adapted to the same elevation as Cusco, and I suffered none of the ill effects that tourists experience when they first arrive in the Inca capital.

My awareness of this kind of adaptation was heightened five years later when I spent nine months teaching at the National University of Cusco on a Fulbright lectureship. One morning, after teaching my class, I was leaving the university when I saw the city bus pulling away from the curb barely fifty yards away. Not wanting to wait for the next one, I ran to catch it and jumped on the step at the open rear door and grabbed the pole inside the bus.

After I literally "caught" the bus, a moment of terror gripped me.

"You stupid idiot," I thought. *"This is not Urbana, Illinois! It's Cusco, at 11,200 feet above sea level!"*

By the time I pondered my impulsive (and seemingly regrettable) decision to run down a moving vehicle at this altitude, my position on the bus was secure. Taking a deep breath, I exhaled, but in a moment of uncommon self-awareness, I noticed that I was not winded. Breathing normally thereafter, I realized that my body had adapted to the altitude of Cusco! Such adaptation, however, is not permanent, but is lost once one returns to a lower altitude.

Being in Cusco was thrilling. It was the center and the hub of the Inca state. Cusco means "navel" in Quechua, and indeed it was. But it was more; it was the center of the Inca infrastructure, and from it, roads fanned out in all directions to channel armies to the provinces and receive tribute back from conquered territories. On these roads, Inca armies moved the length of the Andes to create an empire more than two thousand miles long through some of the most variegated terrain on Earth—a land from sea level upward to heights of 22,000 feet. Although most of this terrain was not so excessively high, much of the highland Andean population lives at elevations exceeding 10,000 feet above sea level.

I arrived in Cusco about three weeks before the southern hemisphere's winter solstice in June. Although the days were sunny and warm, the nights were cold because the air did not hold the heat. Daily temperature swings at this altitude can vary as much as 30 degrees F. during the winter months.

The necessity of solar warmth to mitigate the bone-chilling cold of high altitude was not lost on the Incas. Although they venerated several deities, they also worshiped the sun, and I had no trouble understanding that belief while I was in Cusco. Most of the days were sunny, but chilly. Walking in the sunshine warmed the skin and the body, but a step into the shade revealed that the ambient temperature was much colder, bringing chills and shivers to my body along with a strong desire to return to the sunshine.

On two of the days I was in Cusco, no sun penetrated the gray sky and the temperature chilled my unprotected extremities. Going outside into the Andean air on those days was miserable. My bulky knit sweater provided sufficient warmth during the sunny days, and comfort against the cold of the Andean nights, but it was insufficient to keep me warm on the days without sunshine.

Rather than visiting the sights of the city on those days, I spent my time in the tourist hotel lobby drinking tea and writing postcards to relatives and letters to my new girlfriend in Urbana. I was not staying there, but during my extended time in the lobby, I discovered that the hotel served a fare associated with British tea time in the late afternoon, and I enjoyed the tea and light sandwiches at a reasonable cost in a setting that I could not normally afford. The British had built the hotel and apparently introduced the practice, but it remained long after the Peruvian government took over its ownership and management.

The warmth of the flames in the fireplace during those cold days took the chill off the lobby, but even a brief visit outside brought shudders and again reminded me of why the Incas worshiped the sun. It was clear that at this altitude, only the sun provided the needed warmth from cold outside on overcast and cold winter days.

I discovered a restaurant on the Plaza de Armas that was part of an ancient Inca building. Tightly fitted stones in a masonry wall and a trapezoidal niche characteristic of Inca stonework formed one of its interior sides, and it provided a relaxed setting to eat and contemplate the atmosphere of the Inca capital by pondering its architecture. I liked the setting as stimulation for the imagination, as well as its menu for sustenance for the body, and I enjoyed eating there. After one or two meals, I discovered that young, English-speaking expatriates also hung out there. They traded stories of their experiences and about others who were teaching English to the youth of Cusco.

RETRACING INCA STEPS THROUGH THEIR CAPITAL

One of my colleagues in Ayacucho had briefed me about the important archaeological sites to see in Cusco, and a visit to the fortress of Sacsayhuamán topped my list. When the Chankas threatened Cusco in the early fifteenth century during the reign of Inca Viracocha, he abandoned the capital and left its defense to his younger son, Cusi Yupanqui. Yupanqui strengthened the defenses of Cusco by expanding the site of Sacsayhuamán into a fortress above the city to the north. Yupanqui repulsed the Chankas twice, successfully defended Cusco, and began an expansion of the empire through conquest that soon included the Ayacucho area.[1]

One of my Ayacucho colleagues told me that it was easy to climb up to Sacsayhuamán because it was directly above the city to the north. So, on one of my first days in Cusco, I started walking west along the covered portions of the Huatanay River that ran through (and now under) Cusco, and proceeded to the base of the hill upon which the fortress was built. The slope was steep and I climbed through a forest of eucalyptus trees. Highly valued for their rapid growth, Peru had imported them from Australia and they had thrived in the Andes, served to check erosion, and provided a scarce resource—wood.

Even without the trees, I mused about how difficult it was to climb up the slope. Any attackers approaching the fortress from the city below faced a suicidal ascent if its defenders rolled boulders down on them.

About halfway up the slope, I came across a modern road made of concrete, and followed it. Eventually, it merged with the well-worn path that was the usual tourist route to the site.

Although most of my ascent would have seemed formidable for an attacking army, the opposite side of the fortress was equally challenging for a different reason. A zigzag pattern of walls rose on three different terraces above a flat plain. Using huge stones that were shaped precisely to fit a particular spot in the wall, junctures were so carefully crafted that not even a knife blade could fit between them.[2]

The remains of the quarry for many of the stones lay about ninety yards across a flat plain, with a few small caves pockmarking the outcrop there. These caves, according to a local travel guide, supposedly led down into the city so that when it was attacked, its inhabitants could retreat into them and find their way up into the fortress. Although a tantalizing and fascinating story, I subsequently learned from local archaeologists that the tale, no matter how appealing, was untrue and reminds us to be cautious about believing the stories concocted by tourist guides. Even if the tunnels did exist, it was unlikely that they survived the devastating earthquakes that shook Cusco through the centuries. Nevertheless, the enigma of the tunnels' existence and use still fascinates visitors.

At one spot in the lower wall of the fortress, the Incas built a narrow doorway so that defenders could escape to a higher terrace via a stone stairway. Another wall shielded each higher terrace so that once attackers breached the lowest wall, the defenders could retreat behind another fortified wall to a higher level, regroup, and continue to protect their position.

I finished my exploration of Sacsayhuamán, and found my way back down to the city along the trail that I should have taken to reach the fortress in the first place. It passed along the road that I had encountered on my way up to the fortress. As the road turned a corner, a church, San Cristobal, stood in front of another Inca wall that supported a very large platform, called Colcampata. Along the wall supporting the platform, builders had constructed trapezoidal niches that were typical of Inca construction, and a trapezoidal doorway with a stairway that led to the top of the platform. Blocked by an iron gate, one could alternatively access the top of the platform farther up the road from which I had come. Although the wall was constructed with rough, polygonally shaped stones—another classic characteristic of Inca buildings—a smaller Inca structure constructed with more precisely shaped stones lay farther back on the platform and out of sight from below.

Believed to be the palace of the first Inca, Manco Capac, Colcampata was also the site of a modern house built on top of this platform. Set back away from the edge of the retaining wall, it was close enough to have a stunning view of the city and the Cusco Valley (fig. 7.1).

In front of Colcampata was the church of San Cristobal, and at this point, I turned off the road to go down one of the colonial streets, past the rear of the cathedral, and emerged on the central plaza, the Plaza de Armas. Fronted by the cathedral along part of one side, the Jesuit church and the university's law school occupied another side. Like the plaza in Ayacucho, almost the entire outer perimeter of the plaza was covered with an arcade. Walking along it and detouring into the adjoining

FIGURE 7.1. The city of Cusco from Colcampata. The long white building in the center of the image faces the Plaza of San Francisco, and the church of San Francisco lies to the right of it. The central plaza of Cusco, the Plaza de Armas, can be seen in the lower left corner.

streets, one could see the remains of the Inca walls below the colonial construction.

Although Inca walls pervade the streets of central Cusco, Spanish colonial architecture, especially that of the churches, sometimes were built on top of Inca ruins, dominate the central city. Overviews of Cusco from Sacsayhuamán above the city revealed that churches are the tallest structures in the old city, a pattern still found throughout much of Europe that symbolizes the role of the church as the dominant institution in medieval society.

The Plaza de Armas also displays this ecclesiastical dominance. As in Ayacucho and other colonial cities, the city is structured around a central plaza with the offices of the main political and religious institutions of the state located around its perimeter. Unlike the Inca period in which the religious institution *was* the state, and the Inca was viewed as a descendant of the sun, the Spanish conquest replaced Inca religion and political structure with the Spanish crown on the one hand and the Catholic Church on the other.

During the colonial period, Spanish priests tried to adapt and contextualize Christianity to Inca, and especially Andean, beliefs. Inside the cathedral, immense paintings portray the life of Christ, biblical scenes, and the lives of the saints. During the colonial period, priests used paintings as a way to communicate the events of the Bible and the acts of the saints, creating spectacular scenes on gigantic canvases that adorned the walls of the churches, monasteries, and convents in colonial Andean cities such as Cusco (Peru), Quito (Ecuador), and Potosí (Bolivia).

One of these paintings in the Cusco cathedral illustrates the syncretism of Spanish and Andean beliefs by dramatizing the value of the guinea pig as an Andean ritual food. Doubtless trying to communicate the significance of the Last Supper as the archetype of the Catholic mass, the painter portrayed a dressed guinea pig on a plate on the table in front of Jesus in a painting modeled after Leonardo da Vinci's rendering of the Last Supper. The Last Supper was, of course, a Jewish Passover meal, but the artist was apparently trying to contextualize the meal in an Andean context. The painting underscored the ritual importance of the Last Supper as the basis of the Roman Catholic mass by using a familiar Andean ritual practice as a visual metaphor, and thus linking Andean beliefs to Roman Catholic ones.

Walking south away from the front of the cathedral and across the plaza, one street took me to the tourist hotel that fronts another small plaza. On its far side lies the house of "El Inca," Garcilaso de la Vega.

Garcilaso was the son of an Inca princess and a Spanish conquistador, and known principally for his seventeenth-century work called the *Royal Commentaries of the Incas*.[3] Although several descriptions of Inca life and history were written in the early colonial period, Garcilaso's is the best known, and much of the popular knowledge about the Incas comes from that work. More recent research on early colonial history and archaeology, however, has altered interpretations of Inca history based upon Garcilaso's work that tended to idealize Inca society.

Continuing up the hill to the south beyond the tourist hotel, I encountered the Plaza of San Francisco, one of the largest plazas in Cusco and one of several in the center of the old city. Dominated by the massive church of San Francisco at one corner, I wandered into the monastery next to it and walked around. Most impressive were the immense paintings of the life of Saint Francis on the walls inside the portico that surrounded the patio on each of two floors.

Not being familiar with the life of Saint Francis, I did not understand the meanings of the individual paintings. Nevertheless, these lifelike images were obviously intended to communicate the significance of his life to illiterate laymen and monastic noviciates in a visual way.

I had come to the Inca capital to learn about its past, but my experience in Quinua led me to want to learn something about Inca pottery to aid me in answering my research questions. So, after visiting the San Francisco church and monastery, I turned down a side street to find the archaeology museum. Besides the resettlement of the people of Acos in and around Quinua, could the Inca administration have had an effect on the production of Quinua pottery after their conquest and the resettlement of the Acos Indians there? Many examples of pottery with Inca designs have been found outside of Cusco, but they are often not as carefully made and executed as the Inca pottery from Cusco. Archaeologists believe that these vessels were made by local potters to replicate imperial pottery with instructions from Inca administrators. Did this practice occur in Quinua, and might there be some evidence of it in the modern pottery of the Quinua? So, I visited the archaeology museum in Cusco noting vessel shapes, taking photographs, and copying designs that I thought might relate to modern Quinua pottery.

Another approach to investigating the possible Inca influence on Quinua pottery was to visit the daily market in Cusco. So, after visiting the archaeology museum, I returned to the Plaza of San Francisco and headed for the market. I had visited the market in Abancay, photographed the

FIGURE 7.2. A pottery seller in the Cusco market.

vessels there, and tried to get as much information as I could from the vendors. I wanted to do the same in Cusco, to discover where the vessels were
from and whether there were any from Acos, and photograph as many as
I could (fig. 7.2). Vendors thought I was crazy, but I did get some information about where the pottery was made. Acos was not one of those places.

At the time, I did not know whether my documentation of the market
pottery in Abancay and Cusco was relevant to my project, but it was a
"fall-back" data set, since I believed that the information collected on pottery making in Quinua was insufficient, and I was already convinced that
my Quinua study was a failure. So, I had hoped that a visit to the Cusco
market might provide some evidence of similarity between the pottery
sold there and that of Quinua. Unfortunately, the shapes sold in the Cusco
market, and the little decoration that existed on them, bore no similarity at all to those of Quinua. Surprisingly, these shapes and decoration
also bore no similarity to the Inca pottery displayed in the archaeological
museum that I had visited earlier. Nevertheless, Quinua pottery still stood
out as a unique tradition, and unrelated to inhabitants of the Cusco region
during the Inca period.

The Spanish built their city on top of the buildings in the Inca capital,
and walking down almost every street from the central plaza, I saw Inca

FIGURE 7.3. A street in Cusco looking south toward the Plaza de Armas. The polygonal wall in Figure 7.4 is on the left side of the street in the center of the image.

FIGURE 7.4. An Inca polygonal wall on an Inca street (see fig. 7.3).

walls constructed with tightly fitted stones. In places where the colonial architecture appeared to obscure the Inca structures, a closer look often revealed Inca walls at their base. Tilting slightly inward toward the interior of the structure, the walls were so stable that when earthquakes struck Cusco after the conquest, the Inca walls survived, whereas much of the colonial superstructure above them collapsed and had to be rebuilt.

Behind the cathedral, a narrow Inca street leads northward toward the church of San Blas (fig. 7.3). Along that street one finds polygonal stones that form a massive Inca wall. The individual size and shape of each of these stones again reveals that Inca stone masons trimmed each stone to fit into a unique position in the wall; one of most interesting stones displayed twelve distinct sides (fig. 7.4).

Everywhere colorful Quechua women scurried about with their full calf-length skirts, colorful blouses, and distinct hats. Women of each community wore a unique type of clothing and hat. Some were topped with white wide-brimmed hats with black bands marking their residence farther down the Cusco Valley in the towns of San Sebastián and San Jerónimo (see fig. 6.2). Others wore brown bowler hats indicative of communities nearer to the Peru-Bolivian Altiplano that lay 160 miles to the southeast. Women from Chinchero north of Cusco wore colorful, blouse-like wool jackets and a hat with a flat top larger than the base that in profile looked like an upside-down truncated pyramid. A distinctive type of poncho marked the men of each community.

A rather narrow street led east away from the central plaza along the north side of the Jesuit church. With Inca walls on each side, the wall on the left formed the outer wall of the Temple of Chosen Women, an Inca convent in which women under a vow of chastity prepared ritual food, maintained the sacred fire, and wove garments for ritual use and for the supreme Inca.[4] At the end of this narrow street, another street with Inca walls continued. Walking along it to its end, I encountered a small plaza fronted by a church and more Inca walls. Seemingly just one of many colonial churches in Cusco, this church, called Santo Domingo, was actually built on the site of the Inca's sacred Temple of the Sun. The Spanish destroyed the temple, and the Dominican friars built their church on the site. Nothing remains of the ancient temple under the church, but near the altar, a door leads to the outside that allows tourists to see the curved wall that held the gold image of the sun which the Incas venerated.[5]

A large colonial door outside the rear of the Dominican church leads into the Order's cloisters. At first, they seemed like just any other colonial cloister found in Cusco, except that the colonial construction had been removed, revealing only the Inca walls and a series of rooms facing a central courtyard. These structures were the Coricancha, the golden enclosure adjacent to the original sun temple.[6]

Inca structures in Cusco were constructed of stone walls, sometimes using adobe blocks on their upper courses, but the roofs were made of thatch supported by a wood infrastructure, which, like all Inca roof structures, were susceptible to fire. As in other parts of Spanish America, the Spanish often built their churches on the sites of pagan temples to attract the natives to attend their services. With a new church constructed over the ruins of the actual sun temple, the Dominicans then plastered over the walls of the neighboring golden enclosure (Coricancha) and incorporated its doors and windows into their cloisters. As a consequence, the golden enclosure and its colonially plastered facade remained covered by the construction of the monastery.[7]

It was not until the earthquake of 1650 that the underlying Inca structures emerged, revealing the colonial construction of the individual cloisters which were actually the renovated and plastered rooms of the original golden enclosure portion of the Inca sun temple. Unlike other earthquake damage in Cusco, the Inca structures in the cloisters were then cleared to display part of their former glory, and the colonial additions to the cloisters were not rebuilt.[8]

The Incas positioned a large trapezoidal niche that faced the courtyard on the exterior of one of these former cloisters. The niche faced northeast and was reputed to be the seat of the Inca during the winter solstice where he witnessed the rising of the sun. Holes through the upper corners and edges of the niche apparently anchored gold accouterments to surround the Inca with symbols of his sacred position and power.[9]

The walls of the temple originally were covered with sheets of gold and a climb to the second floor of the cloister provided a view of the Inca walls from above. Although it would seem to be an unimportant perspective, the topmost course of the walls revealed T-shaped depressions pecked into the stone with the base of the "T" touching the outer edge of the walls. Tabs of the sheets of gold apparently were folded down over the top of the wall and then hammered into these depressions presumably to hold them against the exterior before the roof timbers and thatch of the ancient roof were added.[10]

All the rooms of the golden enclosure faced a central court that became the patio of the cloisters of the Dominican monastery. During the Inca empire, the courtyard was filled with "life-size figures made in gold and silver"[11] such as maize plants, the most valued Andean crop. Excavations of the courtyard by the National Institute of Culture in 1972–1973, however, found no gold. All had been removed by the Spanish during their conquest of the city.[12]

The sun temple was the focal point of a number of lines of shrines (called *ceques*) that radiated outward from Cusco linking multiple ritual locations.[13] These ceques paralleled the transportation infrastructure of Inca roads and bridges that also extended outward from the city. If I had been an Inca nobleman, retracing the steps of the Inca to Cusco would have ended here at the center of the Inca Empire, the Temple of the Sun. Although I had not trekked on the ancient roads during my journey to Cusco, traveling to the village of Acos away from Cusco, I would travel in a direction of several other ceques that would also retrace the steps of the Incas on or very near their roads. The initial portion of the next segment of my journey would involve a different form of transportation, a modern rail system, that followed the general path of one of the ancient Inca roads.

LEAVING CUSCO

Although I enjoyed my stay in Cusco, it was just a stop on my journey to my ultimate destination, the village of Acos south-southwest of the city. So, after a few days in Cusco, I looked for a way to get to Acos. I inquired about transportation, but no buses traveled there. The only way to get there was to climb into the back of a truck full of rural peasants who used this mode of transportation to travel to many parts of the Andes—especially those distant from main roads and population centers. Trucks to Acos, I was told, left from Rimacpampa, a small plaza just north of the Church of Santo Domingo with its remains of the Inca Temple of the Sun. I inquired at a store on the plaza, but no one knew of any trucks that went to Acos from there.

During my interactions with the young expatriates in Cusco, I met a young married couple who were Peace Corps volunteers and were working in a village called Sangarará, not far from Acos. They suggested that I take the train and have the conductor stop it where it crosses the road to Acos, and then board a truck to get to Acos.

Cusco is the rail head for two different railway lines, and each leaves from a different terminal. One line is a narrow-gauge line and begins across the street from the market, only a few blocks south of the main square of the city, the Plaza de Armas. This line heads up over the pass into the Pampa de Anta crossing its eastern end before it descendsng into the Sacred Valley of the Incas, where the name of the river changes from the Vilcanota upstream to the Urubamba River downstream. Moving down the valley, the railway passes through the town of Ollantaytambo with its Inca streets, walls, and fortress (see fig. 6.2). Small, but located on a small promontory at the bottom edge of the mountain slope, the fortress has high terraces that Inca craftsman created by hewing huge boulders fitted on-site into a unique position using the multisided style characteristic of so many Inca walls.

From Ollantaytambo, the rail line follows the Urubamba River to Machu Picchu. In 1967, it went on to the town of Quillabamba in the jungle north of Machu Picchu. In the years since then, however, the rail line beyond Machu Picchu has been abandoned.

The other rail line, a standard gauge, leaves from a station near the east end of the central city at the bottom of Avenida Sol. From there, trains head east down the Cusco Valley and then south into the Vilcanota River Valley (see fig. 6.2). At that point, the line goes upriver to the Altiplano, and beyond to the city of Puno on the shore of Lake Titicaca (see fig. 2.1).

At Puno, it continues west up over the mountains and down to the city of Arequipa nearer to the Pacific coast. From Arequipa, one must get a bus, or a *colectivo* (a car that takes multiple passengers to a common destination), to go to Lima or to southern Peru and Chile in the opposite direction. Alternatively, from Puno one could take a steamship across the lake to the Bolivian port of Guaqui, where another train line went to La Paz, the capital of Bolivia. More recently, however, the steamer no longer runs and one must find other means to get to Bolivia, such as a bus or a colectivo overland or a hydrofoil across the lake.

I needed to take the standard-gauge railway line toward Puno to get nearer to Acos. So, I went to the train station and told the agent where I wanted to go. After buying my ticket, he told me that I should be sure to tell the conductor where I wanted to depart the train because the point at which the rail line crossed the road to Acos was not a regular stop.

A FRIGHTENING PAUSE

The next morning, I walked to the station early and boarded the train. I told the conductor that I wanted to get off where the rail line crosses the road to Acos, and he said that he would inform me where that was, and would signal the engineer to stop the train (fig. 7.5).

I was very nervous and feared that the conductor would forget about me. So, I repeatedly reminded him. He reassured me again and again that he would let me know about my stop. After about two hours, the train stopped, and the conductor informed me that I should disembark.

I stepped down from the train with my backpack, and the train pulled away. I was left standing by the side of the tracks alone; no one else got off the train. There was no station, no platform, no waiting area—nothing indicated that it was a regular stop. No house, no village, and no human being were in sight. It was just a place where the railroad line crossed a road.

I was standing in a narrow valley barely a third of a mile across. On the east side, the mountains rose so steeply that ascending them seemed impossible. They stretched up and down the valley as far as I could see. On the west side of the valley, another high range extended in both directions and, like those on the other side, were very steep. In front of me, however, a stream entered the valley and a gravel road snaked its way up along the side of a stream nudged in between two mountains. Across the river behind me, the road from Cusco to Puno paralleled the train track.

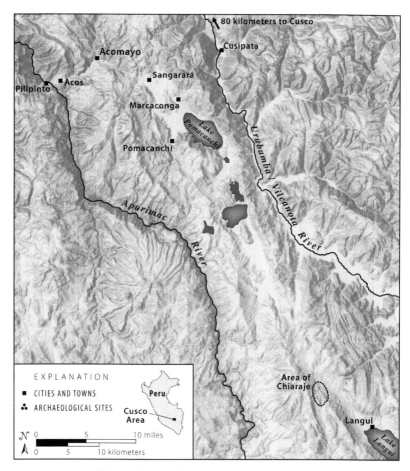

FIGURE 7.5. Map of the area between the Vilcanota River and Apurimac River showing the location of Acos, other nearby communities, and the location of the *Chiaraje* battle in 1973. (Map by Chelsea M. Feeney)

Not a little fear and apprehension gripped me. I had no idea whether I was in the proper location or not, but the conductor said that I should wait and a truck would come along and take me to Acos. I was beginning to doubt his veracity.

Watching the traffic on the dusty Cusco/Puno road on the other side of the river, I hoped, with each passing vehicle, that one would come my way. Being alone in a strange place, I contemplated what it would be like to spend the frigid Andean night beside the railroad tracks in my sleeping bag.

Fortunately, before long, a truck turned off the Cusco/Puno road and headed toward me, just as the conductor had predicted. I flagged it down and asked the driver if he was going to Acos. He was not, but was on his way to Acomayo, only part of the distance to my destination (fig. 7.5). Any ride to a town farther along the road to Acos was better than staying in the isolated spot in which I currently found myself. So, I climbed aboard the back of the truck and it departed for Acomayo.

CHAPTER 8

Nearing My Destination

AFTER A BUMPY AND DUSTY RIDE on the back of a truck, I arrived in Acomayo in the early afternoon. Because no vehicles were going to Acos that day, I needed a place to sleep and inquired about accommodations for the night. Fortunately, Acomayo was a provincial capital and had a small hotel. The price was cheap, but trudging upstairs to what I thought was a private room, I was greeted instead with a large space with ten single beds; it was more like a hostel or military barracks than a hotel room. Though I had experienced this kind of accommodation two years previously in Belize, I was surprised, disappointed, and more than a little concerned about the security of sleeping in a room with nine others.

I left my backpack in the room and took my camera into the streets of the town. It happened that I arrived on the day that the local government was sponsoring a celebration of peasant life, and a contest for the best musical group was in full swing. Each group consisted of musicians playing various combinations of a harp, a drum, an Andean flute, and one or two violins. The celebration also involved a competition for the title of "Miss Indigenous Beauty." Young women and musical groups waited in the streets dressed in their local ethnic finery ready to compete for the title in the auditorium of the local school (fig. 8.1). The reds, yellows, and blues of their ponchos, blouses, and skirts stood out against the whitewashed buildings, and the shadows of the bright sunlight bathed the walls of the narrow streets with deep purple. Standing in the deep shade to shield myself from the intense sunlight, my body shivered with a chill that marked the approach of the winter solstice.

FIGURE 8.1. Musicians waiting in the street to participate in the indigenous music festival in Acomayo.

I found refuge from the cold in the school auditorium. My seat provided respite from the chill of the Andean air, but I also wanted to watch the competition hoping to hear some of the musical groups. Andean music uses a different tonal scale than European-derived music, and even with the lack of precise tuning of the instruments, it had come to symbolize Andean life for me, and I enjoyed it.

Unfortunately, I happened to enter the auditorium during the beauty competition, and the presentation and announcements were in Quechua, which I didn't understand, rather than Spanish. Further, sitting in a room out of the Andean sun, I was still cold. So, I left the auditorium and wandered down the street to the market where vendors sold Andean tubers, *chuñu* (freeze-dried potatoes), squash, quinoa, and other crops. I strolled amidst buyers and sellers wearing clothing of brown, red, tan, and black moving across the background of the market. Men wore brightly colored woven ponchos. Women walked to and fro with their colored blouses and black, mid-calf-length skirts (fig. 8.2). Both men and women wore brightly colored shawls on their backs called *mantas*—a square cloth usually made with a tapestry technique and used to carry a small child, produce to and from the market, or anything that would fit into it. Since the peasants of

FIGURE 8.2. The Acomayo market.

each town wore clothing of a unique style, I could see that the buyers and sellers came from several different communities.

The next day I found a truck going to Acos, the destination of my long journey. I was relieved that finally I was within reach of the village from which the Incas had exiled its inhabitants to Quinua more than five centuries before. Unfortunately, I arrived at the departure site too late for a comfortable position within the wooden box-like frame that enclosed the cargo area. I climbed aboard, but the only space remaining was the top of the left rear corner of the wooden box with only enough space on the inside to place my feet on the spare tire.

The unpaved, narrow road to Acos was bumpy, and required holding onto the wooden frame around the cargo area to keep from falling off onto the road below. Fortunately, I could grab the side and rear edges of the frame with my hands and use my feet to push on the spare tire to raise my body and lessen the impact of the bumps on my tailbone. In spite of this occasionally painful inconvenience, my position did provide a first-class view of the beautiful Andean scenery that would have been impossible to see from deep inside the mass of humanity squeezed into the interior of the cargo area and screened from the outside by the wooden frame around its perimeter.

About thirty minutes into the journey, some passengers disembarked, leaving more space in the back of the truck. After that, I could slide down and sit on the upright end of the spare tire slightly below my former position.

As the truck swung around hairpin turns down into the valley, one of my traveling companions asked where I was going.

"Acos," I replied.

He slowly extended his arm and pointed down the valley.

"There's Acos," he said.

My head followed the direction of his finger, and in the distance I could see a small village perched on a small plateau at the end of the long valley into which we were descending. The valley was the erosion product of the drainage of a small river, but at the plateau, the river was deflected and entered a narrow canyon with steep sides. Since movement along the river was impossible at this point, the road went up and over a plateau before it disappeared beyond. Even from some distance away, I could see that the elevation of Acos was much lower than my present position (fig. 8.3).

FIGURE 8.3. View of Acos (on the plateau in the center of the image) from my position on the back of a truck on the road from Acomayo to Acos. The Acomayo River enters the Apurimac River through a canyon marked by the steep face on the mountain slightly to the left of center of the image. The archaeological site of Marca Urqu, the site from which the Acos probably defended themselves against Inca Pachacuti, lies on the right side of the mountain and faces the village of Acos.

My companion continued, "Beyond it lies Pillpinto, on the other side of the Apurimac River. That's the end of the road."

His final phrase, "the end of the road," echoed through my brain and reinforced my sense of the isolated nature of the place. I had already traveled five days from Ayacucho, not counting my days in Cusco. If I added my stops in Abancay and in Cusco, I had been gone almost two weeks, but I was finally nearing my destination. I didn't know what awaited me in Acos. But it was near the end of the road, and it seemed frighteningly remote. Any travel beyond Pillpinto could only be done on foot or horseback.

ARRIVAL IN ACOS

Although the trip to Acos was mostly downhill, the road zigzagged up to the plateau as we neared the village. As the truck raced across it, I looked around and noted that Acos was surrounded by abundant agricultural land with large areas of both level and intensively terraced fields (fig. 8.4).

FIGURE 8.4. Views of terracing in the Acos Valley from the top of the fortress south of Acos. The elevation of Acos, and its extensive terracing indicates that it was an important producer of maize.

When we reached the village, the truck stopped to empty some of its passengers, and I descended from my perch on top of the upright spare tire. I went into the nearest store to ask about a place to stay, but I quickly learned that, unlike Acomayo, there was no public accommodation, and no place to eat. Hearing my queries to the store owner, a schoolteacher extended an invitation to stay in his house. I thanked him and followed him up the street, where he offered me the floor of his simple living room next to his household altar. I inflated my air mattress and rolled out my sleeping bag on top of it.

I left my host's house and walked around the village talking to people who knew enough Spanish to converse with me. Much to my disappointment, within an hour I learned that no pottery was made in Acos and none had been produced there in recent memory. No potters were reported anywhere in the Province of Acomayo, the province in which Acos lies, and my informants reported that the nearest pottery-making communities were two remote hamlets called Charamoray and Yanque, three days' walk to the west.[1] My quest to discover the potential source of pottery making in Quinua had come to a dead end. What should I do? Should I return to Quinua with nothing?

With no data to compare pottery making in Acos with that in Quinua, I had no evidence to establish a historical relationship between these two communities using its pottery. Because of the five days of arduous travel from Ayacucho, an immediate return seemed unwise without learning more about Acos, its landscape, and its ancient past. Familiarity with the area might provide insight about the Inca conquest of the village and about the exile of its population to the Ayacucho region recounted by the sixteenth-century writer Sarmiento de Gamboa.[2]

A SURPRISING DISCOVERY

On the way into town I had seen a large archaeological site on the mountain south of Acos with the side facing it covered with ruined terraces. So, the next day, my first task was to investigate the site (see fig. 8.3).[3]

I walked south toward the mountain and followed a path to the top. As I climbed, I moved through collapsed and eroded terraces and noted large concentrations of ceramics on the surface. They were heaviest near the summit but extended down the terraces. Those ceramics turned out to be types (one of which was called Killke) associated with a population that occupied the area immediately before the Inca conquest and continued being used during the empire's early years when Pachacuti began to rule as the ninth Inca. They did not resemble Quinua pottery at all.

Along the upper terraces of the mountain and at its summit, ruined rectangular structures were evident everywhere. At the east end of the summit, the ancient inhabitants had built a small rectangular platform with two terraced levels each about eighteen inches high. At one side of the topmost level were the remains of a small square room, much smaller than the area of the top of the platform but just large enough for a person to stand inside. I stepped into it and I had a commanding view of the Acomayo Valley to the east and the pass that leads into the high plain around Sangarará from which I had come. To the north, I could see the entire Acos plateau, and a portion of the Apurimac Valley to the west. The structure's small size and location, with views of much of the surrounding area, indicated that it was probably a sentry position.

The archaeological site on this mountain was strategically located, easily defended, and was appropriately called Marca Urqu, which means "mountain defender" in Quechua. Accessibility was restricted by very steep slopes on all sides. On the north, the steepness of the slope, walls, and terraces made any attack on the fortress difficult. Fallen walls of rectangular structures on the summit and extensive ceramics on the terraces indicated that the site was used for habitation and defense rather than agriculture, unlike those terraces across the plateau to the north (fig. 8.4).

The position and defensible character of *Marca Urqu* is consistent with the narrative written by a late-sixteenth-century writer, Sarmiento de Gamboa, who described the conquest of the Acos people by the ninth Inca, Inca Yupanqui [Pachacuti]. Sarmiento said that the two headmen of Acos openly opposed the Inca and resisted him forcefully. As a result, Pachacuti fought them with great military might, but they fiercely defended themselves, and in the process, wounded him in the head with a stone. Consequently, Pachacuti spent a great deal of time fighting them, and did not stop until he had conquered them. He killed almost all of the people of Acos, but those who survived, he pardoned, and then exiled them to the edges of Huamanga (the old name of Ayacucho) where they were called Acos—the area around the village of Quinua, 172 miles to the northwest, where I had begun my journey.[4]

Sarmiento's narrative not only links the people of Quinua with the village of Acos, but it implies that the people of Acos occupied a position that was sufficiently defensible to resist Pachacuti's aggression for a lengthy period before they succumbed to his conquest. The site of Marca Urqu best matched the location of which Sarmiento speaks (see fig. 8.3). It is the one location from which the Acos people could have defended themselves and resisted Pachacuti's attempt to defeat them. Its strategic location with panoramic views in three directions provided ample warning of approaching armies. Sight in the fourth direction (south) was blocked by a mountain separated from the site by a steep ravine. Second, terraces on the north side and steep slopes on the other sides provided security. Third, the quantity of pottery on the site implied that people were living there over a period of time. Finally, the pottery (Killke and associated styles) dated to the time immediately before the Inca Empire emerged, and to its early days, and thus corresponded to the period when Pachacuti would have attacked them.[5]

FURTHER LINKS WITH THE PAST

Local inhabitants in Acos also told me that a ruined town called Atu Huasi ("House of the Fox") with oval structures and human burials was located on the mountain north of Acos. This site presumably also was defensible and could also have resisted the Inca attack. Further, its inhabitants could observe activity in the Apurimac River valley to the west, the Acomayo River valley to the east, as well as activity on the Acos plateau itself. The people of Acos also said that the Spanish dug for gold on the pampa or *pajonal* on the top of the mountain (called *Curi Urqu,* or "Gold Mountain"). Could the Inca have wanted the territory around Acos because it also might have been a source of gold? Gold was associated with *Inti,* the sun god, and sheets of it covered the walls of the Temple of the Sun in Cusco.

Sarmiento said that Acos was governed by two headmen (Ocacique and Otoquasi), and this bipartite leadership may reflect a twofold division of the community related to its defensive locations. One may have been the site of Atu Huasi on the mountain of Curi Urqu north of Acos, and the other may have been the site of Marca Urqu south of Acos.[6] The similarity of the name of one headman (*Otoquasi*) in Sarmiento's account and the name of one of these sites (Atu Huasi) used by the inhabitants of Acos suggest that the sites and the names in Sarmiento's account may be historically related.

Besides simple revenge, imperial expansion, and perhaps gold, why else might Pachacuti be so interested in conquering the people of Acos?

First, the Acos plateau lies along a major corridor from the Apurimac River to the plain of Sangarará (see figs. 7.5 and 8.3). From Sangarará, it is but a simple trek down to the Vilcanota Valley that leads eventually to Cusco. Pachacuti might have wanted to move his army through their territory and cross the Apurimac. In any event, the people of Acos resisted his intentions, and he fought them, eventually conquering them.

Second, the site of Marca Urqu lies at the point where the Apurimac River emerges from a narrow canyon with near vertical walls. This position suggests that the site might also have been the bridgehead spanning the Apurimac. Given its position in the corridor from the Apurimac River to the Vilcanota River, a bridge across the Apurimac at Acos might have been one of the main ports of entry into the region west of the Apurimac because of the ease of crossing. Writing in the early seventeenth century, another writer, Guaman Poma de Ayala, said that "Acos Inca" was the administrator of the bridges.[7] Pachacuti may have wanted to conquer the people of Acos because they possessed bridge-building skills.

If the people of Acos already possessed bridge-building and bridge-maintaining skills, then they would be very useful to Inca imperial expansion. Bridges across deep gorges provided critical components of the Inca road system. Crossing them also required a toll to control those who used the bridges, and users presumably were recorded on a series of knotted cords (called a *quipu*) that encoded information that was passed on to authorities. Bridges thus were strategic places, and the Inca trusted those charged with the responsibility of their construction, maintenance, and administration. Presumably, even after the conquest of Acos, the remainder of its population earned the confidence of the Inca to perform such important tasks.

Finally, at 9,564 feet above sea level, Acos lies at an elevation that is relatively low by Andean standards. The extensive agricultural land around it and the elaborate terraces above it suggest that Acos produced a significant amount of maize. Maize was (and is) a critical crop in the Andes, and unlike root crops (such as potatoes and other Andean tubers), it can be stored for long periods of time. It was also a significant item of tribute. So, the prospect of maize tribute as well as bridge-building skills also may have influenced Pachacuti's desire to conquer Acos.

After I climbed to the top of Marca Urqu, and looked down toward Acos, I had an excellent view of the village, and noted other features of the landscape that were worth investigating. Acos is built on a series of terraces on the north side of the valley. On the northern edge of the village, a large mound in a circular-shaped cultivated field contrasted with the surrounding terrain. Since this mound did not have the configuration of the slope of the mountain or was terraced, I surmised that it must be artificial and probably was another archaeological site. There was no standing architecture on the mound, but the walls may have been removed and the rocks from them placed in the piles in and around it.

After I descended Marca Urqu and hiked back to Acos, I walked up the street to locate the mound, and in doing so, I had to climb up several terraces. After crossing over the stone fence around the mound, I examined its surface, and found pottery that was totally unlike the pottery from Marca Urqu. A comparison of its style with that from Cusco suggested that it predated the Inca period by at least a millennium.[8] This provisional dating suggested that the Acos had a longtime depth and a location that was favored because of the presence of a spring there, flat agricultural land on the plateau, and extensive terracing made possible by the gentle slopes around the community.

I returned to the street, walking down the terraces to the plaza. Along the way, I picked up one sherd of Imperial Inca polychrome pottery. From all of my survey over the terrain around Acos, it was the only evidence of Imperial Inca occupation that I found compared to the pre-Inca and early Inca occupation present on Marca Urqu.[9]

INCA BATTLES: A VIEW FROM THE PRESENT

Cultural patterns in the present often can help interpret the past, and a modern-day ritual conflict helped me understand Pachacuti's attack on Acos, and Inca warfare in general. During my Fulbright lectureship at the University of Cusco five years later in 1972–1973, a friend of me and my wife learned about a ritual battle (called *Chiaraje*) that would take place on New Year's Day in an area about forty miles southeast of Acos. Fought by men from two communities in the high puna northwest of the town of Langui, it was said that if someone was killed in the battle, the crops would flourish. Since the puna is associated with the mountain spirits (or the Mountain God), this battle did not appear to be just a ritual, but rather a sacrificial conflict presumably to propitiate the spirits (or the god) of the mountains. I was curious to know more about it.[10]

So, early in the morning on New Year's Day in 1973, my wife and I left Cusco in our friends' Volkswagen van. After descending from 11,000 feet at Cusco to the Vilcanota Valley at 10,000 feet, we followed the valley up toward La Raya, a pass at 14,327 feet that separates the drainage of the Vilcanota River from those rivers that empty into Lake Titicaca on the Peru-Bolivian Altiplano.

Long before we reached the pass, however, we left the valley and followed a road up a narrow valley into the high puna grassland to the west. Eventually, we entered a large, broad valley at an elevation of about 13,000 feet. In the distance, widely separated green fields of Andean tubers, black patches of llama corrals, recently plowed fields, and an occasional adobe house stood out against the tan and green ichu grasses on the lower slopes of the mountains. Settlement was sparse, but it appeared that subsistence was based upon root crops and herding.

Our destination lay at the top of the mountains across the valley to the west, but to get there, the road first turned north to follow a gentle slope as it ascended to traverse the steeper slopes of the mountains on the far side. Along the way, we passed the isolated houses, corrals, and both cultivated and uncultivated fields that we had seen from the other side of the valley. As we moved higher, the settlements and the fields disappeared with just llamas grazing on the slopes.

Finally, as the road reached the far side of the valley, we could see tiny black specks on the top of a mountain to the west indicating that we were nearing our destination. We could not drive to the site of the battle, so we stopped and parked along a wide spot in the road.

Our wives remained in our van and we followed a single-vehicle track as we walked upward to the top of the range. Each step was exhausting and painful, and we had to rest frequently. Having lived for four and a half months at the 11,000-foot elevation of Cusco, I was surprised that I had so much trouble walking along a track that ascended so gradually. I had thought I had adapted to high attitude, but I actually had no idea about the precise elevation of my ascent. With elevations now available on Google Earth, I discovered later that we had left our vehicle at approximately 14,300 feet above sea level and that our destination was more than 15,000 feet above sea level. The slow pace of my ascent suddenly became more understandable. No wonder I was winded!

Ultimately, we began to make out the detail of what had appeared to be specks from a distance. The mountaintop was actually a highly elevated portion of a ridge filled with men in red ponchos and women in black skirts. Horses and mules grazed on the slope below.

We eventually reached a pass into the valley to the west, and as we did, the people on the mountaintop north of us rushed down the slope toward us yelling and cursing as they went. Frightened that they would attack us, we stood there frozen with fear. But, when a man on horseback passed in front of us, we realized that we were not their targets. As we turned to see where he was going, we saw another group of men streaming in our direction from another mountain in the distance to the south.

Behind the man on horseback came a small army of men with slings. A few stopped and we asked to take their picture before they continued on to the battle line (fig. 8.5). They were not only friendly, unlike our initial impression, but I even convinced one to sell me his sling.

The battle itself took place along a front line about two hundred feet apart with combatants using slings to hurl stones at the other side. Anxious to get some pictures, I followed the men into battle, staying well behind them out of range from the projectiles slung from the opposing side. One man on a horse carried a whip with a hexagonal brass nut attached to its end, and, riding into the fray, he used it to strike at anyone within range.

Slowly approaching from the rear of the advancing fighters, I found a promontory overlooking the conflict and sat there aiming my camera

FIGURE 8.5. Three men with slings pausing just before they engage the opposing community in the ritual battle of *Chiaraje*.

FIGURE 8.6. With his sling loaded with a rock, a participant in the *Chiaraje* battle pauses before hurling the rock at the opposing side.

FIGURE 8.7. Young men engaged in various stages of using their slings during the *Chiaraje* battle. The man on the right is placing a rock in his sling. The man on the left is spinning it, and the man in the center has just released a rock aimed at the opposing side.

with its 200 mm lens toward the battle line in a large depression below me. I captured some telling images of the fighters next to me: one with a rock in his sling ready to use it (fig. 8.6), and another of three men in various stages of preparing and spinning a sling prior to sending a projectile off to the opposing side (fig. 8.7).

I felt some guilt as I sat on my perch photographing a spectacle in which the goal was to injure, maim, or kill someone. I could do nothing about it, but I was fascinated by the conflict. When we arrived at the battlefield and the fighters rushed toward the front line, they were cursing. What could drive the men of these communities to fight one another so brutally? Ideology is a powerful motivator for fighting, to protect honor, and to defend and protect one's territory and kin. But this was a ritual battle fought on predetermined days each year. Why was all this hostility directed toward a neighboring community at a scheduled time and place? The location of the battle was critical because the landscape was high enough to be in the sacred space of the Mountain God. Yet, even at 15,000 feet, fighting was still possible for these men who were not as constrained by the altitude as I was.

I looked down on the parallel battle lines and realized how fortunate I was for placing myself out of range of the rocks hurled from the slings on the other side. Busy photographing the fray and trying to get as many interesting images as possible, I was jarred into reality when I discovered that the men on my side of the conflict were retreating from a sudden advance of their opponents. Up to this point, I was safely behind the front lines, taking pictures outside of danger.

Frightened again because I knew that I could not sustain running to the rear with the retreating fighters at this altitude, I had to think quickly and decide upon a course of action. I knew that the opposing side was not after me, but I could still be hit by a stray rock hurled from their slings. So, I determined that if I could just get out of the way of the advancing onslaught from the opposing side, I could avoid having a lithic projectile make an unwelcome contact with my body.

So, I ran over the top of the ridge at right angles to the retreating fighters and then down the other side toward the valley from which we had come. After I ran a short distance (which is all I could manage at that altitude), I turned to be sure I was away from the front line and that no one would be slinging a stone in my direction. Fortunately, I was alone and no one had come over the ridge behind me.

I waited until I thought the front line of battle had passed, then climbed back up to the top of the ridge to see what was happening. The battle had ceased and the men from both sides were retreating to their respective mountaintops.

I had been alone taking pictures behind the front line and had not seen my friend who had accompanied me. Now, in the distance, he was moving toward the mountaintop near the spot where we had ascended from our vehicle. The fighters from that community were climbing ahead of him, and some had already reached the summit.

In the other direction, roughly a mile away, I could see their adversaries climbing up to their position (called a *pukara*, or fortress) on another mountaintop. From my vantage point, they seemed like a retreating army of tiny red ants marching up the slope of their hill to return to the safety of their nest. I could only make out their human form through my telephoto lens.

Walking back along the ridge on which I had come, I continued down the slope to the pass that separated the valley from which we came and the one to the west. Ahead of me was the mountaintop fortress of the retreating fighters, and I carefully climbed to the top. Since its position was higher and steeper than the surrounding terrain, and exceeded 15,000 feet above sea level, I was winded with every step.

As I reached the top of the mountain, what had appeared to be ants from our trek up the mountain turned out to be a group of perhaps fifty people. Women in black shawls and skirts sat with cooking pots filled with food, dispensing it to the men in red ponchos who had just retreated from the battle. Some poured chicha into cups for the fighters to refresh themselves.

The men had thrown their slings and ponchos over their shoulders and were taking a break—presumably before another encounter with the opposing community from the mountaintop to the south. Wandering through the small crowd, I saw no serious injuries, except a man with a bump the size of a tennis ball on one of his cheek bones. On a ridge below, other women tended the horses used in the fray, along with the mules that had transported the food and chicha to the site.

We asked when the men would return to the battle, and they said they would not fight again for several hours. Rather than wait for a new conflict, we decided to walk down the mountain to our van and return to Cusco so that we could arrive home before dark.

This battle was probably similar to those in which the Incas engaged their enemies when they conquered new territories. There were, of course, no horses or mules before the arrival of the Spanish, but both the modern Chiaraje battle and Inca battles used slings to hurl stones at one another. Rather than a brass-tipped whip wielded by horseback rider, Inca warriors probably employed clubs with bronze heads for close combat.

In the late sixteenth century, historian Sarmiento de Gamboa wrote that Inca Pachacuti was hit in the head with a stone during the battle to conquer the people of Acos. After witnessing the modern battle of Chiaraje, Pachacuti's injury likely resulted from a stone hurled from a sling of one of the Acos defenders. Given the size of the bump on the cheekbone of one of the combatants that I saw after the battle, Pachacuti's injury was likely very painful. His anger directed against the people of Acos thus was understandable and helped explain why he persisted in fighting them, conquering them, and then exiling the survivors.

THE CULMINATION OF THE ACOS JOURNEY

After spending three days investigating the area around Acos, I decided that I should return to Cusco. I had finally fulfilled the purpose of my journey across the Andes. I had retraced the steps of the conquering Incas who had exiled the defeated Acos Indians to Quinua in the fifteenth century, and I had visited their village of origin. Even though I did not actually travel on Inca roads or cross Inca bridges, the experience of making the trip gave me an appreciation of the gargantuan task that the Incas accomplished in conquering and exiling the people of Acos.

My trip had been a long, difficult journey, and it made me appreciate even more what it took to relocate conquered groups during the expansion of the Inca Empire. Even with modern transportation, five days were required to travel from Ayacucho to Acos, but how long did Pachacuti require to resettle the Acos survivors northeast of Ayacucho? Using the narrow Andean trails and bridges meant that armies, llama trains, and exiles must have stretched out for miles along the roads, requiring far more than the five days it took me to get to Acos. The entire process must have taken weeks, if not months, and required provisions to sustain both the army and exiles alike.

Since the people of Acos made no pottery and it was not made anywhere nearby, it appeared that if any survivors remained after Pachacuti conquered them, none were potters. Even though I did not find potters nearby, I had learned a great deal about Acos and its environs. I had discovered one site, Marca Urqu, from which people of Acos probably defended themselves against the Inca's conquering army. This site, its strategic location within the landscape of Acos, and the pottery on its surface appeared to link the archaeology of the Acos area to its ethnohistory as described by Sarmiento. Indeed, Marca Urqu appeared to be the site where the Acos Indians defended themselves against the attack by Inca Pachacuti early in the fifteenth century.

CHAPTER 9

Returning to Cusco

EARLY THE NEXT MORNING, I packed my backpack, said goodbye to my host and his family, and thanked them for their hospitality. I walked down to the plaza to catch a ride on a truck coming from the town of Pillpinto.

On my return trip I wanted to meet up with the Peace Corps volunteer that I met in Cusco who, with his wife, was working in the village of Sangarará roughly halfway between Acos and the Cusco-Puno road (see fig. 7.5). When I had told them about my trip, they asked me to stop in Sangarará and see them. They would not return for several days, but since I was spending time in Acos, a stop in Sangarará on my way back to Cusco should coincide with their return.

For this leg of my trip, I did not need to stay overnight in Acomayo because the truck was on its way to Cusco and would drop me in Sangarará. As before, riding on a truck meant that there were no seats—only a space to stand in the rather large cargo area in the rear. I found a cramped space and sat on my backpack. My position was definitely not first-class, and not comfortable. Because of my position deep inside the rear of the truck, this leg of my journey was not as scenic as my trip to Acos when I was perched precariously on the corner of the wooden box enclosing the cargo area.

Travel on Andean roads was not only dangerous because of their narrowness and treacherous locations, but riding on the back of a truck meant almost certain death if your vehicle went over the edge and rolled down the slope. Because of these risks, one of the rules of the road in the Andes was to have traffic move in one direction on one day and in the opposite direction on the following day. So, if I was going toward Cusco on one day, and made an overnight stop, I could only get transportation in that same direction two days later. So, every other day one could catch a truck going in the desired direction.

After a brief trip across the plateau on which Acos lies, the truck descended into the valley and then climbed the other side through harvested fields and terraces to the pass that separated the valley from the high plain around Sangarará (see fig. 7.5). Even though this plain was very flat, it was more than 12,350 feet above sea level. Too cold to grow maize, its inhabitants cultivated barley, potatoes, a bitter variety of potatoes that required processing before eating, and other Andean tubers. The land was wet and swampy in places but was full of grass that served as pasture for cattle, sheep, and llamas.

Sangarará lies in the center of the western part of the plain. So, after going over the pass, the travel time to the village was brief, and soon the truck stopped in the middle of the village. After climbing out of the truck, my first priority was to find my Peace Corps friends. They were not there, but I was told that they would return the next day when the traffic came from Cusco.

I had counted on my friends' hospitality for meals and a place to stay. Needless to say, I was disappointed that they had not returned, but their delay meant that I needed to find shelter and something to eat for that day and evening. I soon learned that there was no hotel and no eating place in the village. I could go without food for a day, but facing the Andean winter night at this altitude would be a challenge because the outside temperature would drop below freezing. It was not a comforting thought, and I was not eager to sleep outside under those conditions. I had my sleeping bag and air mattress, but I had never slept outside in the Andes, much less in the winter. So, I was out of luck for even the most basic of necessities.

Spending the night at the police station was the most obvious option, thinking that I would ask to sleep in a cell for the night. It was hardly a desirable place, but it was secure, inside, and away from the harshest temperatures of the Andean night.

So, I went into the police station and told them that I was waiting for my friends, the Peace Corps volunteers, and asked the officer at the desk if I could sleep in a cell. He said yes and asked me to follow him. Instead of a jail cell, he took me to the sleeping quarters of his men and told me I could sleep there. I began to unload my backpack and unroll my air mattress and sleeping bag on the floor. I had started inflating the air mattress when one of the men asked me to stop and took me over to a bed and said I could sleep there. He was leaving the post for a few days and explained that his bed would not be used that night. I didn't need my mattress or sleeping bag, and I could crawl under layers of toasty-warm wool blankets.

It was still early in the afternoon with plenty of daylight left, so I left my belongings in the police dormitory and took my camera and went out for a walk. I meandered to the edge of the village. It was early June, and stalks of harvested barley were awaiting processing on a makeshift threshing floor. Men had already pounded some of the stalks with poles to remove the grains, and as I arrived, they were forking off the straw into a pile leaving the grains on the ground that the women then winnowed in the wind. The yellow chaff blew off to the side as the grain fell into a pile that subsequently was gathered up into large wool sacks with stripes of black, brown, white, and beige woven into their fabric.

Off to the side, two men and a woman were taking a break from their post-harvesting activities and were drinking cane alcohol (*aguardiente*) dispensed from a bottle into small glasses, with two large ceramic vessels of homemade maize beer (*chicha*) to one side (fig. 9.1). One was stoppered with the hoof of a cow, and it seemed a most unlikely use for that part of the animal. They offered me a drink of the cane alcohol, but I politely

FIGURE 9.1. Taking a break from threshing barley and making *chuñu*, these workers near Sangarará pause to drink cane alcohol poured out by the man on the right.

FIGURE 9.2. A woman pressing out the moisture from bitter potatoes to make *chuñu*. Alternate freezing and thawing and then repeated pressing results in a dehydrated product that can be stored for long periods of time.

refused—not willing to risk even the slightest inebriation at this high altitude. I had tangled with aguardiente previously in Quinua, and I was uncertain about the effects that even one drink would have on me at the altitude of Sangarará.

Another woman was preparing freeze-dried *chuñu* from a variety of bitter potatoes. These tubers were small, had a bitter taste, and were not eaten without processing. The Andean people, however, developed a way to make them palatable and preserve them without spoilage. The process is best carried out at high altitudes where the temperature drops below freezing at night. Tubers are spread out on the ground and then trampled with bare feet, breaking the cell walls, and expelling the water (fig. 9.2). Overnight, the subfreezing temperatures rupture the tuber's remaining cells. The next day, the warm rays of the sun melt the frozen water, the water drains out of them, and they are trampled again. This cycle is repeated until all of the water is expelled from the tubers and they are dry.

This preparation of chuñu involves the unintentional addition of other ubiquitous materials such as dirt and those bodily substances found between the toes. The end result may be just bagged "as is" and called "black chuñu" or washed in a stream and called "white chuñu." This process creates a product that can be stored for long periods of time and can buffer food scarcity when the supplies of other crops are exhausted before the next harvest.

Chuñu is added to soups and stews, and after cooking, the taste and texture are like a small dumpling, but in its dried raw state, it has the appearance and texture of thick, lumpy, dark-gray Styrofoam and is tasteless. Although I ate it in soups without hesitation, knowing how it is made kept me from being a great fan of it.

I took some additional photographs of the barley threshing and then wandered back into the village, walking down one of the streets to the plaza and the church. One young man told me about the church's bell tower and I walked toward it and climbed to the top to photograph the village set against the jagged maroon and brown tones of the mountain scenery, and the azure blue of the Andean sky behind it.

A WELCOME MEAL

After descending the tower, I strolled down one of the dusty streets and came upon a man separating fava beans from their pods in front of his house. He had spread out several mantas, the square shawls of native woven cloth, used to carry everything from babies to produce from the market. Now, he was using them to keep the beans off the dirt on the street.

Fava beans are one of those plants that the Spanish brought to Peru. They grow as a series of single pods attached along the length of a three- to four-foot vertical stalk. Because the plants are productive and tolerant of the cold and high altitudes, Andean peoples began to cultivate them sometime during the colonial period. Unlike Andean root crops (except freeze-dried chuñu), they can be stored easily without spoiling.

When these fields are harvested, the stalks are tied in bundles, and taken to the house lot, where the pods are removed from the stalks. Then, the beans must be separated from the pods, leaves, and fragments of the stems.

I knelt down on one of the pieces of cloth opposite him and started helping him sort the beans by picking out the husks and detritus and throwing the cleaned beans into a pile. With two of us working, we moved through the stack of unshucked beans quickly.

It was the end of the day, and daylight was waning. We soon finished the task, and I rose to my feet, brushed myself off, and was about to return to the police station to spend the night. As I did so, the man gestured to me, bringing the tips of all five fingers together and raising them to repeatedly point to his mouth. I was a bit puzzled by the meaning of this gesture and tried to communicate in Spanish, but with nods and smiles, he repeated the action, and I surmised that he wanted me to stay and eat with him. This was a puzzling course of events since I knew very little Quechua, and my companion knew no Spanish—at least not enough to speak it. However, the thought of eating with the man pleased me as I had no other prospects of food that evening, and there would be no supper except for crackers, cookies, and canned food from the local store. Even then, I would have to purchase a can opener and eating utensils to consume that fare, if the store sold them.

I hesitated to make a move, but he motioned for me to follow and led me into his modest house of mud brick that was similar to many others in the village. It was dark, dingy, and cluttered on the inside with a raised hearth in the rear. He spoke to his wife in Quechua, and then ushered me into a tiny room at the back just inside the rear door that was open to the patio.

We sat across from one another in silence. Soon, his wife gave us each a bowl of boiled root crops in their skins: potatoes and two other Andean root crops called *oca* and *añu*. No eating utensils came with the meal, but even eating with my hands, I welcomed the food. Some of the tubers still had pieces of dirt on them, and it crunched between my teeth when I chewed, but I didn't care. The añu, an Andean tuber related biologically to a common garden flower known in North America as nasturtium, was succulent, delicious, and slightly sweet. After chewing, it slid easily down my throat. Unfortunately, there were only one or two of those in my bowl. Unlike the añu, however, the potatoes stuck to the inside of my throat. Either having the same problem as I did with the potatoes, or sensing my discomfort with them, he offered me water to wash them down. Suspicious about the water quality, I didn't accept it. I would have preferred chicha because it would have been safer with fewer bacteria and amoebas, but no maize grows at this altitude and no pepper trees existed to supply the raw material for the brew. Nevertheless, I had seen chicha being served at the threshing floor at the edge of the village.

I felt awkward about not being able to talk during a meal. In my own culture, eating in a home is a social occasion, a time to connect emotionally, and establish trust and rapport, but my attempts were frustrated, and our failure to communicate continued. Nevertheless, he seemed content with my presence and comfortable to entertain a guest with whom he could not converse. So, we sat in silence with an occasional attempt on my part to express myself. Somehow, despite the frustration of the failure to know each other's language, his invitation and seeming expression of generosity transcended our inability to talk with one another.

I was very grateful for the meal and for his hospitality, and expressed this gratitude in Spanish remarking about how delicious it was. Considering that the only other option for supper was soda crackers and canned tuna from the local store in front of the police station, it was deeply appreciated.

After finishing my meal, I rose, again thanked my host profusely in Spanish, expressed my appreciation to his wife who cooked the food, and turned to leave. I exited the house and walked down the street toward the police station. By this time, it was twilight and the bluish-black mountains were silhouetted against the canvas of a darkening blue sky and the glow of the setting sun.

His generous hospitality puzzled me until I started teaching a few years later. Rapport is critical for doing anthropological fieldwork, and one of the ways of establishing it consists of doing something helpful for the people with whom you are working. From my other field experiences both before and since, I realized that even the simplest act of kindness and help is usually greatly appreciated. Sometimes, however, speakers of native American languages and wearers of peasant clothing are so despised that any act of identification with them implies respect and appreciation for them—rarely given by people of higher status.

For an anthropologist to learn about a culture, it is necessary to participate in it, and such attempts are often greeted with gratitude and appreciation. Any person of higher status in Peru would not even think of eating with a peasant family. That I helped this man with his fava beans must have implied my respect and appreciation for him, and thus he invited me to eat with him.

But another explanation may also be at work here. In Andean culture, harvesting is communal, and family, friends, and neighbors help with the tasks required. Such labor is not without compensation because custom requires that the host provide coca leaves, maize beer (chicha), and food for the group in return for their labor. As any anthropologist knows, reciprocity is a fundamental universal principle of human social relationships.

I returned to the police station ready to turn in for the night. I found the post bunkhouse, along with the bed that I had been given, and crawled under its wool blankets. Wrapped in the warmth of the bed covers away from the cold of the Andean night, I fell asleep.

RETURN TO THE VILCANOTA VALLEY

I awoke the next morning when the shift changed because of the bustle of activity in the sleeping quarters. I crawled out of the bed, pulled on my pants, and before I put on my shoes, I checked inside them for nighttime visitors such as scorpions, spiders, or other unwelcome guests.

I picked up my razor, shaving brush, and soap, and stumbled into the courtyard to the water spigot. The morning air was still very cold, and although I was aware of the great daily variation in temperature, understanding that fact cognitively is not the same as understanding it experientially. The sun still hid behind the mountains on the other side of the pampa, but its light outlined their summits with a golden fringe while blackness enveloped the shadow of the mountains in front of me as well as the courtyard of the police station.

A washbasin lay beneath the spigot, obviously used by the policemen to wash. But, as I looked down and picked it up, I saw that it was frozen solid with at least two inches of solid ice. I tried to upend the basin to remove the ice, but it was useless.

There was no point in continuing. Even if there was unfrozen water under the ice, and the pipes leading to the spigot were not frozen, the thought of shaving in water close to freezing forewarned me of a masochistic experience that I did not want to endure.

I went back into the dormitory and returned to my bed. I must have slept well because when I awoke again, the bright morning sun was streaming through the windows. The police had left the room, and I was alone. So, I decided it was time to arise and meet the day. Perhaps my second attempt at personal grooming would be more successful than the first.

My second visit to the courtyard was more productive and I found that the morning sunshine had melted the ice in the basin. The water was frigid, but at least the content of the basin was liquid and not solid. Shaving was possible and I endured the experience washing and shaving in ice water. Because the water was so cold, it transformed me from a groggy state to wide awake in a shocking, eye-opening instant.

I emerged from the police station just as herds of llamas, sheep, and cattle headed out to their pastures for the day (fig. 9.3). The elevation of Sangarará was a bit low for llama herding, and too low for alpacas because

FIGURE 9.3. Llamas and sheep on their way to pasture in the early morning in Sangarará.

their sensitive feet require the softer tundra vegetation that exists at elevations higher than that used for llamas. If alpacas spend too much time at a lower elevation, their feet are susceptible to a fungus disease. At higher elevations, tiny air pockets in their wool insulate the skin by allowing the moisture on the tips of the wool fibers to freeze, protecting and insulating the skin from the cold, snow, and ice. This quality of the wool makes it a prized product for warmth—by locals and outsiders alike.

It was still cold, but the bright blue sky enhanced the color of the green grasses of the valley, and the morning sun lifted my spirits. The yellow of the harvested fields contrasted with the medley of the browns, reds, and grays of the rocks on the mountains.

I went across the street to the only store in town and bought some crackers and cookies for my breakfast.

Anxious to see my friends, I enquired about the transportation from Cusco, and learned that the trucks from there usually arrive during the late morning. It was then that I realized I could not find a truck to Acos in Cusco because the shops in Rimacpampa were not open when the trucks departed so early in the morning, and the shopkeepers would not have known that it was a departure point for Acos.

Finally, a truck brought my Peace Corps friend and his wife. We greeted one another and I collected my backpack from the police station. We walked to their house near the edge of town. It was a two-room affair superficially similar to other houses in the village, but with one important difference. Unlike other houses in which there was no ceiling—just the rafters and the underside of the roof tiles—my friends had stretched sheets of plastic as a ceiling from the top of the walls across the interior of the entire house, and melted the edges together. It rattled in the wind, and I was curious as to why they made this change. They explained that it reduced the dust inside the house and kept it warmer.

They set up a cot for me in the room devoted to living, dining, and preparing their meals, and I unrolled my sleeping bag on it. During the night the wind blew through the tile roof and rattled the plastic above me. Nevertheless, it helped hold the heat inside the house and I slept warmly and peacefully in my sleeping bag.

The next morning, my new friend asked me if I would like to see some archaeological sites. I said yes, and we walked toward the western edge of the valley. There, the boundary between the valley floor and the uplands is rather abrupt, and soon we came upon a rock shelter with some pottery and bones. My host noted that many burials (some with skulls) were associated with Inca pottery in this and other rock shelters. Some skulls had holes drilled into them.

The Incas and their predecessors sometimes drilled or cut holes in the skull (called trephination) and this practice is evident on many skulls recovered in the archaeological record. Perhaps done for medical reasons to deal with a head injury, victims did not always survive the operation. Sometimes, however, the victim recovered, as evidenced by bone growth around the hole. Holes with no growth, however, indicate that the individual did not survive.

We moved along the edge of the valley until we could ascend a low flat ridge at its northwest side. It was a short walk to the top, but it gave a panoramic view of the mountains and valley with a stunning vista of the villages of Sangarará, Marcaconga, and the low mountain in the middle of the valley that separated Marcaconga and Lake Pomacanchi (see fig. 7.5). Although the valley was situated more than 12,000 feet above sea level, it was flat, and I realized why three villages were so close together. It was one of the few areas of relatively flat agricultural land at this elevation.

From our vantage point, I could also see a panorama of the pastures and fields of the valley, bounded by mountains on either side. The peaks to the north and east were spectacular with views unobstructed by the houses of the village and the low hills near it.

Our position also overlooked the pass between the flat plain (pampa) around Sangarará from which we had come, and over the pass to the west, we could see the upper part of the Acomayo Valley that led to Acos. This pass was a critical point between Acos and the Vilcanota River valley to the east. Once one reached the pass from Acos, travel across the flat plain was unimpeded by foot or llama train, and one could easily traverse the distance between the Apurimac River to the west and the Vilcanota valley to the east. The flat plain around Sangarará was a virtual throughway by Andean standards.

The remains of an ancient road crossed this pass at a spot no more than fifty feet from the modern road. Next to the road, and on the pass itself, I could see the foundations of a small structure. One of many along the Inca system of roads, it was probably a way station (*tambo*) for runners that was part of the Inca system of communication. At tambos, one runner stopped and passed his message to another who continued the journey to, or from, Cusco. The combination of the Inca infrastructure of roads, bridges, a system of runners/messengers (called *chaskis*), and tambos helped tie the empire together and allowed the Inca to govern the vast empire that stretched along the spine of the Andes from northern Ecuador to northern Chile and northwest Argentina.

Behind us lay another archaeological site called Quispillaqta, situated in a critical position to control access to the pass below. The structures on the site were both oval and rectangular. Pottery scattered on the surface dated to the period immediately preceding the Inca Empire and during its early years. Although in a crucial position to defend and control the pass, the inhabitants of the site apparently were unable to abate the advance of the Inca troops toward Acos in the early fifteenth century.

After seeing the archaeological sites around Sangarará, there was no reason to stay there longer. The purpose of my journey had been realized, and because of the duration of my trip so far, I did not know how much time was required to return. So, I was anxious to continue my journey back to Quinua.

I decided to leave the following day, but unfortunately, traffic was headed away from Cusco that day, and the only way for me to get to Cusco was to walk across the plain, down to the Cusco-Puno road in the Vilcanota valley, and then flag down a vehicle going to Cusco. The road there was wide enough for traffic to go to and from Cusco on the same day.

My trek on foot took me past the village of Marcaconga and its school. The pupils were outside and drinking something from cups. With a closer look, I saw that they were drinking a mixture of water and powder from large bags marked with the "Alliance for Progress" symbol, emblazoned with the phrase "From the People of the United States of America" in English. The Alliance for Progress was a U.S. program to establish economic cooperation between the United States and Latin America.[1] One aspect of it was sending food to the Latin American poor. The U.S. government bought agricultural commodities like milk powder and flour at set prices to subsidize the price at home and then sent these commodities abroad to feed the poor. Unfortunately, such policies appeared to be more about price supports for farmers at home than feeding the poor abroad because the commodities from the United States did not always match the diet of the recipients, and if it did, it undercut local producers.

The road passed a small mountain in the middle of the valley and tranquil Lake Pomacanchi came into view on its other side (see fig. 7.5). Beyond it, in a valley to the south of the lake, lay the village of Pomacanchi, another sleepy settlement similar to Sangarará and Marcaconga.

A few trucks passed me going in the opposite direction and covered me with dust from the dirt road, but generally, I had the road to myself.

I passed part of Lake Pomacanchi before the road turned down into the valley of the Vilcanota River. The descent was much easier than my walk across the flat valley from Sangarará.

The trek to the Vilcanota valley seemed to take a long time, even though the distance from Sangarará was only about eleven miles. But, with a pack on my back, and an elevation of more than 12,000 feet, the experience was rigorous and required several hours. By contemporary standards, the trek was not very long, but in 1967, few gringo expatriates hiked the Andes carrying a backpack.

This was the route that Inca Pachacuti and his army probably took in their advance on Acos. The relative ease of travel, even considering the altitude, provided an easy but critical link between the Apurimac River and the Vilcanota valley that went to Cusco in one direction, and to the pass that led to Lake Titicaca in the other.

By midafternoon, I reached the Cusco-Puno road, and sat down on its edge to wait for a truck to take me to Cusco. I did not have to wait long because a truck soon appeared. I flagged it down, paid the driver, and climbed into the cargo section from the rear. I was the only passenger. Although the road was an important transportation link from Cusco to Puno in the Altiplano, it was still gravel, and because it was the dry season, the truck kicked up an unending cloud of beige dust that covered me and my belongings.

I eventually arrived in Cusco as a tired and filthy traveler. Not in the mood to have less than the best to rest and get cleaned up, I checked into the tourist hotel for a night so that I could take a bath, get my clothes washed, have a relaxing meal, and generally rest from my adventures. I took a long soaking bath in a warm room and enjoyed a brief respite in relative luxury.

The next day I returned to my former hotel and rented another room for $2.50 a night for each of the subsequent nights that I spent in Cusco.

CHAPTER 10

Returning to Ayacucho

AFTER SEVERAL DAYS in the Inca capital, it was time to leave, and I looked for a way to retrace my journey back to the Ayacucho Valley from which I had come. The overland trip to Cusco and then to Acos had been arduous, over a seemingly scant airline distance of 170 miles, but a journey that stretched out over a period of five days—a disjunction of time and distance that I had not realized before I came to Peru. Even with modern car, bus, train, and truck transportation, the trip from Ayacucho to Acos was a long journey. Its duration over such a short air distance taught me much about the Andes. I had learned about its extremely varied topography from experience. Now, back in Cusco, it was time for find transportation to return to Quinua.

After hours of searching and asking about transportation, I found a company that provided a car that took multiple passengers (a *colectivo*) to Andahuaylas. The service was to take me up over the low pass northwest of the city, over the plain of Anta, down into the deep canyon of the Apurimac River, to Abancay and beyond to Andahuaylas farther west (see fig. 5.2). This route generally retraced the steps of the ninth Inca, Pachacuti, when he crossed the Apurimac River, defeated the Chankas, and then moved northwest in his conquest to the area around Ayacucho. So, I paid my fare, collected my ticket, and was told to report to the office early the next morning.

The next morning I awoke, packed my backpack, and walked up the street to the waiting colectivo opposite the San Francisco church. It was crowded with five passengers, but it was relatively comfortable. I slept for most of the long trip, and when we arrived in Andahuaylas, darkness had already fallen. I was anxious to eat and rest. I still needed to travel to Ayacucho, but I would deal with finding transportation for that last leg of my return journey in the morning.

I soon found what was touted to be the best hotel in town. It was an old colonial structure with the rooms built around a central patio. As in many such buildings, the exterior doorway was gigantic—large enough for horses and a carriage to enter. The entrance was closed with two large thick wooden doors with a smaller door within one of them that could open separately to admit pedestrians.

I paid for my room and inquired about dinner. Soon, a young boy appeared and showed me to my room upstairs. It was spacious and cold, but its most memorable feature was the floor. The boards were broken in places with open knot holes. Pausing during my walk across the floor, I noticed that light appeared through the spaces revealing what appeared to be the lobby below. So, I turned off the light in the room and sure enough, there was no ceiling over the lobby—only the bottom of the floorboards of the rooms above. I could see all the activity in the lobby below with great clarity through the knot holes in the boards on the floor.

Pausing only to drop my backpack and wash my face, I descended to the restaurant at the rear of the lobby. There, the same boy that showed me to my room was my waiter. Because I was tired from my trip, I did not notice that he might have called me *"Padre"* (father), a term reserved for priests, when he showed me to my room. Now, in the restaurant, every response was "Yes, Padre" or "No, Padre" to my queries about the menu.

I was both puzzled and annoyed by his appellation, and I wondered why he thought I was a priest. Were priests the only gringos that stayed in this kind of a hotel? To accept the title he gave me, however, was disingenuous. I would not be in a position to hear his confession, recite a "Hail Mary," or say the rosary, much less officiate at a mass. I did not know enough about Catholicism to pass for a priest.

As I pondered his reasons, and my resistance to being called a priest, I realized that part of the problem was my clothing. As a poor graduate student, my wardrobe was limited. The standard dress for many Peruvians was a sweater, and perhaps a scarf around the neck at night during the cold Andean nights. Because I had traveled halfway across the Andes with a sleeping bag and air mattress in my backpack, little space remained for clothing.

When I left Quinua three weeks previously, I had packed two sweaters and two shirts for my trip to Acos. One sweater was a black crew neck that I wore over a pair of dark green cotton twill trousers. I had donned a gray shirt with the black sweater the morning that I left Cusco for the overland journey to Andahuaylas. The sweater left enough room around the neck to expose the collar of the shirt. It was similar to a priest's collar if one was imaginative and had little exposure to priestly garb.

When my annoyance with the boy's responses reached its limit, I replied with exasperation: "I am not a priest!"

To which he replied: "Sí, Padre!"

Clothing can communicate powerful messages, often with unintended consequences in another culture. I had faced this problem earlier in Ayacucho when I purchased a local felt hat to shade me from the hot Andean sun and its punishing ultraviolet radiation. After several days of astonished looks and snickers, I discovered that I was communicating a message that I was identifying with peasants. Men who were not peasants did not wear hats. Being mistaken for a priest was another matter. I had nothing in common with a priest except a common Christian faith, but in a sense, being called a priest may not have seemed such a bad thing, and it was better than being called a spy. Nevertheless, I was still annoyed because I did not want to misrepresent myself. It would be dishonest to accept that attribution, not just because I was not a priest, but also because I could not perform the duties of one.

I sat down to enjoy one of the great Peruvian dishes on the menu called *lomo saltado*, a fine cut of beef sliced in strips and then fried with potatoes, onions, and tomatoes. I had also ordered "Potatoes Huancayo Style" (*Papas a la Huancayina*), consisting of a boiled potato covered with a luscious cheese and peanut sauce garnished with parsley. The meal was excellent, better than the quality of the hotel.

As I ate, I remembered that my traveling companion between Andahuaylas and Cusco, the cash register salesman, had refused to stay in Andahuaylas, and I finally understood why he wanted to push on from Andahuaylas to Abancay three weeks previously. The hotel in which I found myself was a far cry from the tourist hotels in which I stayed in Abancay and Cusco.

The next day I needed to find transportation back to Ayacucho and explored several ways to make the trip. This portion of the journey to Acos had been both the longest and the most difficult.

I soon discovered that there were regular flights from Andahuaylas to Ayacucho provided by a Peruvian airline. The thought of traveling thirteen hours across the Andes by bus or by car to get to Ayacucho created enough anxiety in me to book a seat immediately for the flight the next day.

For the remainder of the day, I walked around the city and discovered an indigenous art festival. There were many examples of crafts from the Department of Apurimac, including pottery. So, I asked permission to photograph all of the pottery on display.

My curiosity for learning more about pottery, and my desire to collect as much data about local pottery as I could, later served me well. The Andahuaylas area was the Chanka homeland, and in retrospect, I realized that this local exhibition provided some comparative data about the pottery from the descendants of the Chankas. Since Chanka territory may have extended into the Ayacucho Valley before the Inca conquest, Chanka potters also may have influenced pottery made in Quinua. I discovered, however, that the ethnic pottery that I documented in Andahuaylas, like that in Abancay, bore no resemblance in shape and style to that of Quinua.

My flight to Ayacucho departed early the next morning. Since the airport was some distance from the city, I arrived with plenty of lead-time. As I waited my turn to board the aircraft, a family of Quechua peasants came onto the grass strip with their flocks and walked over to the airplane to examine it more closely, inspecting the engine and the wheels as I waited to board.

Finally, I boarded the plane and in less than an hour, I was back in Ayacucho—pleased that I did not have to endure the harrowing thirteen-hour bus ride that I had taken to begin my trip. I wished that I had known about the air connection when I started my journey.

THE PRESENT AND THE PAST

While I was gone on my trip to Acos, two more graduate students from the University of Illinois arrived in Ayacucho to work with Professor Zuidema. A few days later, he took all of us to a remote area in the southeastern part of the valley to examine several archaeological sites. I wanted to go because a community named "Acocro" was located in that area. Like the historic names of the two parts of Quinua, called Hanan Acos and Lurin Acos, and Acos Vinchos, its name, Acocro (Acos Ocros) implied a link to the Acos Indians that the Incas brought to the area in the fifteenth century.[1] I wanted to see that part of the valley that I had only seen from afar (see fig. 2.3).

Traveling along a dusty road in Dr. Zuidema's truck, we passed through a gigantic bed of pure white material thirty feet high. I had never seen anything like this before, and since I was looking for clay sources, I wondered if the material was clay. Some pottery dating from the time of the Wari Empire was made with a white clay, but archaeologists thought that it was made in Cajamarca in northern Peru. So, I wondered if the source of that clay might be found instead in deep deposits such as this one within the Ayacucho Valley.

We stopped and I took a sample for analysis. Back in Urbana, however, I learned that it was not clay at all, but rather a large layer of volcanic ash that had been folded during the uplift of the Andes, and one of the many beds of the ash that blanketed the Ayacucho Valley to great depths. One can still see the remains of a volcanic peak across from Wari in the middle of the valley, and it might have been a source of that ash. Once the drainage in the valley opened up into the Mantaro River to the north, however, the soft, friable beds of ash eroded, leaving deep ravines with long fingers of land between them (see fig. 5.5).

Being near the bottom of the valley, it was very hot. Even though it was the Andean winter, the sun bore down with vengeance at this lower altitude, but we finally finished our reconnaissance.

Famished and very thirsty, we found a local store, but we did not trust the quality of the water used in the bottled soft drink sold there and the store did not stock any other kind. The only reasonably refreshing beverage available was warm pilsner beer, but it was only sold in two-liter bottles. So, we purchased a bottle and shared it under a nearby pepper tree that provided only limited shade.

We dozed and rested between gulps of beer, talking about the archaeological sites that we had just visited and listening to Professor Zuidema hold forth with his vast knowledge of Peruvian ethnohistory. Transfixed on him, his narrative, the beer, and our exhaustion, we were oblivious to our surroundings until we heard bells—an unlikely sound in this remote location. It wasn't until the bells came closer that we realized that they announced the arrival of about twenty llamas laden with agricultural produce (fig. 10.1). In order to keep track of the animals, the drovers placed bells around their necks. We had unknowingly refreshed ourselves next to the main trail into Ayacucho from the southeast used by the llama trains. The store that we had just patronized was strategically placed at the spot where the trail crossed the road on which we had just traveled.

FIGURE 10.1. A llama train laden with bags of produce moving along a trail on the way to the city of Ayacucho.

In the past, Ayacucho was known for its traders, drovers, and muleteers, and this prominence is consistent with what we know about the Ayacucho Valley from history and prehistory. The Barrio of Carmen Alto, on the southwest side of the city of Ayacucho, was formerly known for its muleteers who moved goods overland to and from Ayacucho and the south coast. This economic link extends back into prehistory as indicated by similarity of the pottery from the south coast to pottery in the valley that preceded the development of the Wari state.

The juxtaposition of seeing llamas traveling along a trail to Ayacucho and having just returned from my long and arduous trip to Acos stimulated my thinking about the Inca conquest, and how the Incas accomplished it. Certainly, building roads and bridges was crucial for maintaining control of the empire by the flow of information, people, and goods across the Andes. Supplies for the conquering armies, and tribute from conquered lands, could be transported easily with llama trains that traveled along with them.

The Incas often replaced people in newly conquered areas with groups from more secure areas. Pachacuti's conquest of the Acos Indians south of Cusco and their forced exile to the eastern side of the Ayacucho Valley was part of this practice, but understanding it intellectually and cognitively was quite different from experiencing the rigor of traveling the distance from Acos myself—even with modern transportation. I concluded that Pachacuti's forced movement of the Acos Indians to the Ayacucho Valley over some of the most difficult terrain on earth was no easy task.

The trail that lay before us upon which the llama train had passed appeared to be the main trail from the southeastern end of the valley. It might have been the trail upon which the Incas had advanced to conquer the valley's inhabitants, and then brought the exiled Acos Indians on it to resettle them in the area.

Because my journey to Acos revealed that potters did not live there, I could say little about the relationship of Quinua potters and the people of Acos. Pachacuti had annihilated most of the Acos population, and those that remained, he exiled to the area around Quinua. So, if most of the people of Acos were killed, and the remainder were exiled, then the modern population of Acos would reveal nothing about the pre-Inca population. This meant that there were probably no descendants of the original inhabitants in modern Acos remaining from the Inca conquest. Further, the Spanish crown had concentrated populations into villages in the late sixteenth century during the *Reducciones* (literally, the "Reductions").[2] So, in retrospect, the population of Acos in 1967 probably bore no historical relationship to the one that the Incas conquered in the early fifteenth century. In retrospect, had I known all of these facts at the time, my trip to Acos may have been unnecessary.

Nevertheless, the journey to Acos was a great lesson of the difficulties that the Incas faced in moving their exiles over some of the world's most variegated terrain. No experience with travel in the Andes convinced me more of the monumental task of the Inca relocation of conquered groups. During the first leg of the trip to Andahuaylas, the bus zigzagged up and down mountains from snowstorms to subtropical river valleys with xerophytic vegetation and groves of bananas and oranges. During the next leg of the trip from Andahuaylas to Abancay, the lights of Abancay twinkled in the valley below hours before we arrived by road. The only part of the journey that was not characterized by up and down travel was the relatively short hourlong trip across the flat Plain of Anta, through the Urubamba/ Vilcanota Valley near Cusco, and across the high plain around Sangarará. Not included in the difficulties of such a lengthy trip were the problems with the accouterments of industrial civilization: a punctured gas tank, an overheated radiator, and two flat tires (one with no spare).

Even so, the trip to Acos was a fascinating, challenging, and an incredible adventure. I learned much about the history, geography, archaeology, and culture of the Andes that I could not have learned in any other way. Truly, experience is the best teacher, as all anthropologists know. Reading and learning about the Andes is not the same as actually being there. Reading Sarmiento's description of Pachacuti's conquest of the people of Acos, and their subsequent exile to Quinua is not the same as making the trip to Acos myself, climbing up to the fortress from which they defended themselves against the Inca, and then returning to Quinua. My journey thus helped me understand the consequences of the Inca conquest and their exiled populations in new ways.

CHAPTER 11

The End of the Journey

ALL ADVENTURES come to an end, often for very practical reasons. My money was running out, and I needed to leave Peru. A Peace Corps volunteer had invited me to stop in Panama to see the canal, and I wanted to continue on to Mexico to do some more research in Yucatán. I knew that I could cash a check there at the research institute with which I was affiliated in 1965 and 1966, but I also wanted to get back to Urbana to see my new girlfriend. We had written letters back and forth while I was in Peru, and although we had made no commitment to one another, our relationship had grown through our letter writing, and I had gotten very serious about our future together. Our separation and correspondence convinced me that she was the woman for me, and I wanted to be with her forever.

I could only make plans for my flights to Panama, Yucatán, and the United States in Lima, but I wanted to continue my adventure and satisfy my curiosity about seeing as much of the Andes as I could. So, I considered several options. One was an overland trip by bus to Lima through the central Andean city of Huancayo, or taking a bus over the Andes down to the south coast and then up the Pan American Highway (see fig. 5.2). The lingering memory of my bus ride from Ayacucho to Andahuaylas, in a cramped seat made for someone smaller than I, eliminated this option even before I seriously considered it. Flying was a second option, but I had already made an additional trip to Lima during my time in Ayacucho and I wanted a different kind of experience. A third choice involved taking a *colectivo* to the coast and then to Lima. Colectivos are more expensive than buses, but they are quicker, and more comfortable because five paying passengers share a car to a common destination. Trips through the Andes to the coast would expose me to a different part of Peru, and I would be able to observe the coast in detail.

After considering all of these options, I discovered a fourth possibility. I enjoy riding trains. I traveled by train to and from my home in South Dakota during my undergraduate years near Chicago and during my years in graduate school in Urbana. Although Ayacucho had no rail service, a train to Lima departed from the central Andean city of Huancayo located an air distance of 100 miles northwest of Ayacucho. So, in order to take the train to Lima, I needed to travel to Huancayo.

I found the appropriate colectivo service in Ayacucho and paid my fare. Early the next morning, I walked to the office near the central plaza and boarded a car with four other passengers for direct service to Huancayo. The road was a precarious one, not unlike the ones that I traveled to Cusco and beyond; it was gravel with portions only wide enough for one vehicle. Like many of the roads in the Andes at the time, traffic proceeded in only one direction on alternate days.

The heavy rainy season had washed out parts of the road and resulted in an abundance of landslides that had closed the road, cutting off Ayacucho for days on end. Even traveling during the dry season, I could see the scars of recent road closures with bulldozers still cleaning up the debris. The consequences of careless driving were also notable; a pickup had gone off the road down one of the embankments.

Nevertheless, the time on the colectivo passed quickly and I arrived in Huancayo in due time. After finding a hotel, I inquired about the train to Lima and discovered that it left the following morning. I was excited about the trip, but I was unprepared for the experience of this next adventure, passing through one of the highest railway stations of the world.

I arose early the next morning and headed to the rail station to begin the last leg of my journey. I bought my ticket and boarded the train. As it left Huancayo, it moved through the valley with its fields of harvested grain and maize. An occasional forest of eucalyptus trees brushed the bright-blue sky in the wind of the dry season, and in the breeze of the passing train.

Soon, the train left the valley and began its climb up the westernmost cordierra of the Andes. Because the weather comes from the east across the Amazon rain forest, most of the rainfall has been wrung from the moisture-drenched clouds in the eastern ranges so that most of the western

FIGURE 11.1. At the highest portions of the western cordierra of the Andes, mountain peaks rise directly out of the relatively flat grasslands. At this point, the elevation of the valley floor is more than 15,000 feet above sea level.

range is dry. The only remaining moisture fell as snow on peaks that rose more than 16,000 feet above sea level, creating a zone of snow that seldom disappeared—at least until climate change began to diminish it.

The scene changed when the train arrived in La Oroya, a city built around a copper refinery with its smokestacks belching out smoke and gaseous by-products from the smelting process (see fig. 5.2). The train picked up and disgorged passengers here for the trip up to the westernmost crest of the Andes, and for those traveling to Lima.

After the train left La Oroya and continued to climb, the dry barrenness of the landscape emerged with many rocks among the tan, dry grasses. In the distance, scattered sheep dotted the landscape. As the elevation increased, the snow-capped peaks of the range rose directly out of the high valleys (fig. 11.1). Here, the dry grasses did not just serve as a pasture for sheep as they did at lower elevations, but also for the llamas that grazed among them.

The train slowed and passed a station with a sign that announced "GALERA" in large capital letters. A smaller sign below said "Altura 15,681 Pies." Translated, that's 15,681 feet above sea level, more than 1,000 feet higher than the highest mountain in the continental United States,

FIGURE 11.2. The railway station of Galera at the continental divide informs passengers that it is 15,681 feet above sea level.

Mount Whitney in California, and almost three miles above sea level. I had never experienced any elevation close to that during my Andean journey so far.

The train stopped shortly after my railroad car passed the station. Since the sign rather dramatically illustrated the high elevation of the station, I wanted to take a picture of it. Knowing the dangers of altitude sickness, I was anxious about doing so and wondered whether it was wise to walk back through the train to a spot where I could photograph the sign without passing out. Living more than five months at over 11,000 feet above sea level gave me some confidence of my adjustment to high altitude, but I was also aware that walking at an elevation 4,000 feet above that would create a significant challenge to my body and my lungs. So, I gently got up from my seat and slowly walked back to the end of the car where I opened the top half of the door above the coach's exit stairs, and took a photograph of the sign (fig. 11.2). Returning to my seat, I moved slowly because even with deliberately restraining my movement, I was winded, and I realized that I was better off to stay seated.

Lurching forward, the train started moving again shortly thereafter and entered a tunnel under the peaks of the range. Emerging on the other side, it stopped again in a small railroad yard huddled against the steep slopes of the western face of a snow-covered mountain.

By passing through the tunnel, the train crossed the continental divide that separates the drainage of the rivers that flow into the Atlantic from those that flow into the Pacific. This western portal was near the top of the western slope, where the Rimac River begins and flows down onto the coast to Lima, my destination.

From this point to the end of my journey, the train would descend quickly into the dry desert of the Peruvian coast. In a mere seventy miles, it would drop more than 15,000 feet.

The slope was so steep that the rail line was made with "switchbacks." On roads and highways built on mountainous terrain, hairpin curves are often referred to as switchbacks, but true switchbacks exist only on a railway line. In a topography of steep slopes, hairpin curves cannot be constructed; building switchbacks creates a more compact railway. So, on such grades, the tracks zigzag back and forth down a slope with a spur at each end headed by a switch. The train goes down the slope and onto the spur, and then the brakeman switches the spur onto the descending line. The train continues down the slope with each switch being manually operated. Travel on such a rail line is extended because of the extra time required to operate the switch. The spur length also limits the length of the train that can be switched onto and from each spur.

Eventually, the switchbacks ended and the track descended into the broader valley of Rimac River. Finally, it broke out of the mountains into the foothills of the Andes. As the terrain leveled off on the flat, dry Peruvian coast, the appearance of continuous dense settlements signaled that we were approaching Lima.

After disembarking at the Lima station, I retired to a *pensión* (boardinghouse) in suburban Pueblo Libre, with its quaint colonial setting and garden. The respite there provided tranquility and relaxation from the excitement of the trip from Ayacucho and Huancayo.

And so, my journey ended. There was no greater teacher of Andean ecology than the experience of being there. I will never forget the azure skies and emerald-green fields that I could see from the balcony of my room after the end of the rainy season. Exhausting hikes in the high altitude (sometimes as high as 14,000 feet above sea level) and countless vistas of staggeringly beautiful Andean scenery remain a vivid memory. Visits to countless colorful Andean markets and rubbing my body down with DDT powder to keep off the fleas will be etched in my memory forever.

ANSWERING THE RESEARCH QUESTIONS

I traveled to Peru to discover whether the culture history of the Ayacucho Valley was reflected in its contemporary ethnic pottery. Early in my stay, I had abandoned that research question and a more evolved version of my research design emerged: comparing pottery and raw materials among different communities in the Ayacucho Valley. In retrospect, I would have encountered the same problem carrying out that project that I experienced in studying pottery making in Quinua. Potters did not ply their craft in the rainy season because the cold and rain delayed, if not inhibited, production. Further, many potters were also peasant farmers, and they had agricultural responsibilities during the rainy season. Even if they could make a few pots during such an inauspicious time, the space available in a household was insufficient to store and dry more than a few vessels for firing during favorable weather.

Nevertheless, I discovered that several other communities in the valley made pottery: Huayhuas near the town of Huanta; Ticllas on the other side of the valley; the barrio of Santa Ana in the city of Ayacucho; and Pampay, a hamlet near the town of Luricocha in the northern portion of the valley (see fig. 2.3).[1] The pottery of all of these communities either had no decoration (Ticllas, Santa Ana), simple plastic decoration (Pampay), or painted decoration that was less complex than Quinua (Huayhuas). Quinua potters, however, produced undecorated cooking and storage pottery, and decorated vessels in three distinct painted styles used for eating, drinking, storage, ritual, and carrying water. Quinua potters also made other objects such as churches, bulls, mythological creatures, and candelabras that locals placed on the roofs of their houses. Even with such a superficial comparison between the pottery-making communities in the valley, Quinua pottery was still the most complex, and much of it was deeply embedded in, and reflective of, local ritual.[2]

Did these styles originally come from the population that the ninth Inca Pachacuti resettled from Acos as I once had hypothesized? It is impossible to be certain, but my trip to Acos and my brief reconnaissance there indicated that the population of Acos probably was not the source of Quinua's pottery technology and its painted styles. No potters existed in modern Acos, and the pottery from the probable site of their battle defending themselves against Pachacuti showed no similarity to the pottery from Quinua.

In retrospect, the most convincing evidence that Quinua pottery did not originate from Acos was that no potters existed in any of the other portions of the Ayacucho Valley in which the Incas resettled exiles from Acos. None was made in the nearby community of Acos Vinchos or in the area around Acocro (or Acos Ocros) near the south end of the valley. Another community north of Ayacucho also had Acos as a part of its name (Acobamba), and it fit the location of the relocated Acos Indians described by sixteenth-century writer Cieza de Leon,[3] but it was unknown if pottery was made there.

Between the Wari collapse and the Inca conquest, the Chankas appeared to dominate the area. The Chankas were centered around Anda-huaylas to the south, and their territory included the area west of the Apu-rimac River, continuing west and north to Ayacucho Valley and including what is now the area around Abancay and Andahuaylas.[4] We had visited the mountaintop site of Quehuahuilca across from Wari and it fit the pattern of the location of sites of the Chanka period. Professor Zuidema thought that it might have been a Chanka site, and somehow related to the fall of Wari, but a mountaintop settlement pattern was common elsewhere in southern Peru during the period between Wari and the Inca conquest.

Could Chanka potters have influenced the pottery made in Quinua in 1967? During my visits to the Abancay market, I documented and pho-tographed the vessels there, and during my stop in Andahuaylas, I visited an exhibition of ethnic pottery from that area, and photographed those vessels.[5] Pottery from these areas might have been made by the descen-dants of Chanka potters. None of these vessels, however, were similar in any way to the shape and style of the Quinua pottery, or to Inca pottery.

What then, was the source of the complex pottery tradition in Quinua? Did it have a Spanish origin? Spanish potters used the potter's wheel and glazed their vessels, but Quinua potters did not use either of these techniques. Further, Pizzaro's original settlement in Quinua lasted slightly more than a year before it moved across the valley to a location that eventually became the city of Ayacucho. The only possible portion of Quinua ceramic technology that could have come from Spain was the updraft kiln that probably came from Andalusia, the origin of most of the Spanish immigrants to the New World. Otherwise, Quinua vessels and ceramic technology probably did not come from Hispanic roots.

If, in the unlikely event that potters were part of the Spanish immigra-tion into the valley during the Colonial period, it was more likely that they lived and worked in Ayacucho where the weather was warmer and drier, and would not have limited the frequency and intensity of the craft as it did in Quinua. Further, if Hispanic potters did immigrate to Ayacucho, then they would have had a market for their wares from the Spanish immigrants in the city. This demand probably did not exist in Quinua, and transportation of vessels to Ayacucho would be precarious and result in much breakage. Why not have Spanish potters make pottery close to the most obvious market for those vessels? Taking all of these factors into consideration, it is not likely that Quinua pottery had Spanish roots, although the potters there had adopted the Hispanic cylindrical updraft kiln for an unknown reason.

Could the origin of Quinua pottery come from the Inca conquest? The Incas had conquered the Ayacucho Valley in the early fifteenth century and replaced the population around Quinua with exiles from the village of Acos. Other populations of the Ayacucho Valley were also replaced, but other than this hypothetical source of potters, did Inca potters or Inca administrators influence the decoration of Quinua pottery? Specifically, could the Incas have supervised local potters by requiring them to produce Inca shapes and styles as tribute, or as symbols of the control of the Inca state?

One way I approached this question was to visit the local archaeological museum in Cusco and observe and record the shapes and designs of Inca pottery. In addition, I examined the archaeological reports at the time that described Inca pottery. Inca shapes were nothing like those made in Quinua, but there was some similarity in the design. The Inca fern design found on the sides of large storage jars (called *aryballos*) was used in an abbreviated form in some of the styles of pottery in Quinua, and potters said that this simple design was maize.

Using the symbol of maize on both Quinua and Inca pottery is not surprising. Maize is the most valued crop in the Andes; it can be stored easily, has a wide variety of uses, and was required by the Incas as tribute. But, linking a motif from the present to the past is mitigated by the overwhelming importance of maize in Andean culture, not necessarily because Inca designs influenced the designs on modern Quinua pottery.

A second similarity of Inca and Quinua pottery was even more ephemeral and appeared to consist of one single portion of the fern design. The Inca fern design used multiple lines as a horizontal (or near-horizontal) branch on the stem that ended with a large black dot. On Quinua pottery, what appeared to be a branch of the fern (perhaps a representation of the maize design) was turned ninety degrees as a vertical line with a dot at the end, and then repeated along a horizontal axis around the principal decorative band on water-carrying vessels of one style.

Even knowing that Inca administrators required local potters to produce Inca shapes and designs (sometimes called "colonial Inca" pottery),
these vague and general similarities of the designs on Inca pottery and
those of Quinua pottery were very speculative at best. Further, such similarities were restricted to only one style in Quinua, the white-on-red style.[6]

From where, then, did pottery production in Quinua originate? It is
most likely that Quinua potters descended from those potters that made
vessels for the city of Wari and its empire. My investigation in Quinua
revealed an abundance of clay and temper sources. Extensive clay beds
are interlayered with thick deposits of volcanic ash that were used for
pottery temper. These beds stretch horizontally across the lower slope of
the community.

One thick layer of bed of clay extends horizontally across the landscape below the village and some clay for making pottery is extracted from
this layer. Below that lies a layer of hard, consolidated volcanic ash that
was used to make the supports upon which to form pottery. Underneath
that is another thick layer of clay from which still other potters extracted
their clay. That layer caps another thick bed of volcanic ash that is less
consolidated than the ash layer above, and can be accessed only at the
bottom of the deepest ravines. Potters mined this deposit resulting in a
large, cave-like opening in one of its vertical exposures.

Further, sources of white, red, tan, and black paint around Quinua
were used as raw materials for the execution of the three painted pottery styles in the community. The resources for these paints were likely
those used for many of the Wari and pre-Wari painted styles because most
occurred within the same distance from Wari as they did from many of the
modern potters. Further, the quick-burning brush called *chamizo* is abundant above the village and would have created a hot flame for producing
the highly fired Wari wares. Finally, general features of the painted styles of
Quinua (the Red-and-Black-on-Zoned-White Style, the White-on-Red
Style, and Black-and-White-on-Tan Style) bore superficial resemblances
to at least some of the pre-Wari and Wari styles (Huarpa, the Chakipampa
styles, and perhaps Viñaque).[7]

Are such ancient roots for the raw materials and technology of a contemporary pottery-making community possible? During my more than
four decades of studying pottery making in Ticul, Yucatán, Mexico, I discovered that each of the main sources of raw materials was unique miner-
alogically, and was associated with archaeological evidence from a thousand years previously (the Terminal Classic Period, AD 800–1100).[8] Three

of these raw materials were mined in these ancient sources up until the last decade of the twentieth century. Furthermore, transmission of the craft followed a very conservative kin-based model of house lot inheritance and postnuptial marital residence that provided a pool of potential learners out of which only a few became potters. Shapes and painted styles have changed greatly over the more than four decades that I studied the community, but the technology, raw materials, and social transmission of the craft changed little until the last decade of the twentieth century. Aspects of a pottery-making tradition can persist for many centuries even though the pottery itself might be very different from that of the ancient past.[9]

In spite of all my attempts at comparing Quinua pottery with likely historic and prehistoric antecedents, the comparisons were still indirect, circumstantial, and superficial. Further, at the end of my fieldwork, I was disappointed that the weather had prevented me from collecting sufficient data about the craft in Quinua because so little pottery was made there during the rainy season. As a consequence, I still considered my study of pottery making in Quinua a failure.

In spite of that perception, however, I managed to write a PhD dissertation about potters' design choices based upon an analysis of the most abundant painted vessels from Quinua that I had observed among the potters I had visited, and those that I saw in the markets of Quinua, Huamanguilla, and Ayacucho.[10] I later distilled the dissertation into a published article arguing that the Quinua potters' choices represented those of what is now called a "community of practice" because of internal social interaction in Quinua and differences from another painted White-on-Red style in the valley made in Huayhuas.[11] Surprisingly, that research anticipated and foreshadowed the theoretical trend of technological choice and *châin operatoíre* of design decisions more than twenty years later, although my publication had no influence on the development of that trend.

After years of reflection, I realized my seeming failure to observe sustained pottery production during the rainy season was, in itself, a significant piece of information. Rainy weather significantly affected the intensity and frequency of pottery production depending on the number of days with cloudiness, rain, fog, and high humidity because moisture delayed drying, destroyed drying pots, and inhibited firing. The climate during this time was also too cold to make pottery. Further, many potters were peasant farmers and had agricultural responsibilities during the rainy season. So, making pottery in Quinua was seasonal.

I thus realized that weather and climate could constrain the development of full-time ceramic specialization in Quinua and were probably
important variables in limiting production in areas with a heavy rainy
season elsewhere in the Andes as well. These insights changed my view
of ceramic production as I discovered that what was important was not
just production itself, but rather how it was tied to the environment and
subsistence. These reflections and the events that stimulated them were
pivotal in my thinking at the time and were significant factors that led to
the publication of an article in the international journal *Current Anthropology*.[12] Unfortunately, some commentators knew little about making
pottery and were unfamiliar with the molecular structure of clay minerals
that requires drying before firing in order to maintain the integrity of the
vessel form, and to avoid breakage during firing because of the formation
of steam within the vessel walls. I wrote a summary response to my critics
in a subsequent issue of the journal,[13] and that essay became the basis for
the development of my widely cited book *Ceramic Theory and Cultural
Process* dealing with the relationship of ceramics to the environment and
the rest of culture based upon my research in Quinua, Yucatán, and Guatemala, and cross-cultural comparisons between them and other communities of potters ("communities of practice") in the literature.[14] Moreover,
a survey of the ethnographic literature of pottery making in the Andes
revealed that production also ceased during the rainy season.[15]

Archaeologists have tended to believe that full-time craft specialization in general, and that of full-time pottery production in particular,
were a consequence of the development of state-level society. My work in
Quinua, however, indicated that full-time pottery production probably
did not occur in the Andes during the Wari and Inca civilizations because
the annual rainy season and lack of indoor space for protecting drying
vessels from damage prevented the development of full-time household
production. Even the making of roof tiles and fired bricks on a massive clay
deposit below the archaeological site of Cata-casa-llaqta on the southern
edge of the city of Cusco ceased production during the rainy season in
1972–1973. Andean households probably could not provide the amount
of drying space to accommodate pottery made throughout the rainy season. Furthermore, storing drying pots indoors in households creates risks
of breakage from children, animals, and clumsy adults, to say nothing of
the general spatial pressures of living.

One of the reasons that archaeologists believe pottery production in
the Andes was full-time resulted from what could best be described as

sampling bias. Studies of pottery making in the Andes (and elsewhere) were done in the dry season when Andean peasants were making pots. If the craft were studied in the rainy season, as I did, there would be little or nothing to report. Consequently, in climates with a substantial rainy season, it is very difficult, if not impossible, to practice the craft year around, and produce masses of pottery without large, covered indoor spaces to dry and fire it.[16] Otherwise, pottery production is seasonal and intermittent. The discovery of this pattern was seminal to my own research and career. As I researched the literature for my book *Ceramic Theory and Cultural Process*, I discovered that many social and cultural anthropologists had noted and/or described the seasonality of pottery making in climates throughout the world, but few, if any, archaeologists have taken these data into account in their theories of craft production and specialization in complex societies, and even after years of the publication of the book, they still don't.

When I studied pottery making in the Valley of Guatemala in 1970, I discovered that pottery making was concentrated in areas of poor agricultural land. There were three linguistic islands of speakers of a Maya language called Central Pokomam. For those who lived on the poorest agricultural land, the women made pottery, whereas those communities living on excellent agricultural land did not make any pottery at all. It was clear from this comparison that pottery was not an indicator of culture history, but the result of many interacting factors, not the least of which was the quality of the agricultural land around the community.[17]

Reflecting on my Quinua data after that Guatemala experience, I discovered through maps, aerial photographs, and the images that I took in Quinua, that potters also lived on poor agricultural land, or were landless. Later, Bill Mitchell wrote that those living on poor agricultural land also practiced other crafts besides making pottery.[18] The source of this marginality was complex, involving erosion and lack of access to irrigation, but the erosion did expose a number of raw materials that potters could use to make pottery. This observation became critical in writing my article in *Current Anthropology*, and raised the question of how ecological relationships affected the production and distribution of pottery.

I was also able to publish several other articles from my experience in Quinua. I published one of the first (if not *the* first) mineralogical analyses of contemporary pottery materials in the Andes, as well as a description of pottery production in Quinua.[19] Later, I analyzed the design fields and symmetry patterns of designs on water-carrying vessels that I had observed. I found that those patterns reflected the structure in the community such as the vertical zonation of the ecological zones in the valley, and the bilateral political structure of the community based upon the two irrigation systems. The bilateral symmetry of the design motifs also reflected the Andean pattern of the dual inheritance of each individual.[20]

The deathblow to my belief that my Quinua research was a failure came from the publication of my book by Cambridge University Press. That work summarized my data on Quinua pottery production within the context of the local environment, and the history and prehistory of the area.[21] So, in spite of my initial and naive sense of failure, my research was successful—if measured by the publications from it and the insights that unpredictably contributed to understanding of the past. With the creativity stimulated by my self-perceived failure, I discovered important data and insights about the interrelationships of pottery production with culture, subsistence scheduling, and the environment, and their role in interpreting ceramic production in the past. Pottery is not simply the product of culture because of the plasticity of the medium. Rather, it is also the result of the interaction of the potters' culture with the raw materials and the environment including weather and climate.

REFLECTIONS ON A JOURNEY

My journey across the Andes was not just a unique adventure, and a trip to do my dissertation research, but it was a great learning experience and pilgrimage into my inner cultural self that challenged me intellectually, culturally, and emotionally—a journey that taught me about myself, my culture, and my own worldview, and challenged my comfortable middle-class values by confronting my ethnocentrism. I learned the importance of seeing culture and society in its geographical, historical, and prehistorical context and that such holism could only be accomplished by firsthand experience—as anthropologists put it, by participant-observation.

Such a methodology is full of challenges, and anthropologists engage the subject of their study 24/7. Although this engagement itself can be challenging, few experiences create more discomfort in another culture as different foods and debilitating illness. Challenges to one's palette often bring the pain of embracing the "other" too closely. Whereas seeing one's faculties diminished certainly is disheartening because of the Andean drinking ritual, when one's health seems threatened, the experience of another culture raises even more questions and doubts about the wisdom of immersing oneself in the culture and participating in its practices.

As a consequence, I realized that the emotional and physical risks of travel and research in Peru led to a transformed mind and spirit, as Casagrande said. Even though my journey ended, what I learned has stayed with me throughout my career and made a unique contribution to the field.

Did my experience in Peru fulfill the purposes of my National Defense Foreign Language Fellowship? It did indeed! I learned much more Spanish than I had known previously, and learned it in its cultural context. I learned much about the culture, history, geography, and environment of Peru and how that context contributes to understanding the prehistoric past. In retrospect, I also gained much experiential knowledge about why the Shining Path guerrilla movement was so appealing to some Peruvians some twenty years later, and understood the hopelessness of those who believed that revolutionary change was the only way for social and political change.

Probably most important, my experience in Peru provided stories, insight, and practical experiences that informed my teaching and helped students successfully engage foreign cultures. Indeed, my courses contributed a bit to hundreds of students who became more culturally informed teachers, development workers, AIDS workers, attorneys, military officers, physicians, nurses, pastors, missionaries, social workers, government and public health officials, college and university professors, and even one opera singer.

EPILOGUE

The places described in this book have changed greatly since 1967. In verifying locations, distances, and elevations, I used "Google Earth," and in the process, I was surprised to see the great changes in many of the locations described here during the subsequent fifty years. Quinua and the Ayacucho area have grown dramatically and are almost unrecognizable with urban sprawl and many paved roads. Urban growth around the city of Ayacucho has swallowed up the important archaeological sites of Conchopata (under the airport and its environs) and Acuchimay (above the city to the south), and is very close to overrunning Ñawim Pukio (located east of the city). Such sprawl is also creeping toward the location of the sixteenth-century Battle of Chupas which challenged the Spanish control of their colonial settlements in Peru, but whose victory placed those settlements securely under the Spanish crown.

Quinua also has changed immensely, and these changes have been documented by William P. Mitchell who has done research in the community for more than forty years.[22]

Roads now go into formerly remote areas where none existed in 1967. Although the road to Acos no longer ends at Pillpinto on the Apurimac River, the town itself seems to have changed little. Sangarará has increased in size, and I no longer recognize the village from its aerial view. A station platform now appears on the Cusco-Puno rail line where it crosses the road to Acos where I wondered if I would have to spend the night alone beside the railroad tracks (see fig. 7.5).

The scholarly research on the prehistory and ethnohistory of the areas covered by this work has expanded greatly with a large number of books and articles about Wari, the Chankas, and the Incas. Wherever possible, I have tried to update my references of this research in the annotations to provide sources for the interested reader.

Finally, the changes in Peru have paralleled the changes in me as a result of my initial journey to Peru retracing Inca steps. As novelist John Steinbeck said in *Travels with Charley*: "We do not take a trip; a trip takes us."[23]

Notes

CHAPTER 1

1. Joseph B. Casagrande, *In the Company of Man* (New York: Harper and Brothers, 1960), xii.

2. Casagrande, *In the Company of Man*, xii. In the original, the bracketed sentence appears after the remainder of the quote but without the brackets.

3. Dean E. Arnold, *Sak lu'um in Maya Culture and Its Possible Relationship to Maya Blue*, Research Report No. 2 (Urbana: University of Illinois, Department of Anthropology, 1967).

4. Maya potters' indigenous knowledge *seemed* almost unfathomable at the time, and I collected vast amounts of data that I put together into a book more than fifty years later entitled *Maya Potters' Indigenous Knowledge: Cognition, Engagement and Practice* (Boulder: University Press of Colorado, 2018). These data could have easily been my PhD dissertation, but I discovered later that after forty-three years of research among the potters in Ticul, I learned much more about potters' indigenous knowledge since 1965.

5. Some scholars write *Incas* as *Inkas* so as not to use the Spanish orthography of colonialism, and to conform to a more phonetic orthography consistent with the integrity of the Quechua language that the Incas spread throughout much of the Andes. I have retained the traditional form here because it is more familiar to readers.

6. The word *campesinos* is translated as "peasants." Although a disparaging word for some, the term "peasant" is actually an anthropological term that refers to people who use traditional agriculture for subsistence and/or are craftspersons and participate in the larger economy of the nation.

7. Paul Tournier, *The Adventure of Living* (New York: Harper and Brothers, 1965).

CHAPTER 2

1. Presently, the earliest evidence for human occupation in the Americas that is widely accepted by archaeologists is found at several sites in South America, but only one of them, Huaca Prieta, is located in Peru. Gustavo G. Politis and Luciano Prates, "The Pre-Clovis Peopling of South America," *SAA Archaeological Record* 19 (2019): 40–44.

2. R. T. Zuidema, "Algunas Problemas Etnohistoricos del Departamento de Ayacucho," *Wamani: Órgano de la Asociación Peruana de Antropólogos, Filial-Ayacucho* 1 (1966): 68–75; Steve J. Stern, *Peru's Indian Peoples and the Challenge of Spanish Conquest: Huamanga to 1640* (Madison: University of Wisconsin Press, 1993), 20.

3. "Oceans & Law of the Sea," Division for Ocean Affairs and Law of the Sea, United Nations, last modified February 2, 2020. https://www.un.org/Depts/los/convention_agreements/convention_overview_convention.htm.

4. Pedro Cieza de Leon, *The Incas of Cieza de Leon* [*Crónica del Perú*, 1553], trans. Harriet de Onis, ed. Victor Wolfgang von Hagen (Norman: University of Oklahoma Press, 1959), 121–22; Stern, *Peru's Indian Peoples*, 28.

5. Stern, *Peru's Indian Peoples*, 28.

6. *Libro de Cabildo de la Ciudad San Juan de la Frontera de Huamanga 1539–1547*, *Documentos Regionales de la Etnología y Etnohistoria Andinas*, no. 3 (Lima: Ediciones de la Casa de la Cultura del Peru, 1966), 7, 8, 33. Cieza de Leon, writing in 1553, says that San Juan de la Frontera originally was founded as early as the ninth of January (Cieza de Leon, *The Incas*, 124), whereas others say that it was founded as late as the seventh of March (Pedro de Rivera and Antonio de Chaves y de Guevara, "Relación de la Ciudad de Guamanga y sus Términos: Año de 1586," in *Relaciónes Geográficas de Indias* , [Madrid: Ministerio de Fomento, 1881], 1:106).

7. Stern, *Peru's Indian Peoples*, 28.

8. *Libro de Cabildo*, 9, 29–31.

9. Rivera and Chavez y de Guevara, "Relación de la Ciudad de Guamanga," 106; *Libro de Cabildo*, 9, 29–31.

10. *Libro de Cabildo*, 33; Rivera and Chavez y de Guevara, "Relación de la Ciudad de Guamanga," 106.

11. *Libro de Cabildo*, 12, 28–33, 140; Stern, *Peru's Indian Peoples*, 28.

12. Cieza de Leon, *The Incas*, 123; Stern, *Peru's Indian Peoples*, 28; *Libro de Cabildo*, 31.

13. *Libro de Cabildo*, 10; Rivera and Chavez y de Guevara, "Relación de la Ciudad de Guamanga," 107.

14. Stern, *Peru's Indian Peoples*, 28.

15. William H. Isbell, "Wari and Tiwanaku: International Identities in the Central Andean Middle Horizon," in *Handbook of South American Archaeology*, ed. Helaine Silverman and William Harris Isbell (New York: Springer, 2008), 731–59.

16. I was attacked and bit by a dog in Cusco in 1972, but was not given additional vaccinations at that time. In preparation for another trip to a Third World country about two decades later, however, my blood was tested for the rabies antibodies. Much to my surprise, I learned that some of the antibodies acquired as a result of the vaccine given to me in 1967 still remained, but I still needed a booster.

17. Clement R. Markham, *Markham in Peru: The Travels of Clement R. Markham, 1852–1853*, ed. Peter Blanchard (Austin: University of Texas Press, 1991), 71.

18. For a review of the use and medicinal value of coca in the Andes, see Amy Sue Biondich and Jeremy D. Joslin, "Coca: High Altitude Remedy of the Ancient Incas," *Wilderness & Environmental Medicine* 26 (2015): 567–71.

19. Tom Blickman, "Coca Leaf: Myths and Reality," Transnational Institute, August 5, 2014, https://www.tni.org/en/primer/coca-leaf-myths-and -reality.

20. Rachel Carson, *The Silent Spring* (New York: Houghton Mifflin Company, 1962).

21. DDT use was banned via a treaty known as the Stockholm Convention on "Persistent Organic Polutants" (POPs), except in those locations where it was necessary to control malaria-infected mosquitoes. "DDT—A Brief History and Status," United States Environmental Protection Agency, accessed April 19, 2020, https://www.epa.gov/ingredients -used-pesticide-products/ddt-brief-history-and-status.

22. William. H. Isbell and K. J. Schreiber, "Was Huari a State?," *American Antiquity* 43 (1978): 372–89; Isbell, "Wari and Tiwanaku," 752.

23. Dorothy Menzel, "Style and Time in the Middle Horizon," *Ñawpa Pacha* 2 (1964): 1–105.

24. Isbell, "Wari and Tiwanaku," 153; Gordon F. McEwan, ed., *Pikillacta: The Wari Empire in Cuzco* (Iowa City: University of Iowa Press, 2005), 741–42; William H. Isbell, "Huari Administration and the Orthogonal Cellular Architecture Horizon" in *Huari Administrative Structure: Prehistoric Monumental Architecture and State Government*, ed. William H. Isbell and Gordon F. McEwan (Washington, DC: Dumbarton Oaks Research Library and Collection, 1991), 310; Isbell and Schreiber, "Was Huari a State?"; Katharina J. Schreiber, "From State to Empire: The Expansion of Wari Outside the Ayacucho Basin," in *The Origins and Development of the Andean State*, ed. Jonathan Haas, Sheila Pozorski, and Thomas Pozorski (Cambridge: Cambridge University Press, 1987), 91–96; Schreiber, "Jincamocco: A Huari Administrative Center in the South Central Highlands of Peru," in Isbell and McEwan, *Huari Administrative Structure*, 199–213.

25. Ice cores from the Quelccaya Ice Cap, on a mountain east-southeast of Cusco, reveal that southern Peru experienced at least two major droughts between approximately AD 1000–1050. L. G. Thompson et al.,

"A 1500-Year Record of Tropical Precipitation in Ice Cores from the Quelccaya Ice Cap, Peru," *Science* 229 (1985): 973.
26. Menzel, "Style and Time," 8–21, 40–46.

CHAPTER 3

1. Isbell and Schreiber, "Was Huari a State?," 372–89; Enrique Bragayrac and
Enrique Gonzalez Carre, "Investigaciones en Wari," *Gaceta Arqueológica
Andina: Informativo Bimenstral Instituto Andino de Estudios Arqueológicos*
1, 4–5 (1982): 8; William H. Isbell, C. Brewster-Wray, and Lynda Spickard,
"Architecture and Spatial Organization at Huari," in Isbell and McEwan,
Huari Administrative Structure, 24, 51; Isbell, "Wari and Tiwanaku," 731,
750.
2. McEwan, *Pikillacta*; Isbell, "Huari Administration and the Orthogonal
Cellular Architecture Horizon," in Isbell and McEwan, *Huari Administrative Structure,*" 310; Schreiber, "From State to Empire"; Schreiber, "Jincamocco"; Isbell, "Wari and Tiwanaku," 741–43.
3. Isbell, Brewster-Wray, and Spickard, "Architecture and Spatial Organization at Huari," 51.
4. Isbell, "Wari and Tiwanaku," 750–51.
5. Menzel, "Style and Time," 69; Martha B. Anders, "Wamanga Pottery:
Symbolic Resistance and Subversion in Middle Horizon Epoch 2 Ceramics
from the Planned Wari Site of Azángaro (Ayacucho, Peru)," in *Cultures in
Conflict: Current Archaeological Perspectives,* ed. Diana Claire Tkaczuk and
Brian C. Vivian (Calgary, Alberta: University of Calgary, Department of
Archaeology, 1989), 7–18; Martha B. Anders, "Structure and Function at
the Planned Site of Azángaro: Cautionary Notes for the Model of Huari as
a Centralized Secular State," in Isbell and McEwan, *Huari Administrative
Structure,* 165–97.
6. Menzel, "Style and Time," 70.
7. Ibid.
8. Jaime Rivera, *Geografía General de Ayacucho (*Ayacucho, Perú: Universidad
Nacional de San Cristóbal de Huamanga, Dirección Universitaria de Investigación, 1971), 41, 43; Dean E. Arnold, *Ecology of Ceramic Production in
an Andean Community* (Cambridge: Cambridge University Press, 2003),
16–19.

CHAPTER 4

1. William P. Mitchell, "Irrigation and Community in the Central Peru-
vian Highlands," *American Anthropologist* 78 (1976): 25–44; Mitchell,
"Dam the Water: The Ecology and Political Economy of Irrigation in the
Ayacucho Valley, Peru," in *Irrigation at High Altitudes: The Social Orga-
nization of Water Control Systems in the Andes,* ed. David Guillet and
William P. Mitchell, Publication Series of the Society for Latin American

Anthropology (Washington, DC: *American Anthropological Association*, 1994), 275–302.
2. William P. Mitchell, "The Hydraulic Hypothesis: A Reappraisal," *Current Anthropology* 14, no. 5 (1973): 532–34.
3. This discussion and the paragraphs that follow summarize Mitchell, "Irrigation and Community," 25–44, and Mitchell, "Dam the Water."
4. Mitchell, "Irrigation and Community," 31.
5. Ibid.
6. Ibid.
7. Ibid.
8. Ibid.
9. Dean E. Arnold, "Native Pottery Making in Quinua, Peru," *Anthropos* 67 (1972): 861–62; Arnold, "Ceramic Ecology in the Ayacucho Basin, Peru: Implications for Prehistory," *Current Anthropology* 16 (1975): 185–203.
10. Mitchell, "Dam the Water," 285–87.
11. Ibid.

CHAPTER 5

1. R. T. Zuidema, *The Ceque System of Cuzco: The Social Organization of the Capital of the Inca* (Leiden: E. J. Brill, 1964).
2. Brian S. Bauer, Lucas C. Kellett, and Miriam Aráoz Silva with contributions by Sabine Hyland and Carlo Socualaya Dávila, *The Chanka: Archaeological Research in Andahuaylas (Aprurimac), Peru*, Monograph 68 (Los Angeles: Cotsen Institute of Archaeology Press, 2010); Brian S. Bauer and Lucas C. Kellett, "Cultural Transformations of the Chanka Homeland (Andahuaylas, Peru) during the Late Intermediate Period (AD 1000–1400)," *Latin American Antiquity* 21, no. 1 (2010): 87–111.
3. Bauer, Kellett, and Aráoz Silva, *The Chanka*; Bauer and Kellett, "Cultural Transformations," 87–111.
4. Ice cores from the Quelccaya Ice Cap, on a mountain east-southeast of Cusco, reveal that southern Peru experienced at least two major droughts between approximately AD 1000 and 1050 (Thompson et al., "A 1500-Year Record of Tropical Precipitation," 973).

CHAPTER 6

1. Sarmiento de Gamboa, *The History of the Incas* [1572], trans. and ed. Brian S. Bauer and Vania Smith (Austin: University of Texas Press, 2007), 135–38.
2. Zuidema, "Algunas Problemas Etnohistoricos," 71.
3. Ibid.; Cieza de Leon, *The Incas*, 119.
4. Noble David Cook y los Estudios de Alejandro Malaga Medina y Therese Bouysse Cassagne, *Tasa de la Visita General de Francisco de Toledo* (Lima, Peru: Universidad Nacional Mayor de San Marcos, Dirección Universitaria de Biblioteca y Publicaciones, 1975), 275.

5. Titulos de Propiedad, Legajo No. 13, Cuaderno No. 354, 1632, Archivo Nacional del Peru, Lima; Derecho Indígena y Encomiendas, Legajo No. 8, Cuaderno No. 186, 1702, Archivo Nacional del Peru, Lima.

6. For a brief description of other communities that make pottery in the valley, see Arnold, *Ecology and Ceramic Production*, 177–87.

7. Sir Clement Markham's historical travelogue provides an account of the battle (Markham, *Markham in Peru*, 74–76).

8. Dean E. Arnold, "Mold-made Potters' Marks from Andahuaylas, Department of Apurimac, Peru," *Ethnos* 37, nos. 1–4 (1972): 81–87.

9. Bauer, Kellett, and Aráoz Silva (*The Chanka*, 3–6) have written a summary of the Chanka War acknowledging the variations in Inca mythology about it that were derived from the various ethnohistorical sources. The relationship of the Chanka War and Inca state development varies according to one's view of the Spanish chronicles (Brian S. Bauer, *The Development of the Inca State* [Austin: University of Texas Press, 1992], 109).

10. Bauer, Kellett, and Aráoz Silva, *The Chanka*, 3–6; Juan de Betanzos, *Narrative of the Incas* [1557], trans. and ed. Roland Hamilton and Dana Buchanan (Austin: University of Texas Press, 1996), chapters 7–8, pp. 21–30; Bauer, *Development of the Inca State*, 5.

11. Sarmiento, *The History of the Incas*, chapter 35, p. 127.

12. Zuidema, "Algunas Problemas Etnohistoricos," 20; Felipe Guaman Poma de Ayala, *The First New Chronicle and Good Government: On the History of the World and the Incas up to 1615*, trans. and ed. Roland Hamilton (Austin: University of Texas Press, 2009), 284.

13. E. G. Squier, *Incidents of Travel and Exploration in the Land of the Incas* (New York: Harper and Brothers, 1877), 548, https://archive.org/details/peruincidentsoft00squi/page/n9. The Inca bridge probably did not cross the Apurimac River at the same location as the present bridge. By comparing Squier's description of the places approaching the bridge with locations on Google Earth, the Inca bridge probably was positioned further down stream from the modern one.

14. Ibid., 547.

15. Ibid., 545–46.

16. Thornton Wilder, *The Bridge of San Luis Rey* (New York: HarperCollins, 1927).

17. Markham, *Markham in Peru*, 83–84.

CHAPTER 7

1. Bauer, Kellett, and Aráoz Silva, *The Chanka*, 4; Betanzos, *Narrative of the Incas*, 21–30.

2. Archaeological research and syntheses of the Spanish chronicles about Cusco have been brought together in a highly illustrated synthetic work of ancient Cusco by Brian Bauer, *Ancient Cuzco: Heartland of the Inca*

(Austin: University of Texas Press, 2004). For the section on Sacsayhuamán, see pp. 98–106.

3. El Inca Garcilaso de la Vega, *Royal Commentaries of the Incas and General
   History of Peru* [1609], trans. Harold V. Livermore (Austin: University
   of Texas Press, 1966 [1609]).

4. Bauer, *Ancient Cuzco*, 128–34, esp. photo on page 130.

5. Ibid., 139–57.

6. Ibid.

7. Ibid.

8. Ibid., 152. The structures of the Coricancha revealed after the 1650 earthquake, and before the 1950 earthquake, can be seen in John H. Rowe's,
   *An Introduction to the Archaeology of Cuzco, Papers of the Peabody Museum
   of American Archaeology and Ethnology*, Harvard University, vol. 27, no. 2
   (1944), plates III and IV.

9. Bauer, *Ancient Cuzco*, 148.

10. Ibid., 143–46.

11. Ibid., 145.

12. Ibid., 145–46.

13. Zuidema, *Ceque System of Cuzco*; Brian S. Bauer, *The Sacred Landscape of
    the Inca: The Cusco Ceque System* (Austin: University of Texas Press, 1998).

CHAPTER 8

1. About twenty years later, Bill Sillar, now of the Institute of Archeology of
   the University of London, studied pottery making in these communities
   for his PhD research (Bill Sillar, *Shaping Culture: Making Pots and Constructing Households: An Ethnoarchaeological Study of Pottery Production,
   Trade and Use in the Andes*, BAR International Series 883 [Oxford: British
   Archaeological Reports, 2000]).

2. Sarmiento, *History of the Incas*, chapter 35.

3. To see a detailed description of the site with images, see Dean E. Arnold,
   "Early Inca Expansion and the Incorporation of Local Ethnic Groups:
   Ethnohistory and Archeological Reconnaissance in the Region of Acos,
   Department of Cuzco, Peru," *Andean Past* 7 (2005): 219–49.

4. Sarmiento, *History of the Incas*, chapter 35.

5. For detailed illustrations of the pottery from this site, see Arnold, "Early
   Inca Expansion," 229, 241–46. Compare these illustrations with those
   of Brian S. Bauer, *The Early Ceramics of the Inca Heartland, Fieldiana
   Anthropology*, New Series 31, Field Museum of Natural History Publication
   1501 (Chicago: Field Museum of Natural History, 1999), 13–60.

6. An image from Google Earth dated August 8, 2017, showed extensive terracing on the west side of the mountain north of Acos.

7. Guaman Poma de Ayala stated that the Acos Indians were "Incas by Privi-
   lege" and that the maintenance of the bridges of the empire was under the

administration of Acos Inca. He illustrated this point with a drawing show-ing *AcosInga* (Acos Inca) in front of the bridge at Guambo (*Guambochaca*). Translated, the inscription on the drawing reads "Governor of the bridges of this kingdom" in Spanish and "General administrator of bridges, Acos Inca" in Quechua (Guaman Poma, *The First New Chronicle and Good Government*, 284).

8. The pottery was a largely undecorated brown ware similar to that found at a site above Cusco called Chanapata that dated to the first millennium BC (see Rowe, "Introduction to the Archaeology of Cuzco," 15–17).

9. For a more detailed description of other archaeological sites around Acos, see Arnold, "Early Inca Expansion," 219–49.

10. *Chiaraje* is still performed, and entering "Chiaraje" into a search engine brings up many websites with the battles from previous years. Several are videos (such as https://www.youtube.com/watch?v'3YtnfXeSn6Q, accessed April 18, 2020) and seem to take place in the same general area as the battle described here. The difference between the battle described here and the web video is that the web video reported that as many as four thousand participated in the battle and that it occurred on January 20, and shows the presence of microwave towers and different ethnic clothing than that worn in 1973.

CHAPTER 9

1. The Alliance for Progress was another U.S. program besides the National Defense Education Act that sought to mitigate the conditions that would lead to communist revolution in Latin America. Steven J. Rabe, "Alliance for Progress," *Oxford Research Encyclopedia of Latin American History*, March 2016, DOI: 10.1093/acrefore/9780199366439.013.95.

CHAPTER 10

1. Zuidema, "Algunas Problemas Etnohistoricos," 71.

2. Daniel W. Gade and Mario Escobar, "Village Settlement and the Colonial Legacy in Southern Peru," *Geographical Review* 72 (1982): 430–49.

CHAPTER 11

1. Pottery was also reportedly made in several hamlets around Luricocha, but production in these hamlets was not verified. See Arnold, *Ceramic Production in an Andean Community*, 179.

2. See Arnold, "Native Pottery Making in Quinua"; Arnold, *Ceramic Production in an Andean Community*.

3. Cieza de Leon, *The Incas*, 119; "Descripción de la Provincia de los Anga-raes," 203.

4. Bauer and Kellett, *Cultural Transformations of the Chanka*; Bauer, Kellett, and Aráoz Silva, *The Chanka*.

5. A photograph of each of the vessels from Abancay, Cusco, Andahuay-las, and the Ayacucho market have been pasted on a 3 × 5 card, grouped by location and placed in two 3 × 5 card files. These and their negatives have been deposited in Wheaton College Archives.

6. For a repertoire of Quinua designs, see Arnold, *Ceramic Production in an Andean Community*, 160–63.

7. Menzel, "Style and Time," 9, 11–13.

8. One of these was the source of the potters' clay (Dean E. Arnold and Bruce F. Bohor, "The Ancient Clay Mine at Yo' K'at, Yucatán," *American Antiquity* 42 [1977]: 575–82), and the other was the source of pottery temper in Ticul (Arnold, "Maya Blue and Palygorskite: A Second Possible Pre-Columbian Source," *Ancient Mesoamerica* 16 [2005]: 51–62).

9. Dean E. Arnold, *Social Change and the Evolution of Ceramic Production and Distribution in a Maya Community* (Boulder: University Press of Colorado, 2008).

10. Dean E. Arnold, "The Emics of Pottery Design from Quinua, Peru" (PhD diss., University of Illinois, Urbana, 1970).

11. Dean E. Arnold, "Social Interaction and Ceramic Design: Community-wide Correlates in Quinua, Peru," in *Pots and Potters: Current Approaches in Ceramic Archaeology*, ed. Prudence M. Rice, Monograph 24 (Los Angeles: Institute of Archaeology University of California, Los Angeles, 1984), 133–61.

12. Arnold, "Ceramic Ecology in the Ayacucho Basin," 185–203.

13. Dean E. Arnold, "Discussion and Criticism: Reply to Haaland and Browman," *Current Anthropology* 16, no. 4 (1975): 637–40.

14. Dean E. Arnold, *Ceramic Theory and Cultural Process* (Cambridge: Cambridge University Press, 1985).

15. Arnold, *Ceramic Production in an Andean Community*, 220–21.

16. In Ticul, Yucatán, it is now possible to make and fire pottery during the rainy season because potters constructed workshops with cement blocks, cement roofs, or roofs of fiber glass or sheet metal that were supported by metal and wooden trusses to create a protected environment for making, drying, and firing pottery (see Dean E. Arnold, *The Evolution of Ceramic Production Organization in a Maya Community* [Boulder: University Press of Colorado, 2015], 243–76).

17. Dean E. Arnold, "Ceramic Variability, Environment and Culture History among the Pokom in the Valley of Guatemala," in *Spatial Organization of Culture*, ed. Ian Hodder (London: Gerald Duckworth, 1978), 39–59.

18. William P. Mitchell, *Peasants on the Edge: Crop, Cult and Crisis in the Andes* (Austin: University of Texas Press, 1991).

19. Dean E. Arnold, "Mineralogical Analyses of Ceramic Materials from Quinua, Department of Ayacucho, Peru," *Archaeometry* 14 (1972): 93–101; Arnold "Native Pottery Making."

20. Dean E. Arnold, "Design Structure and Community Organization in Quinua, Peru," in *Structure and Cognition in Art*, ed. Dorothy Washburn (Cambridge: Cambridge University Press, 1983), 56–73.

21. Arnold, *Ceramic Production in an Andean Community*. This work also showed the patterns of design fields and those of band-and-motif symmetry on Quinua pottery. As a unique community of practice, it also briefly surveyed the differences between Quinua pottery and that from other communities in the valley. I called these different "communities of potters" in my book, but they are best described as different "communities of practice."

22. Among others: Mitchell, *Peasants on the Edge*; Mitchell, "Dam the Water"; William P. Mitchell, "Pressure on Peasant Production and the Transformation of Regional and National Identities," in *Migrants, Regional Identities and Latin American Cities*, ed. Teófilo Altamirano and Lane Ryo Hirabayashi, *Society for Latin American Anthropology Publication Series*, Vol. 13 (Washington, DC: American Anthropological Association), 25–48.

23. John Steinbeck, *Travels with Charley: In Search of America* (New York: Penguin, 1980), 8.

References

Anders, Martha B. "Structure and Function at the Planned Site of Azángaro: Cautionary Notes for the Model of Huari as a Centralized Secular State." In Isbell and McEwan, *Huari Administrative Structure*, 165–97.

———. "Wamanga Pottery: Symbolic Resistance and Subversion in Middle Horizon Epoch 2 Ceramics from the Planned Wari Site of Azángaro (Ayacucho, Peru)." In *Cultures in Conflict: Current Archaeological Perspectives*, edited by Diana Claire Tkaczuk and Brian C. Vivian, 7–18. Calgary, Alberta: University of Calgary, Department of Archaeology, 1989.

Archivo Nacional del Peru, Lima, 1632, Titulos de Propiedad, Legajo No. 13, Cuaderno No. 354.

Archivo Nacional del Peru, Lima, 1702, Derecho Indígena y Encomiendas, Legajo No. 8, Cuaderno No. 186.

Arnold, Dean E. "Ceramic Ecology in the Ayacucho Basin, Peru: Implications for Prehistory." *Current Anthropology* 16 (1975): 185–203.

———. *Ceramic Theory and Cultural Process*. Cambridge: Cambridge University Press, 1985.

———. "Ceramic Variability, Environment and Culture History among the Pokom in the Valley of Guatemala." In *Spatial Organization of Culture*, edited by Ian Hodder, 39–59. London: Gerald Duckworth, 1978.

———. "Design Structure and Community Organization in Quinua, Peru." In *Structure and Cognition in Art*, edited by Dorothy K. Washburn, 56–74. Cambridge: Cambridge University Press, 1983.

———. "Discussion and Criticism: Reply to Haaland and Browman." *Current Anthropology* 16 (1975): 637–40.

———. "Early Inca Expansion and the Incorporation of Local Ethnic Groups: Ethnohistory and Archeological Reconnaissance in the Region of Acos, Department of Cuzco, Peru." *Andean Past* 7 (2005): 219–49.

———. *Ecology of Ceramic Production in an Andean Community*. Cambridge: Cambridge University Press, 1993.

———. "The Emics of Pottery Design from Quinua, Peru." PhD diss., University of Illinois, Urbana, 1970.

———. *The Evolution of Ceramic Production Organization in a Maya Community*. Boulder: University Press of Colorado, 2015.

———. "Maya Blue and Palygorskite: A Second Possible Pre-Columbian Source." *Ancient Mesoamerica* 16 (2005): 51–62.

———. *Maya Potters' Indigenous Knowledge: Cognition, Engagement and Practice*. Boulder: University Press of Colorado, 2018.

———. "Mineralogical Analyses of Ceramic Materials from Quinua, Department of Ayacucho, Peru." *Archaeometry* 14 (1972): 93–101.

———. "Mold-made Potters' Marks from Andahuaylas, Department of Apurimac, Peru." *Ethnos* 37, no. 1-4 (1972): 81–87.

———. "Native Pottery Making in Quinua, Peru." *Anthropos* 67 (1972): 858–72.

———. *Sak lu'um in Maya Culture and Its Possible Relationship to Maya Blue*. Department of Anthropology Research Reports No. 2. Urbana: University of Illinois, 1967.

———. *Social Change and the Evolution of Ceramic Production and Distribution in a Maya Community*. Boulder: University Press of Colorado, 2008.

———. "Social Interaction and Ceramic Design: Community-wide Correlates in Quinua, Peru." In *Pots and Potters: Current Approaches in Ceramic Archaeology*. Monograph 24, edited by Prudence Rice, 133–61. Los Angeles: Institute of Archaeology, University of California, Los Angeles.

Arnold, Dean E., and Bruce F. Bohor. "The Ancient Clay Mine at Yo' K'at, Yucatán." *American Antiquity* 42 (1977): 575–82.

Bauer, Brian S. *Ancient Cuzco: Heartland of the Inca*. Austin: University of Texas Press, 1994.

———. *The Development of the Inca State*. Austin: University of Texas Press, 1992.

———. *The Early Ceramics of the Inca Heartland. Fieldiana Anthropology*, New Series 31, Field Museum of Natural History Publication 1501. Chicago: Field Museum of Natural History, 1999.

———. *The Sacred Landscape of the Inca: The Cusco Ceque System*. Austin: University of Texas Press, 1998.

Bauer, Brian S., and Lucas C. Kellett. "Cultural Transformations of the Chanka Homeland (Andahuaylas, Peru) during the Late Intermediated Period (A.D. 1000–1400)." *Latin American Antiquity* 21, no. 1 (2010): 87–111.

Bauer, Brian S., Lucas C. Kellett, and Miriam Aráoz Silva, with contributions by Sabine Hyland and Carlo Socualaya Dávila. *The Chanka: Archaeological Research in Andahuaylas (Apurimac), Peru*. Monograph 68. Los Angeles: Cotsen Institute of Archaeology Press, 2010.

Betanzos, Juan de. *Narrative of the Incas* [1557]. Translated and edited by Roland Hamilton and Dana Buchanan from the Palma de Mallorca manuscript. Austin: University of Texas Press, 1996.

Biondich, Amy Sue, and Jeremy D. Joslin. "Coca: High Altitude Remedy of the Ancient Incas." *Wilderness & Environmental Medicine* 26 (2015): 567–71.

Blickman, Tom. "Coca Leaf: Myths and Reality." Transnational Institute, August 5, 2014, https://www.tni.org/en/primer/coca-leaf-myths-and-reality.

Bragayrac, Enrique, and Enrique Gonzalez Carre. "Investigaciones en Wari." *Gaceta Arqueológica Andina: Informativo Bimenstral Instituto Andino de Estudios Arqueológicos* 1, 4–5 (1982): 8.

Carson, Rachel. *The Silent Spring.* New York: Houghton Mifflin Company, 1962.

Casagrande, Joseph B. *In the Company of Man.* New York: Harper and Brothers, 1960.

Cieza de Leon, Pedro. *The Incas of Cieza de Leon* [*Crónica del Perú*, Part I, 1553]. Translated by Harriet de Onis. Edited by Victor Wolfgang von Hagen. Norman: University of Oklahoma Press, 1959.

Cook, Noble David, y los Estudios de Alejandro Malaga Medina y Therese Bouysse Cassagne. *Tasa de la Visita General de Francisco de Toledo.* Lima, Peru: Universidad Nacional Mayor de San Marcos, Dirección Universitaria de Biblioteca y Publicaciones, 1975.

"Descripción de la Provincia de los Angaraes" [n.d.]. In *Relaciones Geográficas de Indias-Perú*, por M. Jiménez de la Espada, edición y estudio preliminar por J. U. Martínez Carreras, vol. 1, 201–4. *Biblioteca de Autores Españoles desde la Formación de Lenguaje Hasta Nuestros Dias*, vol. 183. Madrid: Ediciones Atlas, 1965.

Gade, Daniel W., and Mario Escobar. "Village Settlement and the Colonial Legacy in Southern Peru." *Geographical Review* 72 (1982): 430–49.

Garcilaso de la Vega, El Inca. *Royal Commentaries of the Incas and General History of Peru* [1609]. Translated and with an introduction by Harold V. Livermore. Austin: University of Texas Press, 1966.

Guaman Poma de Ayala, Felipe. *The First New Chronicle and Good Government: On the History of the World and the Incas up to 1615* [ca. 1615]. Translated and edited by Roland Hamilton. Austin: University of Texas Press, 2009.

Isbell, William H. "Huari Administration and the Orthogonal Cellular Architecture Horizon." In Isbell and McEwan, *Huari Administrative Structure*, 293–315.

———. "Wari and Tiwanaku: International Identities in the Central Andean Middle Horizon." In *Handbook of South American Archaeology*, edited by Helaine Silverman and William Harris Isbell, 731–59. New York: Springer, 2008.

Isbell, William. H., C. Brewster-Wray, and Lynda Spickard. "Architecture and Spatial Organization at Huari." In Isbell and McEwan, *Huari Administrative Structure*, 19–52.

Isbell, William H., and Gordon F. McEwan, eds. *Huari Administrative Structure: Prehistoric Monumental Architecture and State Government.* Washington, DC: Dumbarton Oaks Research Library and Collection, 1991.

Isbell, William H., and K. J. Schreiber. "Was Huari a State?" *American Antiquity* 43 (1978): 372–89.

Libro de Cabildo de la Ciudad San Juan de la Frontera Huamanga 1539–1547. Transcribed by Raul Rivera Serna. *Documentos Regionales de la Etnología y Etnohistoria Andinas*, no. 3. Lima: Ediciones de la Casa de la Cultura del Peru, 1966.

Markham, Clement R. *Markham in Peru: The Travels of Clement R. Markham, 1852–1853*, edited by Peter Blanchard. Austin: University of Texas Press, 1991.

McEwan, Gordon F., ed. *Pikillacta: The Wari Empire in Cuzco.* Iowa City: University of Iowa Press, 2005.

Menzel, Dorothy. "Style and Time in the Middle Horizon." *Ñawpa Pacha* 2 (1964): 1–105.

Mitchell, William P. "Dam the Water: The Ecology and Political Economy of Irrigation in the Ayacucho Valley, Peru." In *Irrigation at High Altitudes: The Social Organization of Water Control Systems in the Andes*, edited by David Guillet and William P. Mitchell, 275–302. Society for Latin American Anthropology, Publication Series, vol. 12. Washington, DC: American Anthropological Association, 1994.

———. "The Hydraulic Hypothesis: A Reappraisal." *Current Anthropology* 14, no. 5 (1973): 532–34.

———. "Irrigation and Community in the Central Peruvian Highlands." *American Anthropologist* 78 (1976): 25–44.

———. *Peasants on the Edge: Crop, Cult and Crisis in the Andes.* Austin: University of Texas Press, 1991.

———. "Pressure on Peasant Production and the Transformation of Regional and National Identities." In *Migrants, Regional Identities and Latin American Cities*, edited by Teófilo Altamirano and Lane Ryo Hirabayashi, Society for Latin American Anthropology Publication Series, vol. 13, 25–48. Washington, DC: American Anthropological Association, 1997.

Politis, Gustavo G., and Luciano Prates. "The Pre-Clovis Peopling of South America." *SAA Archaeological Record* 19 (2019): 40–44.

Rabe, Stephen G. "Alliance for Progress." *Oxford Research Encyclopedia of Latin American History*, March 2016. DOI:10.1093/acrefore/9780199366439.013.95.

Rivera, Jaime. *Geografía General de Ayacucho.* Ayacucho, Perú: Universidad Nacional de San Cristóbal de Huamanga, Dirección Universitaria de Investigación, 1971.

Rivera, Pedro de, and Antonio de Chaves y de Guevara. "Relación de la Ciudad de Guamanga y sus Términos: Año de 1586." In *Relaciónes Geográficas de Indias.* Vol. I: Perú, 105–39. Madrid: Ministerio de Fomento, 1881.

Rowe, John H. An Introduction to the Archaeology of Cuzco. *Papers of the Peabody Museum of American Archaeology and Ethnology, Harvard University*, vol. 27, no. 8. Cambridge, MA: Peabody Museum, Harvard University, 1944.

Sarmiento de Gamboa, Pedro. *History of the Incas* [1572]. Translated and edited by Brian S. Bauer and Vania Smith, with an introduction by Brian S. Bauer and Jean-Jacques Decoster. Austin: University of Texas Press, 2007.

Schreiber, Katharina J. "Jincamocco: A Huari Administrative Center in the South-Central Highlands of Peru." In Isbell and McEwan, *Huari Administrative Structure*, 199–213.

———. "From State to Empire: The Expansion of Wari Outside the Ayacucho Basin." In *The Origins and Development of the Andean State*, edited by Jonathan Haas, Sheila Pozorski, and Thomas Pozorski, 91–96. Cambridge: Cambridge University Press, 1987.

Sillar, Bill. *Shaping Culture: Making Pots and Constructing Households. An Ethnoarchaeological Study of Pottery Production, Trade and Use in the Andes.* BAR International Series 883. Oxford: British Archaeological Reports, 2000.

Squier, E. G. *Incidents of Travel and Exploration in the Land of the Incas.* New York: Harper and Brothers, 1877. https://archive.org/details /peruincidentsoftoosqui/page/n9.

Steinbeck, John. *Travels with Charley: In Search of America.* New York: Penguin, 1980.

Stern, Steve J. *Peru's Indian Peoples and the Challenge of Spanish Conquest: Huamanga to 1640.* 2nd ed. Madison: University of Wisconsin Press, 1993.

Thompson, L. G., E. Mosley-Thompson, J. F. Bolzan, and B. R. Koci. "A 1500-Year Record of Tropical Precipitation in Ice Cores from the Quelccaya Ice Cap, Peru." *Science* 229 (1985): 971–73.

Tournier, Paul. *The Adventure of Living.* New York: Harper and Brothers, 1965.

United Nations. "Oceans & Law of the Sea: Division for Ocean Affairs and Law of the Sea." Last modified February 2, 2020. https://www.un.org/Depts/los /convention_agreements/convention_overview_convention.htm.

United States Environmental Protection Agency. "DDT: A Brief History and Status." Accessed April 19, 2020. https://www.epa.gov/ingredients-used -pesticide-products/ddt-brief-history-and-status.

Wilder, Thornton. *The Bridge of San Luis Rey.* New York: HarperCollins, 1927, reprinted 2004.

YouTube. "Chiaraje-Canas-Chumbivilcas-Espinar-Cusco." January 24, 2008. https://www.youtube.com/watch?v=3YtnfXeSn6Q.

Zuidema, R. T. "Algunas Problemas Etnohistoricos del Departamento de Ayacucho." *Wamani: Órgano de la Asociación Peruana de Antropólogos, Filial-Ayacucho* 1 (1966): 68–75.

———. *The Ceque System of Cuzco: The Social Organization of the Capital of the Inca.* Leiden: E. J. Brill, 1964.

Index

Entries printed in *italic* type refer to figures or illustrations.

Abancay (city), *90*, 110–13

Acción Popular (political party), 72, 109–10

Acocro (town), *16*, 173, 184

Acomayo (town), *138*, 139, 140

Acomayo River, *143*

Acos (village), *90*, 105–10, 136–39, 140–49, 156, 183–84

Acos Indians, and Inca Empire, 103–4, 115–16, 130, 146–56, 175–76, 199–200n7

Acos Vinchos (village), *16*, 80

Acuchimay (archaeological site), *16*, 30, 89

Adventure of Living, The (Tournier 1965), 4

agriculture: harvesting as communal in Andean culture, 164; and irrigation in Quinua, 70–76; and terracing in Acos Valley, 144, 148. *See also* barley; maize; potatoes; quinoa

Alaska, and Alcan Highway, 118

alcoholic beverages, cultural and social context of consumption in Peruvian Andes, 49–51, 68–70, 114, 159, 161

Alliance for Progress, 168, 200n1

alpacas, 52, 53, 165–66

altitude: and cooking of food, 42; effects of on residents of Ayacucho, 22; and personal hygiene in Quinua, 48; and railway stations in Peruvian Andes, 180–81; and travel to Acos, 107, 110, 124–25

Andahuaylas (city), *90*, 105, 107, 108, 170–73

Andes: climate of, 14–15, 48, 106, 179–80, 195n25, 197n4; early experiences of fieldwork in, 4–5; observations of from flight to Lima, 7; relationship of coastal desert to neighboring highlands of, 14. *See also* Peru; transportation

Anta (village), 104, *121*

Anta Indians, 116

Anta Plain (pampa), 116, 120, 121, 136, 170, 176

anthropology: education and early research in, 1–6; and development of research questions, 9; and participation of anthropologists in local cultures, 164, 190; and use of term "peasant," 193n6. *See also* fieldwork; pottery

Aprista (member of APRA political party), 109